Housing in America

Housing is a fundamental need and universal part of human living that shapes our lives in profound ways that go far beyond basic sheltering. Where we live can determine our self-image, social status, health and safety, quality of public services, access to jobs, and transportation options. But the reality for many in America is that housing choices are constrained: costs are unaffordable, discriminatory practices remain, and physical features do not align with needs. As a society, we recognize the significant role housing plays in our overall quality of life and the stability of our communities. We have made a national commitment to decent housing for all yet this promise remains unrealized.

Housing in America provides a broad overview of the field of housing, with the objective of fostering an informed and engaged citizenry. The evolution of housing norms and policy is explored in a historical context while underscoring the human and cultural dimensions of housing program choices. Specific topics covered include: why housing matters; housing and culture; housing frameworks and political ideologies; housing and opportunities; housing and the economy; housing discrimination; and housing affordability. Readers will gain an understanding of the basic debates within the field of housing, consider the motivations and performance of various interventions, and critically examine persistent patterns of racial and class inequality.

With an exploration of theoretical frameworks, short case studies, reflective exercises, and strong visuals, this introductory text explores improving housing choices in America.

Marijoan Bull, PhD, AICP, is a practicing urban planner and Associate Professor Emerita of Geography and Regional Planning at Westfield State University, USA. In her career of over thirty years she has focused on making urban planning the work of all, and engaging the public in the design of a just and sustainable future.

Alina Gross, PhD, is an Assistant Professor of Geography and Regional Planning at Westfield State University, USA where she teaches students the importance of cultural diversity and community inclusion in the context of becoming effective planners and engaged citizens. Her teaching, research, and professional planning work focuses on housing, public participation, and community-based planning.

Housing in America

An Introduction

Marijoan Bull and Alina Gross

Routledge
Taylor & Francis Group

NEW YORK AND LONDON

First published 2018
by Routledge
711 Third Avenue, New York, NY 10017

and by Routledge
2 Park Square, Milton Park, Abingdon, Oxon, OX14 4RN

Routledge is an imprint of the Taylor & Francis Group, an informa business

© 2018 Taylor & Francis

Library of Congress Cataloging-in-Publication Data
Names: Bull, Marijoan, author. | Gross, Alina, author.
Title: Housing in America / Marijoan Bull and Alina Gross.
Description: New York, NY : Routledge, 2018.
Identifiers: LCCN 2017050178 | ISBN 9781138233638 (hardback) | ISBN 9781138233645 (pbk.)
Subjects: LCSH: Housing—United States.
Classification: LCC HD7293 .B84 2018 | DDC 363.50973—dc23
LC record available at https://lccn.loc.gov/2017050178

ISBN: 978-1-138-23363-8 (hbk)
ISBN: 978-1-138-23364-5 (pbk)
ISBN: 978-1-315-30913-2 (ebk)

Typeset in Warnock Pro
by Apex CoVantage, LLC

Contents

Introduction
Housing in America

Housing is a fundamental and universal part of human living. While often simplified as "having a roof over our heads," the truth is that housing shapes our lives in many ways, ways that go far beyond basic sheltering. We wrote this book because access to adequate, affordable, and accessible housing touches the lives of every American, and we believe communities cannot flourish when there is a lack of decent housing for residents. The lack of stable, suitable housing comes at a cost. Children, families, and communities are diminished and stunted, as housing is tied to our physical, emotional, social, and economic well-being. It is our belief that the many dimensions of housing in America must be better understood. We hope this book educates on housing, and, in turn, encourages and enables more people to support actions toward ensuring housing for all.

This text provides a broad overview of the field of housing, with the objective of fostering an informed citizenry. For many in America, housing choices are constrained by excessive costs, discriminatory and racist practices, and physical features unaligned with needs. In this book, we discuss these challenges in attaining housing, as well as the historical context and cultural frameworks underlying the American approach to meeting housing needs. Our goal is to take readers on a journey through the many dimensions of housing, having them emerge with an understanding of the critical role of housing in America. The chapters of this textbook offer a basic understanding of the important issues those living in the United States may face in their quest to secure housing, and highlight the factors contributing to housing inequities.

Chapter 1, Unique Qualities of Housing, introduces the reasons why housing matters. This chapter walks through the ways that one's residence limits or expands one's life circumstances and discusses housing as one of the largest purchases a household can make, connecting households with a bundle of services. We also examine how housing connects with our self-image and can have an emotional and psychological component. The importance of housing for individuals, communities, and the nation are investigated.

Chapter 2, Housing and Culture, looks at American cultural values and how they have shaped the types of housing constructed and sought after in the United States. This includes patterns of household formation, the use of space in the home, and material culture preferences. This chapter examines the intersection of housing and culture by considering the American cultural values of independence, individualism, privacy, and status, along with the prominence of the nuclear family (parents and children).

Chapter 3, Framing Housing: Disciplinary Approaches and Ideologies, gives an overview of how housing theory has been approached by key thinkers in the field. First, we explore how a variety of academic disciplines approach housing studies, noting the theories, models, and methods of research that are favored. From this discussion, we see that multiple lenses are needed to fully capture the forces at work in housing. Second, we turn to political ideologies and note the general models used by different political orientations when considering how to adequately house Americans. As housing is tied to essential elements of life opportunities, and there are documented inequities in these opportunities, housing interventions are part of the political movement toward providing a level playing field for all.

Chapter 4, History of Federal Involvement in Housing, examines the historical evolution of American government interventions in housing, addressing the major actions taken by the federal government and putting these actions in a historical and cultural context. Given the number of actions covered, it is presented as part 1 and part 2. Broadly, we can say housing policy responds to the major demographic, economic, political, social, and historical forces at play in each period. We will see that housing policy is not limited to actions by housing agencies, but is also affected by actions involving the tax code and banking regulations. Students will take away some important basics on the establishment of a housing finance system with a cornerstone of homeownership, as well as meeting housing needs through supply side (direct government production and subsidizing private production) or demand side (providing vouchers) initiatives. Also covered is how racism was institutionalized through federal guidelines.

Chapter 5, Housing and Discrimination, deals with the quest to provide equal opportunities for all Americans to live in housing of their choice. It covers the role of realtors, banks, and federal agencies in furthering racial and class segregation. Also addressed is the historic pattern of intimidation and violence used against people of color to deny them opportunity and housing choice. While new protections allow for litigation against unequal treatment, research clearly indicates that discriminatory practices based on race, ethnicity, family composition, and other characteristics persist. How this persistent discrimination, in combination with many other factors, contributes to a society segregated by race, ethnicity, and class is also examined.

In Chapter 6, Housing Needs, Affordability, and Federal Responses, we present the evolution of housing needs, including adequacy, accessibility, and affordability. Defining housing needs is a very important and highly debated topic, but if we are to move toward decent housing for all people, we must first grasp the extent of housing needs in this country. A large portion of this chapter addresses the concepts of direct (line item program funding) and indirect federal housing subsidies (tax exemptions and credits). The gaps in how major federal housing programs meet housing needs are explored.

Chapter 7, Housing and Opportunity, looks at the correlation between housing and quality of life outcomes (including education and health) as it relates to building conditions, environmental conditions, and neighborhood conditions. While our housing provides physical shelter, it is also a large determinant of our quality of life because it establishes our access to opportunities or nearness to risks, affecting our lives in both positive and negative ways. Inadequate education perpetuates poverty, and this chapter explores the extent to which racial and class segregation, tied to our semi-regulated housing market, has reinforced severely unequal opportunities. Research also shows that instability in housing, related to excessive cost and profit motives, negatively affects the educational experiences of many children.

Chapter 8, Housing and the Economy, explores how housing functions as an economic engine, noting how housing is produced. For builders, housing is a product to manufacture for profit, for developers it is an investment to generate income, or for financiers housing is an asset to trade. The pursuit by some of housing as a home coexists with the objectives of others to make profits. Most Americans receive housing through the private sector. Topics concerning the private market and housing costs covered here include the relationship between regulations and housing costs, the premise of housing filtering, and the phenomenon of gentrification.

Chapter 9, Public Housing, considers the evolution of public housing, noting its demise, and the realities of current public housing programs and authorities. A preference for the market to meet needs combined with a reluctance for the government to compete with the private sector has made direct government provision of housing a least-favored option. This chapter profiles public housing today, describing the physical dimensions of this part of America's housing stock, and considering whom it serves. A short history of public housing explores the factors researchers have implicated in the failure of parts of public housing. It concludes by assessing the tactical responses to the malfunctions, and the current thinking about public housing.

In Chapter 10, State and Local Housing Initiatives, we discuss the types of actions that lie within the authority of local and state government, including inclusionary zoning, municipal land subsidies, accessory apartments, density bonuses, tax credits, adaptive re-use, infill housing, state revenue bonds, "fair-share" laws, and more. Here we present the major ways states and local communities use their resources and power to address the need for affordable housing. For each of these two levels of government, we consider the planning, funding, and regulatory mechanisms available to further the objective of decent housing for all.

Chapter 11, Homelessness, discusses those in most extreme housing need, the varying issues that may lead to homelessness, and "Housing First," a newer strategy to address homelessness in the United States. This chapter examines the issue of homelessness by offering key statistics, considering a variety of contributing factors, and exploring the ways all can attain and sustain a place to call home. The significant and long-term consequences related to the physical, mental, and emotional stresses of a lack of housing are considered.

Chapter 12, Conclusion, presents concluding thoughts, considering some of the overarching trends, main philosophical debates, and challenges that remain in the quest to provide every American a decent home. After having looked at the many dimensions of housing in America, readers of this chapter will find a summary of the main points of the text and a framing of the basic debates in housing policy. This concluding chapter will remind the reader what we know, what we don't know, and how our political, cultural, social, and economic frameworks shape our responses to the basic human need for housing. It will challenge the reader to assess his/her own conclusions on the national commitment to decent housing for all. Many of us who enjoy safe, stable, and affordable housing take it for granted, and fail to realize such a home remains a dream for many Americans.

Acknowledgments

Our thanks to all those who offered support and inspiration for this work. We would like to thank Routledge for considering housing important enough to publish this book, and those at Routledge who assisted us, Nicole Solano and Krystal LaDuc.

Others worked along with us, providing invaluable feedback on this work and their efforts made it better—thanks to Azelie Fortier for editing assistance and Ted Dobek and Allison Terkelsen for graphics assistance.

Over several years, students in Marijoan's Housing in America course engaged with and responded to ideas and materials, and their feedback has improved this work. Also, chapter reviewers offered many helpful suggestions.

Marijoan thanks Chris for infinite patience and technical assistance.

Alina would like to thank Chris and her parents, Meir and Nava, for their support. She would also like to thank her daughters, Avi and Taly, for being a welcome distraction during the writing process.

Note to Instructors and Students

Our main objective with this work is to educate broadly on housing. We invite your comments and thoughts on the material covered. Please forward your experience with the text, the questions and activities, and your thoughts on changes and additions. We can be reached at: housinginamerica@gmail.com. Thank you.

UNIQUE QUALITIES OF HOUSING

Can you conjure up the image of a quaint "Home Sweet Home" cross-stitch hanging on a wall? While few of us may actually hang such an item, we recognize this motif from its use in cartoons and illustrations to evoke the feeling of being in a place that offers security and warmth, of a familiar place where we are surrounded by those important to us and where we can truly be ourselves. A healthy home provides roots and an acceptance that nourishes us so we can gather the strength to go out into the world. *Home* is a compelling symbol for Americans—it relays a feeling of belonging and refuge that is deeply embedded in our culture. The shared "American Dream" consists of a belief that hard work leads to prosperity, a prosperity made manifest in an iconic image of home. In part, the achievement of the "American Dream" takes the form of owning a single-family home with a yard and a white picket fence (Jackson 1985). Not everyone has a home that is full of warmth and peace, but for all of us the potential for a house to be a home is real. The larger-than-life mythology of home as sacred ground, firmly entrenched in American society, is produced through cultural norms and bolstered by emotive encounters.

Beyond this overall image of a house as a home, we have also assigned symbolic meaning to various parts of a house, such as the foundation, roof, doors, and windows. These parts often serve as metaphors to express sentiments of strength, protection, transition, and warmth—all reinforcing the power of the term *home*. The symbols and metaphors of housing are common in our talk, stories, music, and media. Given that we all share the need for housing and that we spend large amounts of time in our housing, it is not surprising that home is a central theme in our culture. Since we all can relate to the sentiment and emotions surrounding home, these metaphors resonate universally. Even those who don't directly experience the positive elements of home can share a longing for what it represents.

In this book, our approach to housing weaves together the knowledge found in academic disciplines such as sociology, philosophy, economics, and urban planning with the truth found in human expression of our stories. This lays the groundwork for discussions on how best to conceptualize housing and effectively meet housing needs. Ultimately, this exploration is about how our nation can be a place where all Americans have a dwelling that provides the comfort worthy of the name *home*.

In this chapter, we will consider the many roles housing plays in our lives, noting its influence on us as individuals, its significance to neighborhoods and local jobs, and its prominence in the national economy. We also explore the unique qualities of housing, reflecting on how the specific characteristics and significance of housing necessitate an interdisciplinary understanding.

Figure 1.1   Iconic Cross-Stitch
Source: Image by M. Bull, used with permission

Levels of Influence

This textbook explores housing because housing matters. It matters to our individual lives and our communal undertakings. We can organize the influence of housing by examining its power at the personal, community, and national level (Bipartisan Millenial Housing Commission 2002).

Housing Influence on the Personal Level

In American culture, we identify ourselves with our housing, and often use our homes to express our individuality or character. The style, decoration, and quality of the house are seen as extensions of us. These elements are our self-image made evident in the material form of our home. Thus, a prestigious address or opulent house provides social status, and means we are worthy or even better than others, while a dilapidated house or an address in a poor area of town is often associated with people having low self-esteem. Take an example from literature. In Sandra Cisneros's classic book and *New York Times* bestseller, *The House on Mango Street*, Esperanza, a young Latina growing up in Chicago, is ashamed of where she lives. She yearns for a *real* home; for her, this means a well-maintained single-family house with a yard. Early in the story, a teacher passes by and asks where she lives. When Esperanza points to a run-down third-floor apartment, the teacher responds, "You live *there*?" (emphasis in original) and, dejectedly, Esperanza reflects, "The way she said it made me feel like nothing" (Cisneros 1991). The protagonist of this book covets a secure place where she can be content and not judged as inadequate. As readers learn of Esperanza's burning desire for a home that matches the image in her mind's eye, they become aware of the very strong emotional component of housing.

The sentiment evident in this piece of fiction has been concretized by research. Researcher Talja Blokland noted that participants in her study resisted identifying themselves with the place they lived—public housing in New Haven, Connecticut—due to the strong stigma associated with such housing. The residents had internalized the social message that people who live in public housing are failures, so they sought to distance themselves from this pejorative term (2008).

Landscape architecture and urban planning researcher Clare Cooper Marcus has explored these psychological aspects of housing and encourages architects to fully understand the strong link between housing and self. Marcus contends, "the house is very intimately entwined with the psyche" (1999, 305). She notes that we "invest meaning in a place when we are permitted to appropriate and care for it," and goes on to describe a universal drive to personalize space (1990, 54–55). She also notes that, like a person, the house has both a facade and an interior (1999, 301, 309). Sociologists and philosophers have put it this way: "the home as a built artefact, is itself a structure of self-formation, of self-articulation and of self-remembrance" (Jacobs and Malpas 2013). The physical realities of the place and the material objects we add all contribute to the act of self-definition.

The substantial import of a home is, perhaps, best recognized in the absence of a home. In a world where violence, political instability, disaster, and environmental changes are fueling a refugee crisis, the full impact of the loss of home is a significant problem. Within the United States alone, individuals have experienced loss due to natural disasters including hurricanes, floods, and tornadoes, and economic collapse with the associated foreclosures, job losses, and evictions. Responding to such events requires more than simply meeting the primitive shelter needs of those affected. (Chapter 11 also connects these themes to the larger group of **households** in our society who at some point have found themselves homeless.)

The displaced and refugees of the world face the stark reality of having lost their homes. Such a loss is about more than the physical space; gone, too, are the layers of memories and personal experiences that created a home. Research on refugees has shown that the act of beautifying a space through day-to-day modifications is critical to creating home anew, and regaining this feeling of being at home supports healing. According to one researcher,

> Adaptation to new housing situations following an unwelcome move necessitates coming to terms with more than the physical dislocation. The reconstruction of home subsequent to forced displacement is often accompanied by the reconstruction of self and one's relationships to place, family, community, and culture. Making one's intimate surroundings more physically attractive and emotionally satisfying is more than a matter of mere surface adornment. The loss of familiar possessions is more than a material loss.
>
> (Devora 2013, 239)

As places of refuge and places where we are in control, our homes can provide personal safety, privacy, and stability. This translates into support for our mental and physical well-being. By reducing stress, homes directly contribute to better health and longevity. Being able to stay in one place (or at least moving by choice rather than by force) and make it our own, we can mature into our full selves.

Beyond these psychosocial elements, the quality of housing also has a direct impact on individual physical health. Ironically, the very places that should protect us can cause us harm. Whether through material limitations (such as poor lighting or inadequate insulation) or environmental hazards (such as the presence of mold or air pollution), the places we live can affect our physical welfare. This can be especially critical for infants and toddlers, as their body systems are under development (Children 2000). Lead exposure from housing is but one example. According to the National Academy of Sciences, lead exposure is associated with "impaired cognitive function, behavior difficulties, fetal organ development, and other problems . . . low levels of lead in children's blood can cause reduced intelligence, impaired hearing and reduced stature. Yet, lead poisoning is a completely preventable disease" (Children 2000, 1, 21, 11). Given the many hours we spend in our housing, such exposures can present significant risk. In Chapter 7, we explore the need to assess the environmental conditions of housing that are a direct threat to public health.

Housing Influence on the Community Level

The quality and specifics of housing are also important at the neighborhood level. Because a **housing unit** is fixed in place, the surroundings are significant—they are, essentially, a feature of the housing (Reid 2007). The federal Bipartisan Millennial Housing Commission reported that more than a stable home is needed to secure physical and mental well-being. This report outlined how an unsafe and/or declining neighborhood can undermine security and limit opportunity (2002). If crime is high, municipal trash collection spotty, recreational services poor, and local schools failing, then the quality of life for residents is far from ideal—no matter how enriching life is within the abode. The quality of your neighborhood shapes your life experience. For these reasons economists have described housing as essentially a bundle of services (Goodman 1989). Your neighborhood can limit or offer opportunities for employment, transportation, recreation, and shopping. Many studies have documented statistically significant correlations between neighborhood and lifespan.[1]

Neighborhoods matter, as the maintenance of surrounding properties can impact abutting residents. Whether the property next door is painted or repaired affects the desirability of the area. This in turn determines the value of all the properties. A homeowner can see a decline in her/his enjoyment of their property as well as investment if surrounding owners do not maintain their properties. Vacancies and unattended repairs detract from an area and can play a part in turning larger economic forces against ongoing investment (Bipartisan Millenial Housing Commission 2002). This means homeowners or renters can see diminishing neighborhood quality as a reaction to the inaction of others.

As households and families are the building blocks of neighborhoods, communities may suffer when housing undermines the well-being of residents. Families under stress can translate into neighborhoods with dysfunction. Human beings have varied levels of resilience and coping ability for navigating traumatic circumstances. Those deprived of a stable foundation and the healthy social relationships that home can provide may struggle to function in society. Sociologist Matthew Desmond sums this up as follows:

> Residential stability begets a kind of psychological stability which allows people to invest in their home and social relationships. It begets school stability, which increases the chances that children will excel and graduate. And it begets community stability, which encourages neighbors to form strong bonds and take care of their block.
>
> (2016, 296)

Finally, housing plays a significant role in the economic fortunes of a local community. Beyond its more immediate roles as shelter and neighborhood anchor, housing affects communities by providing jobs and contributing real estate property taxes. New construction employs workers such as plumbers, electricians, surveyors, carpenters, real estate agents, and other tradespeople (see Figure 1.2), but so does the renovation or repair of housing. Much of this work represents funds expended in the local or regional economy. While real estate property tax reliance differs across the United States, for many municipalities, this revenue source generates a substantial portion of the funds needed for providing local services such as public education, garbage collection, police and fire protection, and more. In this way residences in a community both provide funds and require services.

Figure 1.2   Housing and the Local Economy

Source: Graphic © Ted Dobek, used with permission

Notes: "The figure for taxes includes revenue from all sources, such as permit and impact fees, for the state government
and all local jurisdictions within the state combined. There are also one-year impacts that include both the
direct and indirect impact of the construction activity itself, and the impact of residents who earn money from
the construction activity spending part of it within the state. Jobs are measured in full-time equivalents—i.e.,
one reported job represents enough work to keep one worker employed full-time for a year, based on average
hours worked per week by full-time employees in the industry. The one-year estimates also assume that construction materials are subject to a state and local sales tax of 7.24 percent, an average (weighted by population)
computed by NAHB across rates for individual states reported by the Tax Foundation." This estimate does not
include the multi-family housing construction or the renovation and repair of all housing types.

Source of Data for Note: National Association of Home Builders, "The Economic Impact of Home Building in a
Typical State Income, Jobs, and Taxes Generated," 2015. Available at: www.nahb.org/~/media/Sites/NAHB/
Economic%20studies/REPORT_state.ashx?la=en

Housing Influence on the National Level

Housing researcher Alex Schwartz calls the national housing sector "a mainstay of the U.S.
economy," accounting for nearly one-fifth of the gross domestic product (GDP) through
direct housing expenditures, construction-related jobs, and housing-associated consumer
goods (Schwartz 2015). This includes construction and remodeling costs, rent and "imputed
rent" payments,[2] home furnishings, and utility costs. Given this, the housing industry is
closely watched, with housing starts (see Box 1.1) routinely referenced as a bellwether for
economic conditions. Through the United States Census Bureau, the Commerce Department issues monthly reports on the national figures of **housing starts**, housing completions,
and building permits issued. The sale of consumer goods such as rugs, furniture, and appli-
ances is closely associated with new housing units and major remodeling. A slowdown in
housing starts means fewer new units and fewer purchases of these durable goods.

In addition, for homeowners, housing can be used to secure loans for large purchases
including college tuition, cars, kitchen remodeling, or luxury items such as boats. The

loan is based on the equity the homeowner has accumulated through the appreciation of the housing during the time of his/her residency. These **equity loans** can contribute to an economic stimulus as borrowers make large purchases and invest in the next generation.

Unique Characteristics of Housing

To fully understand Americans' experiences with housing, and historical and current American housing policies, here we compare housing with other goods or services. Six characteristics of housing set it apart from other items (O'Sullivan 2003). These characteristics are significant when considering the programs adopted to meet housing needs in our country. For now, it is important to understand these characteristics, as we will return to them throughout this book. The six characteristics are (in no particular order):

1. Housing is more than just a product—there are strong emotional and psychosocial components to housing.
2. Housing is heterogeneous—each dwelling unit is unique.
3. Housing is generally the largest purchase a household makes.
4. Housing choices can change but the financial and emotional costs of moving can be high.
5. Housing is durable and typically appreciates over time.
6. Housing is shaped by cultural norms *and* institutional practices.

Housing Is More Than a Product

As discussed earlier, housing choice can be connected to our psyche, self-worth, and identity. As an item in daily use, housing's relationship to us is particularly strong. We often have intense emotive connections to the places we live—we may love our home and it may feel like a sanctuary, or it may be a place that failed to protect us and is associated with feelings of pain. Childhood memories often center on the places where we grew up. Human geographer Yi-Fu Tuan has written extensively on the meaning of home and sense of place. Regarding images of home, he writes,

> The most vivid hauntings are likely to be those of childhood and of childhood's home. Why? Well, consider the following facts. Home is never more a nurturing shelter than to the very young who are well aware of their vulnerability; children's engagement with home has a directness and immediacy that grown-ups, more prone to critical appraisal, have lost.
>
> (2012, 228)

The emotive component of housing is significant when thinking about housing needs and housing choices. In reality, it is embedded in our language—what we all desire is not a house but a *home*. When looking for housing, associations with past places we have lived will play a role, as will the strong cultural message of what makes a true home. As expressed by cultural geographer Tim Cresswell, "in the western world 'home' is an ideal as well as a place" (2004, 115). When looking for housing we are driven by more than the biological necessity—we are shaped by our experiences and cultural messages. In the next chapter, we will consider how cultural ideals of home vary due to family composition and societal priorities.

Housing Is Heterogeneous

The housing **stock**—the housing units of all types within an area—is a collection of unique dwelling units. Housing units can vary in all aspects: style, size, layout,

(a)

Price: $125,000
Features: 2 bedrooms, 1 Bath, Remodeled Kitchen
School District: Standish Elementary
Playground: ½ mile

(b)

Price: $300,000
Features: New 3 bedrooms, 2.5 Baths, Large Deck
School District: Lagrange Elementary
Playground: ½ mile, includes public pool

(c)

Price: $108,000
Features: 1 bedroom, 1 Bath, 3 miles to light rail
School District: Lagrange Elementary
Playground: 3/4 mile

Figure 1.3a, b, c Heterogeneous Housing Stock and Bundles of Services

Source: Images by M. Bull, used with permission

quality of construction and finishes, location, lot characteristics, and price. For instance, a single-family housing search may include looking at a two-story Colonial in one neighborhood, a brick raised ranch on the same street, and a manufactured house in another part of the community. If a rental unit is desired, choices may include a unit in a high-rise building, half of a duplex, a single-family rental, or a unit in a renovated warehouse building.

Box 1.1   Terms to Learn

Home Mortgage: A mortgage refers to all forms of debt for which the property is pledged as security for payment of the debt (U.S. Census); generally, a loan to finance the purchase of a housing unit (can be for investment property as well as personal). There are many different types of mortgages.

Household: All people who occupy a particular housing unit as their usual residence, or who live there at the time of the interview and have no usual residence elsewhere (U.S. Census).

Housing Equity: The value of a house that a homeowner has accrued, calculated by subtracting the amount owed on any mortgages from the estimated total value of the house and land.

Housing Start: Start of construction occurs when excavation begins for the footings or foundation of a building. All housing units in a multifamily building are defined as being started when this excavation begins. Estimates of housing starts include units in structures being totally rebuilt on an existing foundation (U.S. Census). Housing starts are distinct from the issuing of building permits, as a builder may delay the actual construction after receiving a permit.

Housing Stock: The total number of housing units (of all types) in an area.

Housing Tenure: Whether a unit is owner-occupied or renter-occupied. A housing unit (including a cooperative or condominium unit) is owner-occupied if someone whose name is on the deed, mortgage, or contract to purchase lives in the unit. Renter-occupied units include those that are rented for cash and those with no cash rent, such as a life tenancy or units that come free with a job (U.S. Census).

Housing Unit: A house, apartment, group of rooms, or single room occupied or intended for occupancy as separate living quarters. The occupants of each housing unit may be one person living alone, a single family, two or more families living together, or any other group of related or unrelated people who share living arrangements (U.S. Census). Housing units may be vacant or occupied by a household.

The variable among housing tenancies of owning or renting is referred to as **housing tenure**. The U.S. Census Bureau has collected data on housing tenure since 1890, a time when home ownership was not as prevalent as it is today (Mazur and Wilson 2010). Even neighborhoods that are built with standardized "cookie-cutter" designs have unique dwelling units, as the precise location of these duplicates will differ. Remember, buyers acquire more than the house. A home purchase is a complete package, as the house comes with a set of neighborhood qualities and amenities. It is in part the immobility of housing that contributes to the uniqueness of each unit. When choosing housing, households balance various factors such as the size and type of yard, number and size of bedrooms, location relative to employment and/or family, quality of the school district, neighborhood crime rate, cost, and more. Economists have described this as follows: "the household chooses a bundle that maximizes the household's utility subject to its budget constraints" (O'Sullivan 2003, 437). Decisions about where to live can thus be complex, as they are highly influential for residents' quality of life. Altering these features can also be a means of changing the ultimate cost of the housing. Smaller homes, smaller lots, economical finishes, and less desirable locations can make housing more affordable.

Housing Is the Largest Household Purchase

Housing is expensive. The purchase of a home is generally the largest purchase a household makes. This purchase can be 3 to 5 times the annual income of the household (O'Sullivan 2003, 437). As the dwelling is such a large purchase, most households must turn to financing to cover the full cost. A loan to purchase a house is called a **mortgage**, and commits the resident to monthly payments (with interest) over a long period of time, generally 15 to 30 years. Chapter 4 on the history of federal housing policy and Chapter 6 on affordability will describe mortgages and housing costs in more detail.

But it is not just *purchasing* a house that is expensive—in many housing markets, renting a place to live also requires a large portion of a household's income. Housing is just one category of monthly expenses; other expenses are utilities, food, transportation, medicine, clothing, and more. The larger the portion of a budget that must go toward housing costs, the less money is available for other expenses. A general rule of thumb is that low- to moderate-income households can cover routine expenses (and absorb an emergency) if housing costs do not exceed 30 percent of their income (Hulchanski 2013).

The fact that housing is so costly makes it even more critical to households because it is a major ongoing financial obligation. This unique characteristic also represents another feature that can be adjusted to make housing more affordable. In terms of mortgages, changes to the overall loan amount, interest rate, and length of loan can change the monthly payment amount and make it more, or less, affordable (see Chapters 4 and 6 for more details).

Home purchases and housing finance are not only the largest purchases most American households make. For most middle-class American households, an investment in home ownership also becomes the household's major source of wealth. This wealth is generated by the appreciation of housing over time. For most of the past 70 years, households gained wealth when what they owed on the home became a smaller percentage of the home's overall worth. The appreciation could be considerable—according to the Economic Policy Institute, home equity "is a far more important source of wealth [than stocks] for most households," accounting for two-thirds of the wealth of middle-income households (Mishel, Bivens, Gould, and Shierholz 2012, 376). Cultural context is important, however, as studies have shown that homeowners of color do not generally see the same levels of appreciation as white homeowners (Sykes 2008). This reflects the racism and segregation in American society, which are explored more fully in Chapters 5 and 7.

Financial and Emotional Costs of Moving Can Be High

If you make a purchase at a retail store and are unhappy with the item, you simply go back and return it. When it comes to housing, such an exchange is neither easy nor cost-free. Making a change to your housing is a major and, in many ways, disruptive and time-consuming action. If you are unhappy where you are settled, there is a high trans-action cost to move. You may need to have the assistance of professional movers, you will need to find another housing unit that meets your criteria, and you may uproot yourself from your current neighborhood and networks. If you have lived in one location for a long time, moving may come at a personal and emotional cost, as your children change schools and your household changes doctors, church affiliations, neighbors, and more (O'Sullivan 2003, 433, 457).

Further, if you are a renter you may have a lease in place, and thus not be able to move when you desire; or if you are a homeowner you may need to wait for your current house to sell. Even if you want to leave, financially you may not be able to (Rohe and Watson 2007). The implication of this is that moving may be a hurdle to improving your housing. In some circumstances households will be eager to make the move, under other condi-tions households may want to stay in a location to avoid emotional distress. Finally, as will be discussed in Chapter 5, discrimination still exists in housing markets, meaning households of color have more difficulty finding housing opportunities.

In his book *Evicted: Poverty and Profit in the American City*, sociologist Matthew Des-mond reminds us that not all housing change is made by choice. He narrates the stories of households who faced eviction—some on a serial basis. One of the striking realities for these individuals was the amount of time spent finding new housing opportunities, and how landlords use prior evictions to screen out potential tenants (Desmond 2016). For many forced to change housing, it is a great challenge to locate new housing that is both affordable and obtainable. These households struggle to establish and maintain the benefits of housing as home.

Housing Is Durable and Appreciates Over Time

Depending on the period when it was built, housing can last for several hundreds of years. According to the U.S. Census Bureau, the median year of construction of all housing units in the United States was 1974—putting 50 percent of housing units at over 40 years old (2009). Also, a figure recently calculated by the Census indicates that 13 percent of all occupied housing units are 76 years old or more—that is, they were built in 1939 or prior (U. S. Census n.d.). Add to this durability of the housing stock, the fact that new housing units generally represent an addition of only 2 to 3 percent of the housing stock (O'Sulli-van 2003, 439), and we can conclude there is a large market of "used" housing units.

Housing is not a product that can be built quickly. The construction process includes finding a suitable location, obtaining permits, and managing a variety of contractors and service providers. Economists say that the housing supply is relatively *inelastic*, meaning if demand increases supply will lag behind, as construction (or conversion)[3] takes time. This delay factor has the effect of keeping housing costs high (O'Sullivan 2003). This is explored further in Chapter 8.

To serve for decades, housing also requires ongoing maintenance. A lack of mainte-nance will decrease the livability and longevity of housing. As noted above, the general trend is for housing values to appreciate over time, but this in part rests on investment in routine upkeep. This maintenance is an associated cost for the homeowner or for a landlord (who passes the costs to renters). As noted earlier, the racial composition of areas is correlated to housing appreciation. Appreciation does not happen equally throughout markets; in general, in part related to racism, neighborhoods of color experience less appreciation (Goetz 2007).

Given these realities, if we are to meet the demand for affordable housing in good condition, we must look to the vast amount of existing housing, and not rely solely on new construction. In addition, funding repairs and replacements is essential to maintaining decent housing choices.

Housing Is Shaped by Cultural Norms and Institutional Practices

What is adequate or inadequate housing is shaped by our societal norms—those defined by the larger culture, our more immediate community, and even our families. Chapter 2 explores this extensively, comparing the United States with other places and noting the roots and evolution of our current housing standards. In America, "making it" or assimilating into society is equated with becoming a homeowner. Culture, of course, shapes many of our norms. But the reality of housing—the forms it takes, the housing opportunities some individuals have or don't have—is determined by much more. Our economic structure, political institutions, and social mores all play a role in how, where, and in what forms housing is made available and for whom. These institutions can themselves be involved in setting or evolving the cultural definition of housing. Take for example the most recent housing bubble in the United States. In the wake of this catastrophic financial collapse, some began to rethink the cultural fetish of home ownership, questioning whether it still makes financial sense for all households, in light of the contemporary need for job mobility (Kiviat 2010).

Additionally, our social institutions determine the production process, availability, and access households have to housing. Some examples of this covered in this textbook include the role local government plays in the siting of housing types, how banks set mortgage requirements, the practice of racial discrimination by actors in the real estate market, and the housing incentives provided by the tax code.

Conclusion

In this introduction, we have answered the question of why housing matters and considered the many ways housing is significant to our lives. While the idea of housing is often simplified to "having a roof over our heads," in fact housing shapes our lives in profound ways that go far beyond basic protection. It may go beyond shelter to provide stability, privacy, security, agency, and status. Housing is a topic we all have a personal familiarity with, and thus a personal story about, but it is also a major public policy issue.

We also considered housing as a force within neighborhoods, noting its relationship to quality of life and the many ways your residence limits or expands your life circumstances. Housing's weighty role in the economy and its relationship to household wealth was introduced as well. In sum, housing is connected to mental and physical health, and social and economic well-being.

Each of these aspects is relevant to how the United States responds to the ongoing housing needs among households. The emphasis here on the fundamental importance of housing to emotional and physical well-being should be taken forward to the more detailed exploration of housing. We should approach the policy questions around housing needs and government responses by connecting these issues to the lives of individuals and the power of housing to shape us. As more data are presented and more technical aspects of housing are explored, we must continue to see the humanity that is at the center of housing dilemmas.

Questions and Activities

1. Explain what is meant by "a house becoming a home."
2. Consider the rise of home-related reality television shows, including ones on buying, renovating, and decorating property. What does the fact that these shows are so popular say about American society? What aspects of housing discussed in this chapter are reflected in these home shows?
3. Compare the purchase of an automobile with that of a house. Considering the characteristics of housing discussed in the chapter, how are these purchases similar? How are they different?
4. In the chapter, Clare Cooper Marcus is quoted as saying, "we invest meaning in a place when we are permitted to appropriate and care for it." What does she mean by this? Can you give examples from your experience of being able—or unable—to "appropriate" a place?
5. A new area of research is the mental health resilience of disaster survivors. Consider the experience of Americans who have lost their homes—and all the contents—to natural disasters like Hurricane Katrina, Hurricane Sandy, California wildfires, etc. What would such a loss mean for your life? How might you feel about rebuilding? What should disaster response include to address the specifics of the loss of "home"?
6. What percentage of American households do you think are homeowners? Write down a guess and then look up the figure. Are you surprised by the number, or not, and why?
7. Break the class into small groups. Draw an image of what you see as the "ideal home." Compare this among members of your group and discuss—what is the same in each? What is different? Where does your image of an ideal come from?
8. Using a handout with a simple graphic of a home with blanks for labeling the chimney, roof, walls, doors, windows, and foundation, have students label the parts. Next, consider how in our language we use the terms for these parts to capture wider meanings. For each term, brainstorm a list of its metaphorical associations—that is, the feelings, attitudes, or experiences it is used to illustrate.
9. Generate a list of all the phrases and sayings you can think of that use the word "home." What associations with "home" do you see emerging?
10. Chapter Long Assignment: Housing Autobiography as a Digital Story. As a way of grounding the importance and power of housing, have students prepare a housing autobiography about their personal experiences in the form of a digital story. There are many easy software programs for creating these stories (e.g., iMovie, Photo Story 3, PowerPoint with narration, etc.). While it is good to allow for flexibility of topics, start by assigning a story about where they grew up and how living where they did shaped them. The creation of the story can be done in several steps. Step one can be a physical description of the place—have them write out all they can to describe it. Emphasize the need to relay all sensory aspects including sight, smells, touch, sound, emotions, etc. You can do an in-class paired peer review of this step, having the listening student ask specific questions to get more detail for the description. Step two is to have the student consider how this place shaped them—what they had access to, who they interacted with, places

they went, and so on. After writing this, have them translate it into a 3-minute script and prepare images to support the story. Share it (with student permission) in class. Realize up front that not all stories may reflect a healthy home.

Notes

1. See, for example, Janet Currie, 2011, "Health and Residential Location," in *Neighborhood and Life Chances: How Place Matters in Modern America*, 3–17. Philadelphia: University of Pennsylvania Press; Mary Shaw, 2004, "Housing and Public Health," *Annual Review of Public Health* 25: 397–418; David R. Williams and Chiquita Collins, September–October 2001, "Racial Residential Segregation: A Fundamental Cause of Racial Disparities in Health 2001 Association of Schools of Public Health," *Public Health Reports*—116(5): 404–416.
2. Imputed rent accounts for the value of housing homeowners receive. The provision of this housing is calculated based on prevailing rental rates. See: *Housing Services in the National Economic Accounts* by Nicole Mayerhauser and Marshall Reinsdorf, Bureau of Economic Analysis, September 11, 2007, available at: www.bea.gov/methodologies/
3. "Conversions" are the repurposing of nonresidential buildings (e.g., a former warehouse, school, factory, church, or commercial building), making the changes needed to meet the code requirements for dwelling units.

References

Bipartisan Millenial Housing Commission. 2002. "Meeting Our Nation's Housing Challenges: Report of the Bipartisan Millennial Housing Commission." *Report to Congress.*

Blokland, Talja. 2008. "You Got to Remember You Live in Public Housing." *Housing, Theory and Society* 25(1): 31–46.

Children, President's Task Force on Environmental Risks and Safety Risks to. 2000. *Eliminating Childhood Lead Poisoning: A Federal Strategy Targeting Lead Paint Hazards.* Center for Disease Control.

Cisneros, Sandra. 1991. *The House on Mango Street.* New York: Vintage.

Cresswell, Tim. 2004. *Place: A Short Introduction.* Malden, MA: Blackwell Publishing.

Desmond, Matthew. 2016. *Evicted: Poverty and Profit in the American City.* New York: Crown Publishers.

Devora, Nuemark. 2013. "Drawn to Beauty: The Practice of House-Beautification as Homemaking Amongst the Forcibly Displaced." *Housing, Theory and Society* 30(3): 237–261.

Goetz, Edward G. 2007. "Is Housing Tenure the New Neighborhood Dividing Line?" In *Chasing the American Dream: New Perspectives on Affordable Homeownership*, edited by William M. Roher and Harry L. Watson, 96–110. Ithaca, NY: Cornell University Press.

Goodman, Allen C. 1989. "Topics in Empirical Urban Housing Research." In *The Economics of Housing Markets*, edited by Richard F. Muth and Allen C. Goodman, 45–53. New York: Harwood Academic Publishers GmbH.

Hulchanski, David. 2013. "The Concept of Housing Affordability: Six Contemporary Uses of the Housing-Expenditure-to-Income-Ratio." In *The Affordable Housing Reader*, edited by J. Rosie Tighe and Elizabeth J. Mueller, 79–94. New York: Routledge.

Jackson, Kenneth. 1985. *Crabgrass Frontier.* New York: Oxford Univeristy Press.

Jacobs, Keith, and Jeff Malpas. 2013. "Material Objects Identity and the Home: Toward a Relational Housing Research Agenda." *Housing, Theory and Society* 30(3): 281–292.

Kiviat, Barbara. 2010. "The Case Against Homeownership." *TIME*, September 11: 40–46.

Marcus, Clare Cooper. 1990. "Self-Identity and the Home." In *Housing: Symbol, Structure, Site*, edited by Lisa Taylor, 54–55. New York: Cooper Hewitt Museum.

Marcus, Clare Cooper. 1999. "The House as Symbol of Self." In *Classic Readings in Architecture*, edited by Jay M. Stein and Kent F. Spreckelmeyer, 299–321. Boston: McGraw Hill.

Mazur, Christopher, and Ellen Wilson. 2010. "Housing Characteristics: 2010." *2010 Census Briefs, C2010BR-07*. U.S. Department of Commerce Economics and Statistics Administration. U.S. Census Bureau. www.census.gov/prod/cen2010/briefs/c2010br-07.

Mishel, Lawrence, Josh Bivens, Elise Gould, and Heidi Shierholz. 2012. *The State of Working America*, 12th Edition. Economic Policy Institute Book. New York: Cornell Univeristy Press.

O'Sullivan, Arthur. 2003. *Urban Economics*. Boston: McGraw Hill.

Reid, Carolina Katz. 2007. "Locating the American Dream: Assessing the Neighborhood Benefits of Homeownership." In *Chasing the American Dream*, edited by William M. Rohe and Harry L. Watson, 233–262. New York: Cornell University Press.

Rohe, William M., and Harold L. Watson. 2007. *Chasing the American Dream: New Perspectives on Affordable Homeownership*. Ithaca, NY: Cornell University Press.

Schwartz, Alex. 2015. *Housing Policy in the United States*, 3rd Edition. New York: Routledge.

Sykes, Lore Latrice. 2008. "Cashing in on the American Dream: Racial Differences in Housing Values 1970–2000." *Housing, Theory and Society* 25(4): 254–274.

Tuan, Yi-Fu. 2012. "Epilogue: Home as Elsewhere." In *Heimat at the Intersection of Memory and Space*, edited by Friederike Eigle and Jens Kugele, 226–240. Boston: Walter de Grufter GmbH.

U.S. Census. 2009. "Table 988. Housing Units-Characteristics by Tenure and Region: 2009." *Based on American Housing Survey.*

U.S. Census. n.d. "Glossary." Accessed February 7, 2018. www.census.gov/glossary/.

U.S. Census. n.d. "S2504 Physical Housing Characteristics for Occupied Housing Units 2009–2013." *American Community Survey 5-Year Estimates.*

HOUSING AND CULTURE

Housing meets a universal need for shelter, yet this protection comes in many diverse forms. A global survey of housing types would reveal homes of varied materials, different sizes and layouts, and distinct development patterns. The composition of households and the design of communities are, in part, a reflection of cultural preferences and values. Our culture influences who we have living in our homes—spouse, children, pets, elderly parents, friends, renters, or others—and for how long. It also shapes the way we design and inhabit the interiors of our spaces. These same cultural ideals are echoed at the macro level in the manner that residential areas are planned and arranged.

This chapter will examine the intersection of housing and culture by considering the cultural values that have profoundly influenced housing in the United States. The strong American values of independence, individualism, privacy, and status, along with the prominence of the nuclear family (parent/s and children) will be explored. These cultural values will be contrasted with the housing choices of other cultures, and throughout the chapter the implications of the diversity of cultures within American society are considered.

What Is Culture?

To explore the ideas and questions raised by thinking about culture and housing, we must understand the meaning of "culture." A complicated word that can signify many different meanings, *culture* for the purpose of this chapter is the body of customs, beliefs, social forms, and material traits that constitute a group of people's way of life (Rothman 2014; Rubenstein 2016). Culture, then, is more than material objects such as dress or food; it is also the nonmaterial concepts and norms that shape behavior and determine societal structure. When it comes to housing in America, housing tenure, family rituals, home décor, living arrangements, and neighborhood design are all influenced by cultural norms. In this chapter, we will explore the many ways our homes and home lives are reflections of American culture. Of course, speaking of "American" culture is a simplification, as there are regional, ethnic, and religious variations that are not accounted for in this generalized approach.

Cultural Preference for Homeownership

Walt Whitman famously wrote:

> A house to live in is the third great necessity; food and clothing only being before it. And fur-
> thermore, it is in some sense true that a man is not a whole and complete man unless he *owns* a

house and the ground it stands on. Men are created owners of the earth. Each was intended to possess his piece of it; and however the modifications of civilized life have covered this truth, or changed the present phase of it, it is still indicated by the universal instinctive desire for landed property, and by the fuller sense of independent manhood which comes from the possession of it.

(Whitman 1856)

This excerpt highlights the sentiments of the American cultural desire to own a home. Embedded in this desire is the culturally defined right of land ownership that came with colonial dominance and has become legally and politically institutionalized in the United States.

The aspiration for homeownership dates back more than two hundred years to President Thomas Jefferson's ideal of the working farmer as the backbone of early America. At the time of Jefferson's presidency, to be a renter was to be dependent on landlords of a higher social class. Such dependency undermined free choice—especially when it came to exercising the right to vote. On the other hand, a farmer with his own land, and thus the ability to care for his family, had the freedom to vote for what he truly believed was the best candidate or policy—not what he was told to support or what would enrich his benefactor. The belief in independence achieved through land ownership endured throughout the nineteenth century and was part of the motivation that lead to hundreds of thousands of people settling the western frontier where, after the passage of the Homestead Act in 1862, a man (initially not all men) could own the land he worked to improve (Cannato 2010).

In subsequent decades, homeownership continued to be an American ideal, as shown through movements such as the Better Home Campaign (1922) run by the United States Department of Commerce. This campaign, supported with print ads and posters, encouraged American homeownership as well as home beautification and modernization. It urged people to build, remodel, and improve their homes. Herbert Hoover, president during the Better Home Campaign, is quoted as stating:

It is in the home that character and high ideals are best developed. The right kind of home life makes for true success in life and means progress for the nation as a whole. To own a home and to make it convenient and attractive, a home where health and happiness, affection and loyalty prevail, brings out the best that lies in every member of the family. Saving for homeownership for instance develops thrift and self denial: a thing of lasting value is kept in the foreground and all energies are bent toward attaining it.

(Saline Observer 1926)

For Americans, homeownership is more than a fervent cultural preference for independence and control. We have come to associate the tenure of one's home as a statement of character. The elevation of homeownership in American culture has, inevitably, both historically and currently, cast those that rent their home as inferior. Renters are characterized as transitory, lacking community investment, and not as dedicated to maintaining their homes. These beliefs, of course, are not necessarily accurate assessments of those who choose to rent, but such broad generalizations undoubtedly reinforce the prevailing preference for homeownership in the United States. Today, the perceptions of renters versus buyers may differ based on location: in the suburbs renters may be seen as not putting roots down in a community or lacking the resources to buy, while in cities, where renting is more the norm, there is much less judgment (Rohe, VanZandt, and McCarthy 2001).

A recent large-scale survey undertaken after a rebound from the housing crisis of 2008 found that the American preference for homeownership is still strong. When renters were asked if they desired to become homeowners, 72 percent identified it as a personal goal (Hart Research Associates 2013). But the survey (and other research) does indicate that Americans are rethinking their elevation of homeownership, so renting may become more socially acceptable. Among the respondents, 61 percent indicated that renters can be just as successful in achieving the American dream as homeowners—a finding that reflects the beginnings of a fundamental redefining of the American dream. Other researchers have suggested that Americans should rethink homeownership, because of an increased need for job mobility and less certainty around housing appreciation (Mallach 2011). These recent studies submit that low-income households may not always find homeownership to be economically beneficial. It remains to be seen to what degree the cultural values of independence, control, and status will be rewritten if economic realities make renting a more rational choice.

Homeownership rates across countries and cultures vary dramatically. One important study by Huber and Schmidt in 2016 revealed that even within the most highly industrialized economies, homeownership rates range from 44 percent in Switzerland (2011) to 83 percent in Spain (2011), with the United States in the middle at 65 percent (2013). While these rates may also reflect institutional, legal, and economic differences among countries, a recent study suggests that a purely economic analysis is not sufficient to explain the variation. This study showed that cultural norms are strongly correlated with a drive toward homeownership, and a narrow economic model will fail to detect this importance. Greater incomes alone could not explain higher homeownership rates. The study also found that immigrants to the United States (in comparison with non-immigrants of similar circumstances) initially followed the tenure pattern of their cultural heritage, although this faded with residency and along succeeding generations (Huber and Schmidt 2016).

While in the United States homeownership has had ties to economic security, financial opportunity, privacy, individuality, and status, these elements are not necessarily

Figure 2.1 Japanese household made up of an extended family
Source: Image © Alamay, used with permission

motivators for homeownership in other countries. For example, in Japan, where the rate of homeownership is like that in the United States, homeownership is not rooted in a cultural desire for independence or a statement of individualism, but is based in a family-oriented collectivist ideology. For the Japanese, being a homeowner is a way to contribute to the greater good by caring for extended family members. By being able to take in vulnerable family members, the Japanese homeowner spares society the burden of housing and caring for needy persons (Ronald 2004).

House and Household Size

The layout and overall size of American living spaces is indicative of the cultural connection between housing and status, and a preference for privacy and specialty spaces. The physical size of new homes in the United States has steadily grown over time and a different set of expectations for an ideal home has emerged. Today most families prefer that each child has a room of his/her own, as opposed to having siblings share rooms. Home buyers may want multiple bathrooms in the home, providing a bathroom for guests to use that is separate from their own or the bathroom their children use. In general, for many Americans, having extra space and the ability of multiple people to achieve privacy while under the same roof has become a priority. Moreover, specialty, single-use spaces, such as "TV rooms" and formal dining rooms, have increased home sizes. The post–World War II period of affluence brought much change to the norm of housing in America. Table 2.1 summarizes the differences in the typical American home between 1949 and 1999. These differences have contributed to an increase in the size of the average American home.

Interestingly, the American interest in homes with more square footage does *not* reflect a growing family size in America. Over the last 50 years, as homes have become larger in the U.S. family sizes have become smaller (Figure 2.2). All of this is happening while the "traditional" type of family with mom, dad, and children is becoming a smaller percentage of all households. Many nontraditional types of families are on the rise, including single mothers and fathers, couples who choose not to have children, and the elderly living alone.

Figure 2.3 provides a comparison on house size between the United States and several other industrialized countries. The United States average house size is as much as 2 to 3 times greater than other countries.

Table 2.1 Affluence and Changes in the Typical American Home

1949 TYPICAL AMERICAN HOME	1999 TYPICAL AMERICAN HOME
One story	2 stories
2 bedrooms (or less)	3+ bedrooms
1 bathroom	3 bathrooms
No garage	2 car garage
No Air conditioning	Central air conditioning
Heated by Coal	Natural gas
983 sq. ft	2000 sq ft

Source: Summarized from "Legacy of the Housing Act of 1949: The Past, Present, and Future of Federal Housing and Urban Policy" by Robert E. Lang & Rebecca R. Sohmer in *Housing Policy Debate*, 2000, 11(2): 291–298.

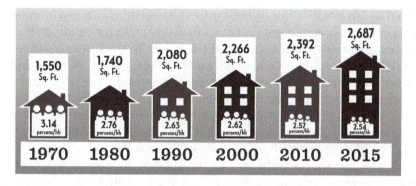

Figure 2.2   Average Household Size versus Average House Size. Graphic© Allison Terkelsen, used with permission

Source: Data from U.S. Census Bureau, Characteristics of New Housing and Families and Living Arrangements

While, on average, homes in the United States are increasing in size, in very recent years there has been a niche movement of tiny houses and "tiny living" in general (The Tiny Life 2015). The tiny house movement involves individuals choosing to significantly downsize the space in which they live from the typical square footage of an American home (averaging about 2,600 square feet) to a home measuring between 100 and 400 square feet. The emphasis is on simpler living in a smaller and more efficient space, saving money, and creating a smaller environmental footprint (The Tiny Life 2015). The concept of tiny homes also emphasizes the flexibility of space, because in such small dwellings, space must serve multiple purposes. Seating areas also serve as storage spaces, bathrooms also serve as laundry areas, and so forth. Tiny living also appears on the HGTV network with *Tiny House Hunters*, and *Tiny House, Big Living*, indicating interest and perhaps some societal traction for this type of lifestyle.

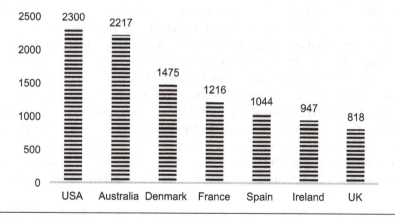

Figure 2.3   Average New House Size by Country (Sq Ft)

Source: Data from 2003–2006 at http://news.bbc.co.uk/2/hi/uk_news/magazine/8201900.stm

Dominance of the Single-Family House

Homeownership is most closely related to the detached (standalone) single-family house of the American suburbs. Such development remains the dominant residential pattern in America (Hayden 2003). While ownership can also occur in attached housing, such as townhouses or row houses and even condominiums in multiunit buildings, the majority of the American housing stock is detached single family units. According to the U.S. Census (2014), single family detached units make up 64 percent of all housing in the United States. Of these units, 84 percent are owner-occupied.

There are many excellent architectural histories of America that tell the story of changing forms of residential development and housing types (see, for example, *Crabgrass Frontier* by Kenneth Jackson, *The Social History of Housing* by Gwendolyn Wright, *Building Suburbia* by Dolores Hayden, and *Bourgeois Utopias* by Robert Fishman). These histories see the rise of the suburbs as one change that embodies Americans' search for a house centered on the nuclear family that was private and near nature (Hayden 2003). The development pattern of exclusively residential neighborhoods with lots providing defined rear yards and frontage on quiet streets fulfilled Americans' ideal of owning and controlling a piece of land. The rear yards became places for private family entertainment, and the front was the public face of these houses, communicating with neighbors and establishing status (Jackson 1985). In her book, *Zoned in the USA*, Sonia Hirt notes the existence and dominance of single-family-only zones or districts in American communities is unique—other industrialized countries do not have similar regulations. Hirt goes on to describe this approach to community planning as the etching of American cultural ideals into the landscape (Hirt 2014).

There was, and is, a diversity of housing types and lifestyles in the United States, but there is no denying that the single-family suburb has played a central role in American life. It is what architectural historian Gwendolyn Wright calls "the model home"—an in-the-flesh example of idealized living that conveys a common social meaning (Wright, *Prescribing the Model Home* 1991). Drawing attention to the role of gender in housing, Wright summarizes how the early suburbs were an extension of the Victorian "cult of domesticity" and the popular view of "home as the man's refuge, the women's protection, a place of peace and inspiration, a reward for diligence and thrift" (Wright 2005, 145). Another historian who has examined American culture, housing, and gender is Dolores Hayden (Hayden 2003; Hayden 2002). In several books, she has described our housing history as one deeply connected to gender prescriptions. The suburban ideal served a world where men went off to work in the city and women were homemakers and caretakers for children. Hayden has written persuasively on how this cultural norm is outdated, yet the housing arrangement persists. The suburban residential pattern makes life for working parents, especially women, more difficult. Long distances between destinations, and women's continued burden of homemaking, add stress to daily life (Hayden 2002). Hayden suggests there is a need for alternatives, where the details of work and the work of home are facilitated through community design, and options to fit many family arrangements are made available.

While offering a refuge of privacy and comfort for residents, it must be remembered that the suburbs developed in an exclusionary manner. Part of the initial appeal of these places had to do with the explicit lack of racial, religious, and class diversity, often enforced by law. Today's suburbs are more diverse, though not assuredly tolerant. Beyond the suburbs there is urban revitalization with new higher density infill development happening. Rural living is also an option. However, the suburbs still appeal to Americans as a place to live.

Use of the Home Space

It seems only natural that food, a daily source of nourishment, should play a large role in the culture of the home. Rituals of food preparation and consumption reflect the culture of households. The sharing of meals is a significant part of developing and reinforcing a household's cultural identity, whether that is a larger cultural connection or one that defines the individual household (Valentine 1999). Food preparation and eating traditions highlight the significance of the home's space, and how use of space can influence our social interactions and family dynamics. Some families may have a ritual of sitting around a table together at dinner while others eat while they watch television. Some families may listen to music as they prepare a meal or perhaps have a less structured eating style where family members prepare food on their own and eat independently. Each family has a different way food is prepared, served, and consumed as well as a varying environment that is created around such food rituals. In addition, the ways that families or family members articulate distinctiveness in their food preparation and rituals in the home also emphasize individuality of that family. This might include, for example, the merging of the different cultural backgrounds of the parents (Valentine 1999).

The way people approach the beautification of their home is influenced by their culture, and it is important to keep in mind that individuals have culturally specific ideas of what beautification means. When people are designing and decorating their homes, they utilize the norms for interpreting space associated with their own culture (Olesen 2012). In turn, people with different backgrounds can experience the same space differently. If your traditional cultural norm is for families to share small spaces or you grew up sharing a smaller space, your memories and emotions may lead you to prefer these spaces. This also means that a space that one person may experience as cozy could feel confining to another person who is used to having more personal space. The same could apply to decorative pieces within the home. Perhaps you grew up in a home with many different items and mementos adorning shelves and walls. What you might find to be a visually beautiful space could be experienced as a space that feels quite cluttered to another person from a varying cultural background. Decorating to reflect an affinity for culture is not restricted to the culture of one's family of origin. For example, those who adopt children from China often decorate their homes with items from Chinese culture to connect their children to their cultural roots (Traver 2007).

It is also evident that people, even unknowingly, utilize ideas and influences from other cultures when making decisions about how they are decorating their home, and popular trends can reflect these patterns as well. This is not surprising given that America is a culturally diverse and globally linked society. For example, historically, the Japanese, being a traditionally floor-seated culture, have used low chairs and tables, pillows, and mats on the floor for seating, and such influences are evident in many American homes. Others may have some Parisian influence in their homes—using the same sort of soft pastel colors that were utilized in palaces belonging to French royalty. Richer and warmer colors in a home could be seen as having some Indian influence—a culture in which reds, oranges, greens, yellows, and purples can play a prominent role. Those who choose a simpler furniture style with natural woods may have some Scandinavian influence, and so forth.

Popular culture is also attuned to the American pursuit of homeownership as a vehicle for independence and status. The Home & Garden Television channel (HGTV) has risen in popularity in recent years, with record high ratings in 2015 (Jones 2016). The shows on HGTV attract more than six million people each month and include shows such as *Flip or Flop*, on buying houses that require significant work, redoing them, and selling them for a profit; *Property Brothers*, on purchasing a home requiring significant renovations to meet buyer's needs and tastes; *Fixer Upper*, on buying, renovating, and decorating homes; and *Ellen's Design Challenge*, focused on the design of furniture. HGTV seems to be popular among the category of "upscale" women between the ages of 25 to 54, finishing in 2015 for the ninth year in a row as the top-rated channel for this group (Jones 2016). The success of these shows indicates the cultural fascination on the part of a portion of American society with controlling personal space and expressing individuality.

Culturally Based Housing Design

Professionals in the field of home design are exploring culturally sensitive housing design—considering the differences of varying cultural groups and creating home designs to support such differences (Hadjiyanni 2005). Such housing could be particularly important for new immigrants who are assimilating to the United States while also wanting to maintain their own cultural practices (Hadjiyanni 2005). An example of a group with varying housing needs based on culture are the Hmong people of Southeast Asia, many of whom immigrated to the United States during the 1980s. Interviews with the Hmong have revealed that living in typical American housing limited their ability to practice their shamanist religious traditions, thereby creating stress in their lives. The Hmong's religious beliefs necessitate that they carry out religious ceremonies in their home at an altar in the house placed across from the main entry. There were additional constraints identified by the Hmong related to cooking, particularly since open American kitchens meant the smells from frying and using spices would permeate the rest of the house—often causing them to cook with propane gas in the basement or outside. Storage of large amounts of food for celebrations as well as large-size cooking utensils in standard-size American kitchens was also identified as a challenge. Examples of some solutions for these challenges for the Hmong could include an altar wall close to the front entry, a kitchen that can be closed off by a Hmong family but kept open by an American family, and a patio that can be used as an outdoor cooking area. These types of design solutions could integrate the needs of Hmong families but are also in line with the mainstream market (Hadjiyanni 2005).

Many other examples of different cultural ways of eating, cooking, sleeping, and praying in the home space are relevant to housing form and layout (Hadjiyanni, Hirani, and Jordan 2012). Immigrant families accustomed to living with extended family (inclusive of relatives beyond parents and children) under one roof may look for homes with additional sleeping areas; other groups may prefer two sitting areas (one for each sex); and still others an outdoor kitchen (Ruiz 2015). Architect Teddy Cruz has documented the modifications Latino immigrants have made to housing in southern California. He suggests local codes and zoning should be rewritten to allow for the culturally functional designs that come from these adaptations (McKone 2011). Ultimately the lesson that most American builders are learning is that home designs should be flexible, so that spaces can be altered to accommodate a variety of cultural preferences and practices. As discussed in Chapter 1, housing is often an expression of identity, and this includes manifestations of cultural identity.

Leaving Home

One aspect of family composition to consider within American culture and beyond, is the expectation of when children should leave their childhood home and establish a home of their own. Both negative and positive generalizations come from the choice of when to leave the family home. Children who leave home earlier can be seen as distant from their parents or families. On the other hand, such behavior may be characterized as particularly independent, successful, and self-sufficient. Those children who stay longer may be characterized as dependent on their parents, lazy, or not having the professional success to establish themselves in their own home. On the plus side, they are considered close with their families, and perhaps as sensible, for saving the money they would otherwise need to put toward rent or a mortgage. The cultural expectations vary among different countries as well as individual households. A recent study (Table 2.2) compares the average age of leaving home in 15 European countries plus Israel (Leopold 2012).

In terms of American young adults leaving their family homes, one of the interesting results that the 2012 U.S. Census revealed was that in the United States, more men and women aged 18 to 34 lived in their parent's home than in the early 2000s (Vespa, Lewis, and Kreider 2013). This delayed "launching" is not a surprise, as this group is undergoing the conventional indicators of adulthood (such as starting a family, leaving home, and establishing stable careers) later, as well.

Nuclear Family

While debated by some, the consensus is that the American norm for families changed from an extended family to a nuclear family during the twentieth century (Ruggles 1994). This change was related to industrialization and work outside the home, education

Table 2.2 Average Age to Leave Home and Distance of a Grown Child's Home from Parents' Home in 15 Countries

COUNTRY	AGE OF LEAVING HOME	DISTANCE (IN MILES)
Denmark	19.9	50.4
Sweden	20.2	50.6
Netherlands	20.0	36.6
Israel	22.1	38.9
Austria	22.2	41.4
France	22.4	40.6
Germany	22.5	45.7
Ireland	22.7	56.2
Czech Republic	23.2	26.3
Belgium	23.5	19.0
Greece	23.9	28.6
Poland	24.1	24.5
Spain	25.2	24.6
Italy	26.1	17.1

Source: Adapted from "The Legacy of Leaving Home: Long-Term Effects of Co-residents on Parent-Child Relationships," *Journal of Marriage and Family* 74: 399–412 (2012), Thomas Leopold.

Figure 2.4   Mom Negotiates the Rent

Source: Cartoon © Roger K. Lewis, used with permission

opening up career opportunities, as well as improved health for the elderly. American senior citizens are said to "prefer the intimacy-at-a-distance that comes from living apart from grown children" (Treas and Mazumdar 2002). Older parent/s live on their own, aging in place, or relocating to retirement villages, assisted living, or nursing homes. We developed these specialized housing arrangements that segregate by age in order to meet our cultural expectations for the elderly to reside independently from family members. These culturally defined arrangements are not without concerns, as independent elderly may have limited funds, feel isolated, lack mobility, and experience undetected medical needs (Joint Center for Housing Studies 2014). Those who are unable to live independently are housed in institutions that have been negatively characterized as "warehousing the elderly" (Stewart 2006).

Multigenerational Households

A housing trend challenging the nuclear family housing norm is the increasing number of multigenerational households (households that include two or more adult generations or that include grandparents and grandchildren) in the United States. Nineteen percent of the American population, or a record number of 60.6 million people lived with multiple generations in 2014. This was an increase from 17 percent in 2009 (when the most recent housing recession ended), and 18 percent in 2012 (Pew Research Center 2016; Cohn and Passel 2016). This trend was at a low 12 percent in 1980, but accelerated during the recession in 2007–2009 when unemployment was high and many young adults moved back in with their parents. Multigenerational living, however, has persisted past the recession, most likely due to the associated benefits of being able to pay off loans and debt more easily, to have grandparents provide childcare, and to care for elderly parents at home (Graham and Niederhaus 2013; Carrins 2016). Another explanation for the increase in multigenerational households is growing racial and ethnic diversity in the United States. Asian and Hispanic populations are growing more rapidly than the white population, and those groups are likelier to live in multigenerational households (Cohn and Passel 2016). Changes in family structure may lead to greater diversity of housing options.

Conclusion

The American independent spirit, along with a desire for freedom, privacy, and status, gave rise to housing that fulfilled these cultural ideals. Increasing affluence has shaped the interior layouts of our homes, and cultural diversity within American society has led to remodeling and reuse to accommodate many different cultural practices. The large-scale pattern of residential development also tells a story about American culture. Our agrarian, land-holding roots evolved as the country grew and developed. This country has urban, suburban, and rural areas and hosts a variety of housing types. Yet the single-family home on its own lot retains power as a symbol of American aspirations.

Questions and Activities

1. Reflect on your own experience of living at home and consider the following:
   - How was your home decorated? Were there photographs displayed? A vase of flowers? Framed artwork? Mementos and souvenirs? What visually connected your home to your family's culture(s)?
   - What were your responsibilities in keeping up your home? Were there chores that you were expected to complete as part of living there?
   - How was space used in your home? Did you have your own room? Did you share a room with other family members? What were other notable uses of space?
   - Do you live with your parents currently? Did your parents encourage your living at home as long as possible? Was there a point in time when they encouraged you to move out of the house and find your own place to live?
   - What is your ideal vision of home as you consider the future? Do you want a spacious home that allows for plenty of privacy? Your own separate bathroom that you don't share with others? A guest room for your visitors? Or do you see yourself in a smaller, cozier home?
2. Do you watch any reality shows related to home buying or home improvement on HGTV or another network? Which ones? What appeals to you about these programs?
3. Suburban development has been criticized for being boring and uniform. The chapter discusses the positive aspects of such housing, which appeals to an American sense of an ideal life. Do you believe there are downsides to such housing? If so, explain them and consider if you think the positives outweigh the negatives.
4. Consider, and list, the variety of household types there are (variety in terms of number of members, relationship between members, etc.). Compare the nuclear

family with the extended or multigenerational family. What are the advantages and disadvantages of each? Do we have forms of housing to meet the needs of all household types?

References

Cannato, Vincent J. 2010. "A Home of One's Own." *National Affairs* 3: 69–86, p. 72.

Carrins, Ann. 2016. "Multigenerational Households: The Benefits, and Perils." *The New York Times*, August 12.

Cohn, D'vera, and Jeffrey S. Passel. 2016. "A Record 60.6 Million Americans Live in Multigenerational Households." *Fact Tank*, August 11.

Graham, John L., and Sharon Graham Niederhaus. 2013. *All in the Family: A Practical Guide for Successful Multigenerational Living.* Lanham, MD: Taylor Trade Publishing.

Hadjiyanni, Tasoulla. 2005. "Culturally Sensitive Housing: Considering Difference." *Implications* 3(1): 1–6.

Hadjiyanni, Tasoulla, Aditi Hirani, and Cathy Jordan. 2012. "Toward Culturally Sensitive Housing: Eliminating Health Disparities by Accounting for Health." *Housing and Society* 39(2): 149–164.

Hart Research Associates. 2013. "How Housing Matters: Americans' Attitudes Transformed by the Housing Crisis & Changing Lifestyles." *Report of Survey Findings*. Washington, DC: MacArthur Foundation.

Hayden, Dolores. 2002. *Redesigning the American Dream: The Future of Housing, Work and Family Life Revised and Expanded.* New York: W.W. Norton & Company.

Hayden, Dolores. 2003. *Building Suburbia: Green Fields and Urban Growth 1820–2000.* New York: Vintage House.

Hirt, Sonia A. 2014. *Zoned in the USA: The Origins and Implications of American Land-use Regulation.* Ithaca: Cornell University Press.

Huber, Stefanie J., and Tobias Schmidt. 2016. "Cross-Country Differences in Homeownership: A Cultural Phenomenon." *Working Paper*, Unpublished. https://dl.dropboxusercontent.com/u/9710700/JMPcompanion1_StefanieHuber.pdf.

Jackson, Kenneth T. 1985. *Crabgrass Frontier: The Suburbanization of the United States.* New York: Oxford University Press.

Joint Center for Housing Studies. 2014. *Housing America's Older Adults: Meeting the Needs of an Aging Population.* Cambridge, MA: Harvard University.

Jones, Rachel. 2016. *HGTV Finishes 2015 With Highest-Rated Year Ever*, January 4. Accessed September 29, 2016. www.scrippsnetworksinteractive.com/newsroom/company-news/HGTV-Finishes-2015-With-Highest-Rated-Year-Ever/.

Leopold, Thomas. 2012. "The Legacy of Leaving Home: Long-Term Effects of Coresidents on Parent-Child Relationships." *Journal of Marriage and Family* 74: 399–412.

Mallach, Alan. 2011. "Building Sustainable Ownership: Rethinking Public Policy Toward Lower-Income Homeownership." *Discussion Papers Community Development Studies and Education.* Philadelphia: Federal Reserve Bank of Philadelphia.

McKone, Jonna. 2011. *The City Fix: Case Studies of Latino New Urbanism*, January 20. Accessed November 20, 2016. http://thecityfix.com/blog/case-studies-of-latino-new-urbanism-san-diego-and-hudson/.

Olesen, Bodil Birkebaek. 2012. "Ethnic Objects in Domestic Interiors: Space, Atmosphere and the Making of Home." *Home Cultures* 7(1): 25–42.

Pew Research Center. 2016. *Pew Research Center Analysis of U.S. Decennial Census Data, 1950–2000, and 2006–2014 American Community Survey (IPUMS).* Washington, DC: Pew Research Center.

Rohe, William H., Shannon VanZandt, and George McCarthy. 2001. "Social Benefits and Costs of Homeownership." *Affordable Housing Issues* (Shimberg Center for Affordable Housing, University of Florida) 11(3): 1–4.

Ronald, Richard. 2004. "Homeownership, Ideology and Diversity: Re-evalutaing Concepts of Housing Ideology in the Case of Japan." *Housing, Theory and Society* 21(2): 49–64.

Rothman, Joshua. 2014. *The Meaning of "Culture"*, December 26. Accessed June 22, 2017. www.newyorker.com/books/joshua-rothman/meaning-culture.

Rubenstein, James M. 2016. *Contemporary Human Geography*. Oxford, OH: Pearson Education, Inc.

Ruggles, Steven. 1994. "The Transformation of American Family Structure." *American Historical Review*: 103–128.

Ruiz, Fernando Pagés. 2015. "Building Multiculturally." *Shelterforce*: 5.

Saline Observer. 1926. "Saline Observer." *Digital Michigan Newspapers*. January 21. Accessed November 29, 2016. https://digmichnews.cmich.edu/cgi-bin/michigan?a=d&d=Washtenaw SO19260121.1.5.

Stewart, Charles Jr. 2006. "New Roles for Government: Warehousing the Elderly." *Challenge* 49(4): 73–85.

The Tiny Life. 2015. *What Is the Tiny House Movement?* Accessed September 29, 2016. thetinylife.com.

Traver, Amy E. 2007. "Home(land) Décor: China Adoptive Parents' Consumption of Chinese Cultural Objects for Display in Their Homes." *Qualitative Sociology* 30(1): 201–220.

Treas, Judith, and Shampa Mazumdar. 2002. "Older People in America's Immigrant Families Dilemmas of Dependence, Integration, and Isolation." *Journal of Aging Studies*: 243–258.

Valentine, Gil. 1999. "Eating in: Home, Consumption and Identity." *The Sociological Review* 47(3): 491–524.

Vespa, Jonathan, Jamie M. Lewis, and Rose M. Kreider. 2013. "American's Families and Living Arrangements: 2012." *U.S. Department of Commerce Economics and Statistics Administration, United States Census Bureau*.

Whitman, Walt. 1856. "New York Dissected." *Life Illustrated* 19: 93.

Wright, Gwendolyn. 1991. "Prescribing the Model Home." *Social Research*: 213–225.

Wright, Gwendolyn. 2005. "Women's Aspirations and the Home." In *Gender and Planning: A Reader*, edited by Susan Fainstein and Lisa Servon, 141–155. New Brunswick, NJ: Rutgers University Press.

3

FRAMING HOUSING
Disciplinary Approaches and Ideologies

Many housing researchers produce empirical works documenting affordability, vacancies, physical conditions, housing densities, and much more. These descriptive works are helpful for researchers, along with activists and government officials, in recognizing patterns and recording changes. For instance, researchers have noted slower rates of home-ownership obtainment for households of color, concentrations of subsidized tenants in low-resource neighborhoods, and a mismatch of location between affordable housing and job openings (Sharp and Hall 2014; Andersson, Haltiwanger, Kutzbach, Pollakowski, and Weinberg 2014; McClure, Schwartz, and Taghavi 2015). But this type of work often provides only a partial understanding of the realm of housing (Atkinson and Jacobs 2016). Empirical work does not necessarily answer larger questions, such as: Why did the trend occur? How did residents experience the change? Why did the change happen when it did? Or what can be done to reverse a negative or accelerate a positive housing outcome? Even with widespread agreement on the dimensions of housing-related conditions, researchers may attribute very different causes to the same data.

In order to make sense of housing, one must apply a framework, or context, for the issue being examined. Imagine a camera: if you frame a photo with a wide-angle lens, what you see differs from what you see through a standard or telephoto lens. When you frame a problem, you automatically define what is relevant and narrow the set of solutions, closing out possibilities that exist within different frameworks. All research is based on a specific set of assumptions about how the world works. These assumptions are often implicit in research, but are important to assessing the validity of the findings. Making these assumptions explicit in the form of a theory of housing is an important part of being able to challenge these underlying assumptions and refine them to improve the model (Phillips 2010). Therefore when reading it is critical to ask yourself what framework a researcher is using—it ends up shaping the outcomes.

One way to study housing is to create a model of how we think the system (or systems, as housing is part of a larger framework) works and then test it through research. A model should help us understand the why and how of the fluctuations in housing conditions. It should identify both the direction and magnitude of factors that influence housing outcomes and capture our experiences with housing. Based on the model, system interventions can be designed to achieve certain outcomes. The model indicates connections among parts of the system, and shows how making a change in a characteristic will ultimately lead to a goal. It also provides an opportunity to check assumptions and see if, in fact, the theorized connections exist. In this way housing is no different than other areas of study. Model-building is at the heart of all problem solving.

Figure 3.1 is an example of a conceptual model. It shows how a researcher theorized the process of household decision-making around housing. It notes the factors involved

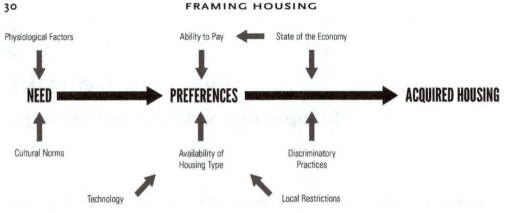

Figure 3.1   Example of Housing Choice Model

Source: Lindamood, Suzanne. "Housing as a Process: A Position Paper on Housing Education," *Housing and Society*, 1974, (2: 22–28)

and the relationship between these factors, including some social, economic, and political factors. It hypothesizes that the process begins with a need that is shaped by both cultural norms and physiology. This gets translated into a housing preference, which is limited by availability. The availability is shaped by other forces, and the preference is constrained by economics and discrimination. Research can test the varied hypothesized relationships and connections that are part of the model and uncover aspects of the housing process not addressed by the model. For example, one might ask where in this model does the self-realization (discussed in Chapter 1) that is part of home appear? And how does this model account for a household prioritizing access to quality schools or jobs?

This example also highlights the challenge of modeling the intricacies of the housing process. This model incorporates only one part of the larger context—absent are decisions made by many other actors (e.g., housing developers, real estate agents, bankers, regulators, etc.) and the pulls and pushes of significant forces outside of the immediate realm of housing (e.g., demographic / life cycle shifts, energy concerns, forces driving cultural norm shifts, existential orientations, etc.).

Some have criticized the realm of housing as being under-theorized; it is suggested that a heavily empirical and practical bias in housing holds the field back (Atkinson and Jacobs 2016). The absence of explicit theory can decrease our ability to learn from the data produced, limiting the effectiveness of interventions and circumscribing our ability to predict end results. Others suggest that housing does not need its own theories, as it is really a part of larger theorized concerns such as poverty. Certainly, housing is nested within a much larger system and does not exist apart from other societal functions. This complexity should not dissuade us from attempting to shed light on households' experiences of housing and to deepen our comprehension, with the goal of achieving an American society where all have a place to call home.

The goal of this chapter is to prepare you to critically approach housing knowledge, recognizing the need to reveal the framework being applied and asking how it shapes the conclusions reached, and then considering what it overlooks. We will explore the housing frameworks within two different arenas, summarizing materials you can delve into more deeply on your own. First, we explore how a variety of academic disciplines approach housing studies, noting the theories, models, and methods of research that are favored. This discussion does not identify a "right" and "wrong" way to view housing, but highlights that there are many approaches with unique strengths and weaknesses and which may be more or less applicable to specific concerns. From this discussion, we see that multiple lenses are needed to fully capture the forces at work in housing. Second, we turn to political ideologies and note the general models used by different political orientations when considering how to adequately house Americans. Political ideologies may privilege one lens over another or favor a type of hybrid that leans toward a more practical position, combining theoretical orientations.

Disciplinary Approaches

Despite acknowledgment that the real world does not operate within separate realms, academics approach the world this way. Here four disciplines are explored as they relate to housing: economics, sociology, philosophy, and urban planning. While others could be added to this list (political science, feminism, geography, anthropology, and more), these are used to highlight distinct and frequently used approaches to studying housing.

Economists, sociologists, philosophers, and urban planners all have models for how the world works. Each model is developed as a means of capturing a very complex reality, and as such, each is a simplification of the world. These models are extensively shaped by the methods of study used within each discipline. Economists favor quantitative methods while sociologists employ interpretive and qualitative approaches to studying the world. These methodologies point to different ways to determine priorities for action and inform ways to achieve change. It is important to note that while we can speak in general terms about the orientation of a discipline, there can be many variations within it. As an example, the vast majority of economists (80 percent or more) subscribe to the orthodox view (explained below) (Phillips 2010)—but other economists have a more radical view (although they understand the dominant paradigm and are keenly aware of the distinctions between it and their own view). The limitations of individual disciplinary frameworks are well known and have invigorated a strong interdisciplinary movement.[1] It can be quite challenging to synthesize different disciplinary approaches into one comprehensive model to guide interventions (Phillips 2010). Yet, this richer approach is clearly a more accurate portrayal of real world happenings.

Economics and Housing

Mainstream economics views housing as a commodity that is produced and consumed. Economists examine the behavior of the consumers of housing and those that seek to profit from providing housing. There is a set of basic principles that are the foundation of the traditional economic model. In the simplest of forms, these include conditions for a perfect market (no monopolies exist, consumers have complete knowledge of choices, and resources can move as needed) and the following (Hays 1995):

1. People act out of self-interest and make rational choices in order to increase their material well-being.
2. The market, in a self-regulating manner, is an efficient and innovative producer, devoting resources (capital, land, labor, funds) as needed to meet demands, maximize profits, and minimize waste (Phillips 2010).
3. Government is best at playing only a supplementary and minimal role in the market. Government interventions in terms of regulations, taxes, or subsidies are best used sparingly and only as necessary to compensate for market limitations or failures.

Using this model, economists view housing as a question of supply and demand. Consumers are making rational choices among competing products, and providers are responding to these demands by offering suitable and competitive products. This model prioritizes efficiency as a goal, and casts the profit motive as a driver of improvement.

Economics studies housing using quantitative analysis, as an example noting the buying habits of certain demographic groups or calculating how different inputs shape the cost of the output. Missing from such an approach are the qualitative experiences of households. It is not possible to capture the emotional and psychological aspects of housing decisions in an equation. Further, accepting only limited government involvement in the market implies that households have equal opportunities to compete for housing. This fails to consider the many ways the present system does not live up to this ideal. Unequal education, a biased justice system, asymmetric wealth accumulation, and active discrimination make the market far from a level playing field where one is guaranteed to reap rewards from work. In addition, those with capital to invest have incentives to take advantage of the shortcomings of the system. Government intervention is necessary as the fundamental need for housing puts "consumers" in a vulnerable position. This vulnerability may be economic or even physical, if housing is built inadequately so investors can save money (Quigley 1999).

Sociology and Housing

It has been said, "economics is about how people make choices; sociology is all about why they don't have any choices to make" (Morris and Winter 1978, 1). This sheds light on sociology's way of seeing the world. Sociologists seek to understand how culture and social institutions (family, religion, schools, government, etc.) shape and constrain people's behavior and choices. Recently sociology has been turning its attention to the area of housing, bringing to it a lens of the social construction of knowledge. For sociology, individuals are products of their social environment. How they experience the world is "influenced by subjective experience and how these experiences are mediated" (Jacobs and Malpas 2013, 36). This model rejects the notion of universal objective truths; rather it contends all experience is subject to interpretation. This interpretation is a product of socialization and institutional processes. Cultural norms, social processes, and language discourses are all mediating influences that intersect with our experience and ultimately shape how we make sense of the world. In this way, we don't have "pure" choices; rather, we have alternatives filtered through these overarching social forces.

Within sociology, housing research focuses on power, conflict, and "problem" construction (Jacobs and Manzi 2000, 40). It asks questions such as: Why are people drawn to homeownership? Is this a natural tendency, or the result of a strong cultural message married to government incentives that make it advantageous over renting (Atkinson and Jacobs 2016)? It asks, who will benefit from certain programs, such as housing vouchers, and how does that affect the promotion of certain approaches? A strong theme in sociology is how social control maintains order and how race, class, gender, social capital, and community function to reproduce and/or reinforce a particular type of society.

Sociologists use interviews, surveys, focus groups, discourse analysis, and participant observation as they seek to portray the housing process. They are reviewing the actions of individual actors within a space produced by social institutions and cultural practices. They may also review documents and discussions to uncover the meaning of words used about housing (Gurney 1999). Sociologists consider the evolution of social forces and seek to explain the individual's actions by examining the wider social context, including the role of institutions.

Philosophy and Housing

The realm of philosophy considers the issue of housing through the lens of ethics. While there are many alternative ethical systems, housing is most often associated with a rights-based system. Under such an approach, there are universal human rights that are at the core of all decision-making.[2] In a rights-based system, all humans are born with natural rights by virtue of their being human. As housing thinker Peter King puts it, "each individual matters as much as another and [. . .] each matters very much" (2000, 29). These rights are to be respected by all others, and by governments and other social institutions. Society both guarantees and protects these rights.

Such human rights are defined in the U.S. Constitution and in other documents such as the General Assembly–adopted 1948 United Nations' (UN) Universal Declaration of Human Rights. While the Constitution does not define housing as a human right, it does enshrine freedom of expression, practice of religion, fair treatment under the law, ownership of property, and more, as basic human rights. Some argue that inasmuch as housing is needed to exercise these explicit rights, then a right to housing is implicit. After all, are you really guaranteed a human right if, due to the lack of shelter and stability, you cannot exercise it? As expressed by sociologist Matthew Desmond, "life and home are so intertwined that it is almost impossible to think about one without the other" (2016, 300). Housing is a prerequisite for the other aspects of life that the Constitution protects.

Article 25 of the UN Universal Declaration of Human Rights states, "Everyone has the right to a standard of living adequate for the health and wellbeing of himself and of his family, including food, clothing, housing and medical care and necessary social services" (Universal Declaration of Human Rights 1948). A right to housing is not necessarily the automatic provision of housing; the right may be a system assuring the availability of decent housing affordable to all income levels. Although an endorsee to the Universal Declaration of Human Rights, the United States is not in full compliance with its principles. In 2009, a United Nations–appointed Special Rapporteur (researcher) on housing visited the United States at the invitation of the federal government. After two weeks of meetings and touring, the special advisor issued a report warning about a rise of income inequality, the foreclosure crisis, dire housing conditions for Native Americans, and the need for participatory and transparent housing policy development. The report called attention to the failure of the United States to provide housing for all and recommended new policies and increased funding (Rolnik 2009).

A human rights framework provides a starting point for housing, but leaves many unanswered specifics. What would the guaranteed housing look like? That is, how large would it be? What amenities would it have? Would there be a level of contribution required to access the housing? How best does society meet this basic human right—is the government responsible to produce, distribute, and manage such housing? Is meeting the need for housing with a minimally determined standard, while others may have access to luxurious housing, consistent with a human rights framework? A right to housing is not necessarily the automatic provision of housing—but an availability of decent housing affordable to all income levels. The answers are not found within the framework; these specifics are worked out through the public policy process. Some suggest that if the response to these housing questions was put in the hands of government, it would undermine the autonomy of people and promote a paternalistic relationship (Fitz-patrick, Bengtsson, and Watts 2014).

Philosophy also considers housing from an ontological point of view, that is, considering the very nature of being. This suggests the function of housing—to have us feel secure and provide a place for nesting—is related to the basic human way of existing in the world. Philosophy notes that we are born seeking a right relationship with the world that would equate with "dwelling" (Jacobs and Malpas 2013). This philosophical framework for housing is rarely engaged at a policy level, and only marginally considered during interdisciplinary attempts to explain housing. Part of this is the practical orientation of many housing works, but also the difficulty of explaining and testing the theory associated with the abstract term "dwelling."

In this philosophical framework, housing appears detached from the reality of physical homelessness, vulnerability to crime, and housing costs that force people to choose between shelter and food. The concept of dwelling has a transcendental feeling about it—one hard to grasp. Philosophers often use phenomenology (learning by examining first-person conscious experiences) as a means of describing the fundamental nature of dwelling. This involves considering the character of consciousness and individual experience—it is quite distinct from traditional scientific research that can be subject to direct observation and testing.

These philosophical ways of framing the human relationship to housing add to our understanding. They are, however, very distinct and are not easily combined with the other frameworks presented.

Urban Planning and Housing

It is important to consider urban planning's view of housing as it is urban planners who are often at the forefront of housing in practice. As a field, urban planning is a social science that has borrowed heavily from other disciplines. Urban planning theory and practice has evolved considerably in its just more than one hundred years as a profession. Planning has roots in physical determinism—the belief that there is a right way to design places to generate a near-utopian existence for all. Planning has left this view behind, as it has its associated successor, the rationalism of modernism. Rationalism similarly puts forth that there is one right way to correct problems that can be found through a careful technical assessment of inputs and outputs. In the end of the twentieth century this approach fell into wide disfavor—not just within planning—as it assumes experts know best, all that matters can be measured, and there is one right way to proceed.

The dominant theoretical framework of contemporary urban planning is that of communicative planning (Healey 1992). Planning in this context is a framework for determining both the ends and the means for improved housing. This is done as a collaborative process that includes relevant stakeholders, and seeks the input of all—those directly affected and those that may be marginalized by societal power structures. Planning combines technical analysis with a publicly accessible, consensus-driven discussion, to determine specific housing goals and methods for meeting these goals. In this way planning links knowledge to action (Friedmann 1988), but is open to different ways of knowing. Urban planning is oriented toward action: the theory is an applied theory, ultimately having its sights set on implementation.

In the process of reviewing quantitative and qualitative data, different options to use in achieving goals are considered. Planning looks to assess the relative strengths and weaknesses of each approach and identify the winners and losers. But more than this, planning claims to act on behalf of the "public interest." This public interest may be more than the mere sum of individual interests. There is wide debate within the field of urban planning about the notion of a common good (Brooks 2002). Some believe it exists and they use a normative approach to determine goals, while others see it emerging from a negotiation among many competing interests. Communicative planning assumes the greater good surfaces in the discourse generated when considering goals and options relative to housing.

Another key characteristic of planning's approach to gaining knowledge about housing is to realize that housing is connected to all other aspects of a functional community. While researchers and practitioners may specialize in housing, there is no escaping the reality of the interdependence among housing, employment, transportation, services, and recreation. All housing goals and options are considered in the light of these interconnections.

From this discussion, we can see the differences in terms of what types of knowledge are sought and what is given value or discarded in the models created by various disciplines. Each adds an element of understanding to our human experience and this complex area of society, some more theoretical and some more practical. Table 3.1 summarizes the goals and approaches for the four disciplinary frameworks presented here. As an open yet questioning thinker, you should bear in mind this discussion of the limitations of models and what can be gained from multiple perspectives.

Political Ideologies

Since housing is a public policy issue, it is also worthwhile to consider the political context for understanding housing. How do conservative, liberal, and radical ideologies differ in how they frame housing issues? Political ideologies reflect a belief system or set of assumptions about human nature, as well as a model for the best way for societal institutions (including the market) to work. These fundamental beliefs are used to choose among different actions or programs for improving society (King 2016). American

Table 3.1 Summary of Four Disciplinary Approaches to Housing

	GOAL	DOMINANT METHODS OF STUDY
Economics	*To meet housing demands in the most efficient manner while rewarding capital*	*Quantitative analysis*
Sociology	*To understand how culture and social institutions influence and constrain the housing behaviors of households*	*Interpretive and qualitative analysis*
Philosophy	*To examine ethical behavior related to housing, and the existential realities of "dwelling"*	*Phenomenology (examining first-person conscious experiences) and reflectivity*
Urban planning	*To identify and meet housing needs through a collaborative process, leading to an integrated and functional community serving all*	*Analytical techniques in combination with qualitative analysis*

political orientations, except for the extreme radical left, share a fundamental acceptance of a capitalist worldview (Hays 1995). This and a commitment to the representative democracy of the Constitution are fundamental guideposts. Differences, however, arise when considering how and when the government should intervene in the market and the degree to which society has established a level playing field for all Americans.

It is interesting to note that today, most of those involved in policymaking will state they seek data-driven solutions. They state that programs or interventions should be designed based on what research or historical precedent indicates will be successful. In fact, however, it is a combination of these findings with their ideology that ultimately shapes policy preferences. Research provides information, yet the data or historical record is interpreted when setting policy by using the assumptions associated with each ideology.

Conservatives and Housing

Conservatives generally align with the adage "less is more" when it comes to government. The belief behind this is that government brings bureaucracy that raises costs, reduces efficiency, and hampers innovation. In this way, the conservative ideology aligns with the economic framework for housing that was outlined above. The belief is that market allocation of resources leads to the best outcomes. Closer examination suggests, in practice, the conservative position is not strictly "no government intervention," but rather government intervention only when it helps the market and protects those with a major investment in the market (Hays 1995). The 2008 federal bailout for financial institutions is cited as an example of action to protect the investment of an established group (Phillips 2010). The private sector has always benefited from some level of financial and legal support from government. What conservatives deliberate on is the nature of that government support—who it is assisting and how it affects who has power. Regarding housing, conservatives feel strongly that direct government production of housing leads to inefficiencies and waste. They contend that the private sector is the preferred provider as it will be more efficient.

Pertaining to human nature and societal institutions, conservatives embrace *meritocracy* as the basis for the distribution of material wealth. Conservatives believe society gets the best from people when they are motivated by their self-interest to perform. Your ability to get housing, or move to a higher quality of housing, is dependent on your hard work. Personal responsibility and discipline are valued traits, and government interventions must promote rather than undermine these traits. In this way, prosperity is an indication of an individual with strong character and poverty, in turn, reflects an individual's inadequacies (Hays 1995).

Liberals and Housing

For liberals, the market, driven solely by profit, often fails. It suffers from a type of tunnel vision that occurs when putting financial gain above people. Government intervention in the market is necessary to protect the public and safeguard the natural environment. Regulations and government programs are needed to manage market outcomes and achieve social change (Phillips 2010). They see the market as a tool for improving society—one we should actively control on our own behalf. Liberals believe inequities of opportunity are not all the product of one's character, but can represent failures of societal institutions and systems. Whether this be unequal access to education or below-living-wage jobs, forces beyond the individual contribute to inequities. Hard work alone will not make up for these shortcomings. Liberals believe society pays a high cost when some are locked out of prosperity. The most direct loss is untapped human talent and abilities. But society must also deal with the associated costs of poor health, high crime, and children falling behind.

Liberals believe the government must create a level playing field for all. This may take the form of the redistribution of wealth through taxes and government supports. Liberals see this as investments in people and a way to overcome the built-in power inequities favoring those with wealth. Liberals are concerned with the strong influence affluent interest groups exert on government to act on their behalf, at the expense of others.

Liberals are, however, willing to work with the private sector—and even promote public-private partnerships. Their worldview favors averting collapse of the market system, and instead modifying it in ways that correct for its inadequacies. They can be pragmatists in their approach to change (Phillips 2010). For this very reason, liberals are criticized by radicals.

Radicals and Housing

The label "radical" can cover a wide range of views. For our purposes, we use it to capture a general socialist and/or Marxist point of view. As noted above, unlike conservatives and liberals, radicals do not believe the system can be managed in a way to improve outcomes; radicals believe the system is the problem. They believe "only by going to the roots (*radical* means 'root') . . . of economic instability and social injustice can problems be solved" (Phillips 2010, 91). Capitalism is this root—it is designed to favor the affluent and exploit wage earners. The affordable housing crisis, homelessness, and the foreclosure meltdown are its products. These negative realities will not be avoided by merely tinkering with minor aspects of the system.

Housing experts Emily Achtenberg and Peter Marcuse, considered radicals, have long written about the need to overhaul the entire system (Achtenberg and Marcuse 1986). They note housing is primarily treated as a means for investors, financial institutions, and the construction industry to make profits—the system primarily serves capital and not people. They write about a "decommodification of housing" intended to "limit the role of profit for decisions affecting housing, substituting instead the basic principle of socially determined need" (Toward the Decommodification of Housing 1986, 477). They call for housing to be treated as a socially created right and society to organize itself in ways to meet the needs of all. They go on to outline alternative forms of housing ownership (cooperatives, land trusts) and a larger role for permanent public ownership and control of land and housing. Housing, they suggest, is "always more than just housing"— it is political and the key questions revolve around "power, inequality, and justice" (Madden and Marcuse 2016, 117, 5).

This approach is echoed by others who believe housing is best recast as a social good and not a commodity, and call for a right-to-housing movement (Bratt, Stone, and Hartman 2006). Another leading critic of the market approach to housing is Marxist geographer David Harvey. Harvey believes the market is no longer a good way for dealing with today's conditions. He favors major changes to remove profits from land development and ownership (2009). Countries with a strong social welfare system that have housing guarantees akin to a right to housing are models for this approach, including Sweden, Finland, and Cuba.

The radical position has not become mainstream in the United States. Some say this is due to the fact the system is specifically designed to gain the support of people by making them believe they are beneficiaries. In fact, it is argued by some that government promotion of homeownership is not what it appears. Rather than a means for households to gain independence and control, the mortgage system binds households in a way that can harm them (Achtenberg and Marcuse 1986). The commitment to a monthly payment for 30 years can rob you of flexibility and end up burdening your budget or—as the foreclosure crisis taught us—unbeknownst to you, the terms of your mortgage may change and exceed your ability to pay. For some, homeownership is "evidence of people's own enslavement to their own domination" (Ronald 2008, 31).

As with our discussion of the frameworks of academic disciplines, these characterizations of conservative, liberal, and radical ideologies are a simplification, and the portrayals here reflect the dominant orientations within each ideology. There is variation within these ideological groupings, and these evolve as new types of challenges are faced.

Most ideologies recognize that today's conditions are far from the basic mythical ideal of the free-market system. Concerns over diminished competition as corporations grow, the widening gap between the rich and poor, the power of special interests, persistent racism, and globalization have led to refinements in ideological positions. Changes in ideologies are likely to continue as the future presents unique and unforeseen circumstances.

Conclusion

In this chapter, we have considered how knowledge is gained about housing and how that knowledge is applied. Research is a way for us to test the models we build to explain the world. Although incredibly valuable, research does not present objective truths—it is shaped by the methods and interpretations of the researchers and decision-makers. By approaching research models, theories, and knowledge with an open and critical mind, we can assess the relative strengths and weaknesses of findings, always moving toward an improved model. Research should be approached with an awareness that bias is built in, assumptions should be made explicit, and findings are to be critically assessed. We also investigated how political ideologies frame housing questions and how those ideologies determine what types of housing initiatives will move forward in society. As we will see in the next chapter, federal housing policy has evolved in alignment with the political ideologies of those in power at the time (Hays 1995).

Questions and Activities

1. Along with some friends, you are moving to a new city. Draw a model of your personal housing search that includes the steps and the influencing factors of how you will go about finding a new place.
2. Given what we have talked about so far in this course and your personal experience with housing, what research questions around housing can you formulate?
3. Choose a discipline not explored in this chapter (anthropology, geography, political science, etc.) and write down what main question you think it would ask about housing and the methods for knowing you think those in the field might use.
4. Explain what is meant by the statement, "Housing is a prerequisite for the other aspects of life that the Constitution protects" (see page 33 in this chapter).
5. Have students search for an article on a current debate/event related to housing. Ask them to summarize the article and identify what, if any, research is used in the

discussion, and if any ideological beliefs are expressed. Can they suggest research that could answer questions raised in the article?

6. Distribute copies of relevant sections of the Universal Declaration of Human Rights and the Convention on the Rights of the Child. Have students read through the documents and develop a list of bullet points of what it would mean for the United States to comply with these standards for housing. Some questions you might pose are: What would have to happen? Who would benefit? What resources would be needed? What decisions would need to be made? Should the United States adopt a right to housing? Consider having a debate on adopting a right to housing.

7. Have students research the requirements of the SNAP program. Any eligible household receives benefits under this federal program. Ask students, how is food different from housing? Explain to students that not all eligible households receive housing assistance and ask why they think this is so.

Notes

1. In addition to interdisciplinary understanding, the concept of transdisciplinary thinking has gained favor. Interdisciplinary thinking claims a combination of the multiple ways of framing an issue is a richer, truer way to make sense of the world. Transdisciplinary thinking suggests that grasping lived experience is best achieved when you approach the issue as it is experienced, and do not reduce it to a combination of separate, incomplete views seen through disparate lenses. Transdisciplinary thinking requires a conscious effort to move past the limitations of discipline-specific methodologies for knowing.

2. Another version of housing as a right sees rights as socially constructed rather than naturally occurring. Under this approach there is of course a diversity of such rights, unique to the society under review. See, for example, "Rights to Housing: Reviewing the Terrain and Exploring a Way Forward," in *Housing, Theory and Society*, edited by Suzanne Fitzpatrick, Bo Bengtsson, and Beth Watts, 2014, 447–463.

References

Achtenberg, Emily Paradise, and Peter Marcuse. 1986. "The Causes of the Housing Problem." In *Critical Perspectives on Housing*, edited by Rachel G. Bratt, Chester Hartman, and Ann Meyerson, 4–11. Philadelphia: Temple University Press.

Achtenberg, Emily Paradise, and Peter Marcuse. 1986. "Toward the Decommodification of Housing." In *Critical Perspectives on Housing*, edited by Rachel G. Bratt, Chester Hartman, and Ann Meyerson, 474–483. Philadelphia: Temple University Press.

Andersson, Fredrik, John C. Haltiwanger, Mark J. Kutzbach, Henry O. Pollakowski, and Daniel O. Weinberg. 2014. "Job Displacement and the Duration of Joblessness: The Role of Spatial Mismatch." *NBER Working Paper No. 20066*. Cambridge, MA: National Bureau of Economic Research.

Atkinson, Rowland, and Keith Jacobs. 2016. *House, Home and Society*. London: Palgrave Macmillan.

Bratt, Rachel G., Michael E. Stone, and Chester W. Hartman. 2006. *A Right to Housing: Foundation for a New Social Agenda*. Philadelphia: Temple University Press.

Brooks, Michael P. 2002. *Planning Theory for Practitioners*. Chicago: American Planning Association.

Desmond, Matthew. 2016. *Evicted: Poverty and Profit in the American City*. New York: Crown Publishers.

Fitzpatrick, Suzanne, Bo Bengtsson, and Beth Watts. 2014. "Rights to Housing: Reviewing the Terrain and Exploring a Way Forward." *Housing, Theory and Society* 31(4): 447–463.

Friedmann, John. 1988. "Reviewing Two Centuries." *Society* 26(1): 7–15.

Gurney, Craig M. 1999. "Lowering the Drawbridge: A Case Study of Analogy and Metaphor in the Social Construction of Home-Ownership." *Urban Studies* 36(10): 1705–1722.

Harvey, David. 2009. *Social Justice and the City*, Revised Edition. Athens, GA: The University of Georgia Press.

Hays, Allen R. 1995. *The Federal Government and Urban Housing*. Albany: State University of New York.

Healey, Patsy. 1992. "Planning Through Debate: The Communicative Turn in Planning Theory." *The Town Planning Review*: 143–162.

Jacobs, Keith, and Jeff Malpas. 2013. "Material Objects, Identity and the Home: Towards a Relational Housing Research Agenda." *Housing, Theory and Society* 30(3): 281–292.

Jacobs, Keith, and Tony Manzi. 2000. "Evaluating the Social Constructionist Paradigm in Housing Research." *Housing, Theory and Society* 17(1): 35–42.

King, Peter. 2000. "Can We Use Rights to Justify Housing Provision?" *Housing, Theory and Society*: 27–34.

King, Peter. 2016. *The Principles of Housing*. New York: Routledge.

Madden, David, and Peter Marcuse. 2016. *In Defense of Housing*. Brooklyn NY: Verso.

McClure, Kirk, Alex F. Schwartz, and Lydia B. Taghavi. 2015. "Housing Choice Voucher Location Patterns a Decade Later." *Housing Policy Debate*: 215–233.

Morris, Earl W., and Mary Winter. 1978. *Housing, Family and Society*. New York: John Wiley and Sons.

Phillips, Barbara E. 2010. *City Lights: Urban-Suburban Life in the Global Society*, 3rd Edition. New York: Oxford University Press.

Quigley, John M. 1999. "Why Should the Government Play a Role in Housing? A View From North America." *Housing, Theory and Society* 16(4): 201–203.

Rolnik, Raquel. 2009. *Report of the Special Rapporteur on Adequate Housing as a Component to an Adequate Standard of Living*. New York: United Nations.

Ronald, Richard. 2008. *The Ideology of Home Ownership: Homeowner Societies and the Role of Housing*. New York: Palgrave MacMillan.

Sharp, Gregory, and Matthew Hall. 2014. "Emerging Forms of Racial Inequality in Homeownership Exit, 1968–2009." *Social Problems*: 427–447.

Universal Declaration of Human Rights. 1948. New York: United Nations.

4

History of Federal
Involvement in Housing

In the first three chapters of this book, we explored the deep importance of housing to each person's quality of life and to a community's welfare, as well as how housing can spur the economy with jobs and buying. Given these realities, it is not surprising that the government is involved in housing. In this chapter, we turn to a history of federal involvement in housing, presenting a generalized chronological account of key roles, programs, and outcomes of federal participation. The federal government has focused heavily on homeownership, and shifts in political control have brought different ideologies to the forefront favoring one approach to affordable housing over another. Here we will discuss how American cultural norms and political ideologies distinguish the involvement of the United States federal government in housing from that of central governments in other countries of the world.

The federal government has played many different roles regarding housing. These include:

1. directly producing housing;
2. subsidizing the production (supply) and consumption (demand) of housing;
3. preparing studies, conducting research, and implementing demonstration projects on housing; and
4. enforcing Fair Housing laws.

(Listokin 1991)

At any given moment, the objectives and programs adopted and funded by the federal government have been shaped by the events and context of the time. Broadly, we can say that housing policy responds to the major demographic, economic, political, social, and historical forces at play in each period. As former Housing and Urban Development (HUD) official Charles Orlebeke saw it, housing policy is shaped by the "debris of tried and canceled programs, experimentation, partisan contention, ideological conflict, and—surely not least—scholarly research, analysis, and debate" (2000, 491). As we discuss the changing federal role in housing, we will note the important events and conditions that influenced the decisions made and helped determine the specifics of federal housing policy and programs. We will see that housing policy is not limited to actions by housing agencies, but is also affected by actions involving tax code and banking regulations. As there is much territory to cover, this chapter is divided into two parts.

Part One

Early Years

Most scholars would mark the early twentieth century as the beginning point for a federal role in housing. Before that, regulations came from local communities interested in safeguarding safety and sanitation. These initial municipal laws addressed the spread of fire, and fairly strict building code regulations were a response to the severe stress that waves of late nineteenth- and early twentieth-century immigration placed on urban housing. The rapid swells of newly settling populations led to deplorable conditions as multiple households shared small, inadequate spaces lacking modern sanitation. Population growth outpaced construction and regulations. For many cities, the late 1800s saw the launch of tenement reform movements. Committees produced long reports documenting the conditions, nonprofits sponsored design competitions for improved tenement buildings, and, ultimately, cities adopted building regulations to ensure safety, sanitation, and "good morals." Many of these initiatives were based on a philosophy of *environmental determinism*—the belief that clean, orderly housing would not only eliminate the spread of disease but also decrease crime and immoral behaviors such as alcoholism, uncleanliness, poor parenting, and unemployment (Vale 2007). Jacob Riis is considered one of the earliest photojournalists because of his work documenting and moralizing on life in these tenements (see his 1890 work, *How the Other Half Lives*). His poignant and stark images of the noxious conditions, captured only after the introduction of flash powder permitted photography in dark spaces, spurred the movement for reform (Davis 2000). Today his work is critiqued for the blatant racism and negative ethnic stereotypes he uses to describe different immigrant groups.

While the 1800s saw federal government programs to promote western settlement—consistent with the cultural preference of land ownership addressed in Chapter 2—for

Figure 4.1   Tenement Conditions in New York City, 1889

Source: Image by Jacob Riis, © Museum of the City of New York, used with permission

the most part, the federal government took a hands-off approach to housing throughout the nineteenth and into the twentieth century, viewing housing as the domain of the private market and only of concern between consumers and producers.

It was World War I that drove the federal government's initial direct involvement in housing. To meet the navy's demands for ships, the federal government passed the Shipping Act of 1917, driven by President Woodrow Wilson. It provided federal funding for the construction of 16,000 homes for shipyard workers in 120 locations (Martens 2009). Under the direction of the short-lived United States Housing Corporation (USHC, 1918–1919) the federal government designed and oversaw the construction of housing—a radical move. At the time, this action was considered a national security necessity because experienced workers and their families would not live in temporary dormitories and rooming houses. High turnover among these key employees was a major concern; those leading the war effort feared the lack of this expertise would undermine efficiency and threaten the fast-paced production schedule. It was agreed that the private sector could not mobilize quickly enough to meet these housing needs and thus the federal government took on this role (Bureau of Industrial Housing and Transportation 1918). These new communities became places where rapid production of the needed vessels could take place. After successfully meeting its goals, and with the end of the war, the USHC ceased to exist (Jackson 1985).

A Different Type of Crisis

The next crisis that motivated federal involvement in housing was not a war but a major economic collapse: the crash of 1929 and the following Great Depression had wide-reaching effects on Americans. While the wealthy experienced a dramatic reversal of fortune, many working-class Americans became unemployed and those who had been homeowners faced foreclosure because the lack of a paycheck meant an inability to keep up with payments on home loans. All sectors of the economy suffered and the housing industry nearly came to a standstill (Jackson 1985). Figure 4.2 reflects some relevant statistics of this period: a steep decline in housing production, a surge in unemployment, declining property values, decimation of small banks, and an alarming rise in foreclosures. Extraordinary loss—of home and employment—was widespread, with households struggling for adequate food and some shelter. Such a dramatic turn of events demanded a major response. The depth and breadth of the crisis overcame any public hostility to federal involvement in housing—in fact, federal leadership and action was viewed as the only approach capable of countering the wide-reaching economic catastrophe (Landis and McClure 2010; Jackson 1985).

The federal legislation of this period, President Franklin D. Roosevelt's New Deal, led to a major restructuring of the housing finance system that had both an immediate and an enduring effect. The main motivations of this time were to put the housing sector back to work and to stop the loss of homes for those facing foreclosure. The changes in the housing finance system were sweeping and became the strong underpinning of the increase in homeownership that followed decades later.

Two significant housing-related components of federal legislation from this period are the Home Owners Loan Corporation (HOLC) and the Federal Housing Administration (FHA). The HOLC was charged with assisting the many homeowners facing foreclosure during this time. The main mechanism used to keep these owners in their homes was the introduction of a new mortgage instrument. Before this time, most mortgages were short-term loans (5–10 years) structured with a *balloon payment*. In

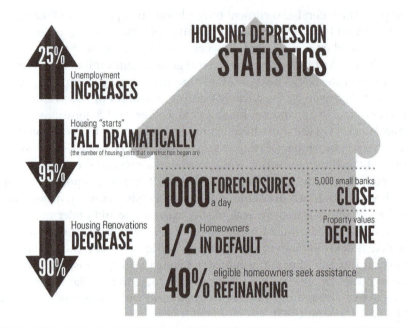

Figure 4.2 Depression Era Housing Related Statistics

Sources: Foreclosures, defaults, starts, and renovations from Jackson, Kenneth T., 1985, Crabgrass Frontier (New York: Oxford University Press), p.193; unemployment rate from von Hoffman, Alexander. 2012. History Lessons for Today's Housing Policy The Political Processes of Making Low-Income Housing Policy. Working Papers, Cambridge MA: Joint Center For Housing Studies Harvard University, p.3; bank closures from Kennedy, Susan Estabrook. 1973. The Banking Crisis of 1933 (Lexington KY: University Press of Kentucky) p.5; and refinancing from Schwartz, Alex F. 2015. Housing Policy in the United States, Third Ed. New York: Routledge, p.71. Graphic © Ted Dobek, used by permission

a balloon payment, the homeowner paid a monthly loan payment toward the amount borrowed (often just the interest on the loan), but at the end of the loan period a major lump sum would be due. These loans also required the borrower to put down large down payments—that is, they could only get a loan to cover 50 to 60 percent of the total housing cost, requiring them to have the cash to pay the other 40 to 50 percent up front (or get an additional mortgage loan). The HOLC developed a new mortgage instrument, the one we know today. These mortgages are loans of much longer terms, at lower interest rates, with lower down payment requirements, and with a *self-amortizing* feature. Self-amortizing means that at the end of the loan period, the borrower has paid in full (there is no balloon payment).

Today's mortgages allow homeowners to repay a hefty loan over an extended period without experiencing an increase in the monthly payment. As an example, today one might seek a mortgage to purchase a $225,000 home. A qualified borrower could take a loan out for 90 percent of the total value, $202,500. The loan payments would be a fixed amount for the duration of the loan, which is, for the majority of Americans, a period of 30 years (U.S. Census Bureau 2013). After 30 years of paying the monthly amount for the term of the loan at an interest rate (a 2016 rate of 3.7 percent of the monthly payment on a $202,500 loan would be approximately $932), the borrower is the outright owner of the property. Table 4.1 summarizes the differences between mortgage instruments before and after the HOLC.

Table 4.1 Comparison of Old and New Mortgage Instruments

OLD MORTGAGE	NEW MORTGAGE
Short term (5–10 years)	Long term (15–30 years)
Balloon payment	Self-amortizing
High down payment (40–50%)	Low down payment (5–10 %)
Low loan to value ratio (50%)	High loan to value Ratio (90–95%)
No consistent building standards	Quality control with construction standards

In 1934, the Federal Housing Administration (FHA) took over where the HOLC had ended. While the HOLC itself was short-lived, it fulfilled its purpose of assisting at-risk homeowners with a new style of mortgage. Through the support of the FHA, the new mortgage became the industry standard. The FHA was primarily designed to stimulate the economy and put people back to work (Jackson 1985). Keeping with a prevailing sentiment that the private sector is best at building housing, the FHA was designed to stimulate private sector activity by making mortgage credit and home improvement loans more available and stable (von Hoffman 2012).

The FHA achieved its purpose not by giving loans to homebuyers but by offering banks insurance on home purchase and home improvement loans they initiated. Consider the change the new mortgage instruments meant for the banking community. They would be loaning larger amounts of money for much longer periods of time (see Table 4.1). It was possible that their available pool of loan funds could be tied up for years, leading to fewer mortgages being issued. Also, the banks had become somewhat timid after the 1929 collapse. To counter the risk banks faced in these larger, longer-term mortgages, the federal government offered to insure the bank against any losses: if a borrower did end up losing a job, or otherwise becoming unable to pay back the loan, the FHA would cover the bank's loss. This cushion encouraged participation by the banks and the decreased risk also decreased interest rates, making home buying more affordable (Jackson 1985).

One of the key features introduced by the FHA was the adoption of criteria for the loans they would insure. The FHA established standards on the quality of the construction of homes to be insured and this led to a noticeable improvement in material standards (Lang and Sohmer 2000). Another key feature of FHA insurance criteria with far-reaching impact was the process used to appraise homes. Appraisals for the value of homes are a critical part of loans because they establish that the property is worth the price being paid. If a borrower were to default, the lender wants to make sure it can sell the property and recoup the full value of the loan.

The FHA appraisal methodology assigned one of four grades to neighborhoods—A, B, C, or D based on a variety of factors. A set of Residential Security Maps (see Chapter 5) were produced for each city representing these neighborhood evaluations with labels and colors in accordance with the grading scale. A legacy of this approach is that certain neighborhoods labeled "D" were coded red on the maps; these were places considered hazardous for loaning (Jackson 1985). Banks were dissuaded from lending in these neighborhoods or did so only by charging borrowers higher interest rates. In general, FHA would not insure loans proposed for these areas. This practice prevented potential buyers from getting loans to purchase in areas labeled D or coded red, and in turn affected sellers by limiting the pool of eligible buyers, or forcing them to sell low. It also made it difficult to obtain home improvement loans in these areas. One of the strongly weighted factors in these evaluations was the race and ethnicity of the households living in the area—if certain groups were living or moving into an area, the rating would be low. Groups considered risky included Black, Mexican, Jewish, and other ethnic households. This practice, known as *redlining* due to the red on the maps, is described in more detail in Chapter 5, Housing and Discrimination.

The ethnic and racial prejudice and discrimination of redlining was incorporated directly from the standard practice of the real estate industry. The FHA was staffed by banking and real estate professionals who brought with them the ideology and guidelines of the industry (Gotham 2000). For real estate professionals, the presence, or increasing presence, of these ethnic and racial groups was associated with a decline in the value of property and thus could lead to housing that was worth less than the loan used for its purchase. These appraisals did not fairly or accurately assess the conditions and potential future of these areas. They disregarded relevant information, such as the repayment histories and incomes of the residents. In addition, they gave prejudice and discrimination legitimacy. By associating property value decline with the presence of certain groups rather than its true source—the attitude of white households and the real estate industry—the neighborhood evaluation criteria gave credence and support to targeted disinvestment and institutionalized discriminatory practices.

The FHA became and remains a major player in the housing market. By 1938, FHA insurance was used for more than one-third of the purchases of new homes (Gotham 2000). Its use and institutionalization of redlining had major and long-term impacts—starving some places of needed financing and preventing certain groups from benefiting from homeownership. The FHA discontinued redlining in the 1960s, yet succeeding generations of the excluded households were denied the wealth creation white households gained from FHA loans (see Chapter 5).

Other key systemic changes of this period were the establishment of the Federal Home Loan Bank (FHLB) system and the Federal National Mortgage Association, or "Fannie Mae." The regional banks established as part of the FHLB system could provide banks with funding to keep mortgages flowing. Fannie Mae (and the later government-sponsored entity known as Freddie Mac) was also designed to provide new capital for banks to loan out as mortgages. With the longer-term mortgage instruments banks could run out of funding, having loaned their capital and tied it up for thirty years; Fannie Mae provides liquidity for lenders by purchasing their mortgage loans. The purchase generates cash for the banks to have as additional mortgage funding. In these initial years, Fannie Mae floated bonds to get the cash for purchasing mortgages, and paid the bond installments with the monthly house payments of the mortgage borrowers.

A second major prong of the housing approach during this period was the launching of a Public Housing program. At first through the U.S. Public Housing Agency, and then later through local Housing Authorities, the federal government covered the cost of the production of housing for working class people facing a temporary financial setback. Chapter 9 will explore this history in depth, but for now, it is important to note the New Deal programs included letting the federal government play a direct role in building housing for those with low incomes. The federal government provided funding for the construction, local authorities assumed control of the site selection and development, and the tenants' rents were used to cover the operating and maintenance costs (von Hoffman 2012). The cost of the housing was kept low through no-frills design (Biles 2000), and public housing was tied to the elimination of blight. In this way the Public Housing program didn't add housing—it just replaced run-down housing with basic publicly owned units.

A National Commitment That Legitimizes Multiple Federal Roles

Housing acts in the 1940s ushered in the next major federal housing initiatives. Like their predecessors, these acts included a variety of approaches to meeting housing needs, and were explicitly crafted to garner political support from a wide variety of groups (Lang and Sohmer 2000; Listokin 1991). The Housing Act of 1949 included four major focus areas: continued FHA funding, rural housing support, urban redevelopment, and public housing. This diversity of approaches appealed to urban and rural concerns, as well as to labor unions interested in federal government involvement, and real estate and construction industry associations favoring a private sector lead (von Hoffman 2012). Approaches outside of homeownership and renting, such as cooperative forms of ownership, were rejected by Congress as socialistic (Radford 2000; Biles 2000).

It is in the Housing Act of 1949 that the federal government first articulated a strong vision for housing. Even today, the preamble (below) is widely quoted as a statement of the federal government's commitment to housing:

> The general welfare and security of the Nation and the health and living standards of its people require housing production and related community development sufficient to remedy the serious housing shortage, the elimination of substandard and other inadequate housing through the clearance of slums and blighted areas, and the realization as soon as feasible of the goal of a decent home and suitable living environment for every American family, this contributing to the development and redevelopment of communities and to the advancement of the growth, wealth, and security of the nation.
>
> (Nenno 1979, 260–261)

The preamble captures the many dimensions of housing that provide the rationale for the federal government to take an active role. It includes elements of an ideology that favors government involvement for only those needs the market fails to address, and an ideology that seeks to keep those with wealth secure. While establishing federal programs, the Act explicitly exhorted the use of the private sector to meet housing needs whenever possible (Listokin 1991).

The housing legislation of the late 1940s was passed amid an acute post–World War II housing shortage. As the end of the war brought returning servicemen and a renewed optimism, marriages led to the formation of numerous new households and a skyrocketing demand for housing units. Some of these new households were forced to find space by moving in with other households—although such "doubling up" can increase interpersonal tensions. There was a very real housing crisis as pent-up demand rose.

The initiatives of the 1940s have been described as establishing two tiers of housing responses—homeownership for some and public housing for others. By this time, however, the FHA had wide popular support, so increasing its involvement in housing was an easy sell (Hays 1995). The redlining of the FHA continued, with people of color and other ethnicities unable to get FHA-insured loans and likely to find the value of property they owned diminished by the negative neighborhood ratings. If a household was a tenant in a redlined area, they might suffer from the landlord's inability to get funds for building improvements at favorable rates. The homeownership programs favored white working and middle class households, while public housing was the federal response for excluded groups in need of affordable housing options.

In addition to the consideration of race and ethnicities in an area, the FHA appraisal manual had a bias favoring newer housing, suburban-style densities, and lots with racial covenants in place (Jackson 1985). The FHA loans of the following years, in combination with the construction of the interstate highway system, made suburbanization possible for white households. The monthly mortgage payments for single family homes outside of urban areas were less costly than urban rentals (Hanchett 2000). The new mortgage instrument, subsidized by the FHA guarantee to the lender (and by income tax deductions for the interest paid on the mortgage—see Chapter 6 for more details) allowed many white households to move to the suburbs as homeowners.

Add to the work of the FHA the benefits of the GI Bill of 1944, and the returning veteran-headed households had access to even more advantageous mortgage options. The Veterans Administration (VA) mortgage program provided direct financing of home-buying loans, with a low to no down-payment requirement. With this benefit, suburban homes were very affordable for veteran households. The housing component of the GI Bill is still in place today and is considered one of the most popular housing programs of the federal government (von Hoffman 2012). Beyond suburban areas, the 1940s federal support for homeownership included opportunities aimed at farmers in rural areas. These housing production efforts eased the post-World War II housing shortage for some (Downs 1974).

The prevailing attitudes of the time, along with the influence of FHA and professional real estate practices, meant these VA opportunities were also exclusionary, mostly serving white veterans. Since the FHA favored neighborhoods with racial covenants on lots, households of color and other groups found they were denied the ability to purchase in these areas. The neighborhoods in which they *could* buy were the very ones to which the FHA had assigned low ratings, making it difficult to receive favorable financing. One example of this is the late 1947–1951 development of Levittown in New York. The case study on page 51 explains how the production of 1,700 houses where potato fields once stood provided affordable homeownership opportunities exclusively for white households.

While white households benefitted from the FHA, VA, and agriculture-related homeownership programs, the other major thrust of this period was on housing in urban areas and housing for low income households. The Housing Act of 1949 included an urban redevelopment strategy, later named Urban Renewal (Biles 2000). Visions of modern, sleek buildings replacing poorly maintained and decrepit buildings were very seductive. Those favoring Urban Renewal saw it as a jobs program with the added benefit of fortifying the property tax base of cities. Urban neighborhoods experiencing decline were targeted for demolition and rebuilding. The legacy of this program is mixed, with the true cost of displacing thousands of people only considered long after the fact. While some Urban Renewal plans included new public housing to replace the removed units, others replaced affordable modest housing with office buildings, retail centers, luxury housing, and convention centers. The program resulted in a net loss of housing units (Lang and Sohmer 2000). The irony is this made access to safe, quality, affordable housing more difficult for those of limited means, exactly contrary to one of the stated intentions of the program. In addition, many of these projects (and the interstate highways sometimes associated with them) isolated neighborhoods within cities, cutting them off from basic services. In the following years, such isolation led to less investment and exacerbated the decline of these neighborhoods. In her groundbreaking critique of Urban Renewal, *The Death and Life of Great American Cities*, journalist Jane Jacobs described the demolition of neighborhoods and modernist reconstruction this way, "This is not the rebuilding of cities. This is the sacking of cities" (quoted in Biles 2000, 153).

Most places chosen for Urban Renewal were neighborhoods occupied by people of color or ethnic groups (Biles 2000). The discrimination in the housing market and professional real estate standards meant these groups had limited housing choices and often lived in areas where landlords failed to invest. Urban Renewal targeted areas of decline, and for these reasons the writer and social critic James Baldwin famously tagged the Urban Renewal program as "Negro Removal" (Morgenthau 1963).

Box 4.1   Urban Renewal and the Destruction of Neighborhoods

Looking back on the many urban renewal projects undertaken during the 1940s–1960s, historians, sociologists, and others have documented how a technical-rational approach, combined with racism and greed, led to the destruction of vital neighborhoods—many of these home to people of color (Thomas and Ritzdorf, Introduction, 1997). City planners of the time measured overcrowding, income, employment, sanitation, and disease; they considered the pre-modern lot layouts and street patterns the reason for disinvestment in cities. They used the terms "slum" and "blight" to label areas in need of "renewal." What they failed to consider were the human costs of losing the social networks and functional cultural communities within these places. Despite being areas where low-income households resided, the people and families living there were connected and cared for each other. For many residents, a very real attachment to these places supported self-actualization, identity development, and satisfaction. Cities selected places strategically located near downtowns to demolish structures and rebuild with buildings touted as bringing in higher tax revenues, or to locate highways that allowed suburban whites easy access to jobs downtown. This story was repeated throughout urban America, and there are many site-specific accounts worth reading. See, for example, Herbert Gans's *The Urban Villagers* (1965), Dawn Bohulano Mabalon's *Little Manila Is in the Heart: The Making of the Pilipina/o American Community in Stockton, CA* (2013), and Samuel Zipp's *Manhattan Projects: The Rise and Fall of Urban Renewal in Cold War New York* (2012).

In Detroit, the predominantly African-American neighborhoods of Black Bottom, Paradise Valley, and Gratiot met a similar fate. These neighborhoods had both low and middle income households. Residents had immediate access to goods and services, including locally owned food stores, bakeries, department stores, entertainment places, restaurants, churches, doctors, lawyers, tailors, and morticians. Business owners served as community leaders, role modeling to youth, and assisting residents through tough times (Thomas 1997). Paradise Valley was a center of jazz, with entertainers such as Duke Ellington, Ella Fitzgerald, and Sarah Vaughn appearing there before multiracial audiences (MacDonald 2012; Grunow 2003). In short, these areas were full of life, and while housing conditions were poor, other aspects of community life were strong.

Detroit, however, was a city segregated through violence, real estate practices, racial covenants, and acts of discrimination. The black population drawn to the city during the "great migration" north was constrained to these neighborhoods. Detroit's urban renewal plans targeted these areas; nonwhite families made up 85 percent of the families affected by urban renewal (Thomas 1997). Eventually these endeavors displaced 9,000 households, and over 350 black-owned businesses (Thomas 1997; MacDonald 2012). Relocation assistance and replacement housing was not provided to all. Given the limited areas black Americans could reside, the loss of these neighborhoods destroyed communities, wiped out assets, and forced many into as bad or worse housing conditions in the few remaining areas open to black Americans.

In the before-and-after images that follow, the replacement of the active Hastings Street—the heart of Black Bottom—with a highway is documented.

Figure 4.3 Hastings Avenue in Detroit Before Urban Renewal

Source: Images © Detroit Historical Society, used with permission

Figure 4.4 Hastings Avenue in Detroit After Urban Renewal

Source: Images © Detroit Historical Society, used with permission

Box 4.2   A Mechanized Crop of Homes: Levittown, NY

The epitome of suburban development made possible with FHA and VA subsidy programs was Levittown, New York. Constructed during 1947–1951, the developer Levitt & Sons built 17,000 homes on 6,000 acres. The simple predominantly Cape Cod–style homes went up outside of New York City on potato fields in Hempstead on Long Island (Ruff 2007). These small (700–800 square feet), single family homes appealed to returning GIs anxious to move out of city apartments or their parents' homes. They were the first step in homeownership for many young families (*Up from the Potato Fields* 1950).

This development had both admirers and detractors. Clearly buyers were happy with it—they waited in line when home availability was announced. Those who critiqued it saw what Malvina Reynolds captured in her 1962 satirical song "Little Boxes":

Little boxes on the hillside,
Little boxes made of ticky tacky,
Little boxes on the hillside,
Little boxes all the same.

(Words and music by Malvina Reynolds, © Copyright 1962 Schroder Music Co. (ASCAP), Renewed 1990. Used by permission. All rights reserved).

Critics saw the sameness of the homes and the sameness of the people, and viewed it as dull and anesthetizing. But sociologist Herbert Gans recognized that it provided new young families with something they sought—"to center their lives around the home and the family, to be among neighbors whom they can trust, to find friends to share leisure hours" (Gans 1967, 413).

Levitt & Sons' President, William Levitt, was one of the first to bring mechanized production to home building. Having had experience with a military housing contract, Levitt brought streamlined procedures and a systematic 27 step process to the non-unionized construction of this and the later Levittowns in Pennsylvania, New Jersey, and beyond. Lumber was precut into packages that were dropped by trucks at foundation locations. Teams of carpenters, followed by electricians and plumbers moved systematically down the blocks of homes, completing a home every 16 minutes! (Ruff 2007). Others took note of Levitt's techniques and much suburban construction was done in the style of large scale mass production.

Levittown is also an example of how FHA and VA programs excluded persons of color. Levitt was unashamed of stating he had deed restrictions limiting occupancy to Caucasians. Historian Arnold Hirsch has documented FHA correspondence with Thurgood Marshall on the issue, with the FHA Commissioner Franklin Richards stating these covenants were a private matter and not an issue for FHA to confront (2006).

Funding for public housing was the fourth component of the 1949 Housing Act, building on the efforts begun in the preceding decade. As public housing siting was in the hands of local level political authorities (generally under white leadership), the white areas in both cities and the suburbs were rarely considered for such housing. These housing initiatives were tied to the elimination of blight and slums, and much of the stock built in the following decades took the form of modern high-rises, designed to keep per-unit construction costs low (Radford 2000). Chapter 9 provides greater details on the story of America's approach to public housing, getting into the specifics of what worked and what didn't.

The late 1940s housing legislation contributed to the development pattern of the following decades—single family housing in the suburbs for white households, and superblock public housing for low income urban households of color. These two distinct tracts of housing support continued during the 1950s and 1960s, with the suburbs expanding and urban areas struggling as white people and jobs relocated out of the cities—a phenomenon known as *white flight* (Orlebeke 2000; Radford 2000). There is irony that in the 1940s and 1950s the federal government's policies were working at cross-purposes. On the one hand, mortgage insurance and highways subsidized suburbanization—directing middle-class people and economic activity away from urban centers—while major federal investments underwrote new urban development seeking to prop up cities (O'Connor 2012).

Figure 4.5   Levittown, New York

Source: Getty Images, by Bernard Hoffman, used with permission

Part Two

Urban Crisis

The next big shift in federal housing involvement comes in the 1960s and is a reaction to the inadequacy of the urban investment strategy. The civil rights movement and extensive urban unrest marked a change in America. Inequalities in housing and jobs between whites and blacks, as well as police violence, fueled riots in such cities as New York; Chicago; Washington, DC; Los Angeles; Detroit; and Newark. More than 150 American cities experienced some form of violent discontent (Downs 1974). The financial conditions of cities were tenuous as jobs and people left for the suburbs, leaving the poor and elderly behind in places with underfunded public services. The gap between the lives of the rich and poor was increasing. President Johnson initiated the War on Poverty and the federal government adopted urban revitalization programs. In addition, key federal actions include the creation of the cabinet-level Department of Housing and Urban Development (HUD) in 1965 and the passing of the 1968 Fair Housing legislation (see Chapter 5). HUD was charged with enforcing non-discrimination laws for housing and continues this work today. Since passage of the original Fair Housing Act, federally protected groups have expanded from the initial categories of "race, color, religion, sex or national origin" to include prohibiting discrimination based on "disability or familial status" (U.S. Department of Housing and Urban Development 2007).

Major shifts were taking place within American society and were mirrored in the political realm. One major theme of this period was a turn toward public participation and empowerment. The displacements forced by urban renewal and demolitions associated with interstate highway construction eventually led to pushback from affected residents. Groups organized and called for resident voice and choice in development decisions. Advisory groups and local boards were formed for this purpose. Some of what was put in place could be categorized as mere window dressing or appeasement, without any real transfer of power to residents (Arnstein 1969). But there are also examples of successful efforts by local groups and tenants of public housing to shape decisions and demand improvements. One housing-related outcome of these efforts is the rise of neighborhood-level Community Development Corporations (CDCs). Senator Robert Kennedy was an early promoter of this effort, getting legislation to include funding for nonprofits established with advisory boards that included private sector leaders (Bedford Stuyvesant Restoration Corporation 2009).

CDCs are place-based nonprofits, working towards improved quality of life for residents. CDCs typically represent the interest of defined neighborhoods, addressing concerns ranging from housing conditions to jobs, crime, and public services. As nonprofits, CDCs get funding from government programs and foundations. Since the 1960s to today, CDCs have evolved, but they continue to play key roles in many areas—both urban and rural—when it comes to housing. CDCs have built housing, rehabbed housing, offered homeownership counseling, advocated for code enforcement of residential buildings, and organized for equality in the distribution of resources. They continue today as effective leaders in the housing arena, often working closely with local governments, banks, and corporations. In fact, in 2015, *Builder* magazine listed Habitat for Humanity, a nonprofit focused on homeownership for low income households, as the largest private housing developer in the country (based on a ranking of the number of housing closings completed) (Croce n.d.).

A second major turn—surprisingly, given the Democratic leadership—was towards private sector involvement. This is clearly captured in President Johnson's 1967 State of the Union address, in which he urged, "We should call upon the genius of the private industry and the most advanced technology to help rebuild our great cities" (quoted in von Hoffman 2012, 26). HUD established a variety of programs that provided subsidies to private developers of housing. Developers could offer affordable rent in some units of multifamily developments, due to the savings generated by federal low-interest construction loans or mortgage insurance. Momentum in housing construction during the late 1960s and early 1970s led to an expansion of the subsidized housing stock under private management (Listokin 1991). Public housing did not fare as well, with low levels of funding slowing new construction and caps on tenants' contributions to public housing rent challenging the ability of management to cover operating costs.

Box 4.3   Clarifying Terms

Affordable housing can be put into two categories:

Public Housing: Housing units that are constructed, managed, and owned by a public entity—most often a local housing authority.

Subsidized Housing: Housing units (often just a portion of the total housing units within a building) that are offered to income eligible households at a reduced rent. This reduced rent is possible because the developer of the housing received a subsidy from the federal government that reduced the cost of constructing the housing units. This subsidy can take many forms: mortgage insurance, a lower interest rate on a construction or mortgage loan, a cash payment generated by selling tax credits. The developer could be a private for-profit corporation, or a nonprofit corporation.

Increased Local Control and a Leaning Toward Demand-Side Funding

By the early 1970s, major shifts were launched under the administration of President Richard Nixon in response to less than stellar performance by some federal housing programs. Public confidence and support for federal housing initiatives plummeted as scandals over poor management, construction cost overruns, and indictments surrounding kickbacks came to light. In 1973, President Nixon declared an 18-month moratorium on housing funding and the federal approach that emerged set a different direction (Biles 2000; U.S. Department of Housing and Urban Development n.d.). The new approach had two main thrusts: one was a repackaging of federal dollars into block grants, and the other was a shift from increasing the supply of housing to influencing the demand (Orlebeke 2000), known as Section 8.

The block grant approach combined more than seven different housing programs into one large pool of funds granted to cities (U.S. Department of Housing and Urban Development, The Community Development Block Grant (CDBG) Program's 40th Anniversary n.d.). The federal government provided broad guidelines of eligible activities, but local authorities could determine the specific projects to be funded. The 1974 Community Development Block Grant program was joined in 1990 by the HOME block grant funds. Both federal block grants provide communities with money that can go to housing production, homeownership support, rehab programs, de-leading programs, and more.

The ideas of combining many programs into one block grant amount was a reaction to the poor management and bureaucracy of the federal government, and a desire for local control. The approach was considered more cost effective and has been embraced. The federal government continues to use the block grant approach for funding local level housing and community development projects.

The Section 8 program (referring to a section of a 1937 Housing Act), shifted funding away from costly subsidies to produce housing with only a small portion of the over-all units restricted to low and moderate-income households, to a program that eligible households used in existing private sector housing units. The program, still active today, allows eligible households to be subsidized in private sector housing.[1]

The largest number of households in the Section 8 program are served by "tenant-based" Housing Choice Vouchers. These vouchers are mobile—a household can take a voucher with them into the private sector to find a unit that meets its needs. The voucher is a commitment from the federal government to pay the landlord the por-tion of the rent that exceeds 30 percent of the tenant's monthly income (more details on housing vouchers are covered in Chapter 6). The rent charged by the owner must be reasonable—that is, must not exceed a cap set for the area—and the housing unit must meet safety standards and pass a quality inspection. The Section 8 program also has "project-based" units—a portion of units within a larger housing project that are made available to income-eligible households, based on a federal subsidy for the project development.

The new approach of vouchers relied on the construction expertise of the private sec-tor and meant facing fewer local battles over the siting of public or subsidized housing. The program was also aligned with the 1970s realization of changing housing needs. By this period, the perceived needs did not concern poor housing quality nearly so much as housing affordability. Another perceived benefit was that vouchers gave more direct choice to the households (Hays 1995). The housing vouchers are "portable"; households can move to different units as their housing needs change over time due to increas-ing or decreasing family size, job relocations, and more. Today, households with Hous-ing Choice Vouchers are the largest portion of low- and moderate-income households receiving HUD assistance (Congressional Budget Office 2015).

The rise of CDCs, discussed previously, led to federal housing-related action during this decade in a non-HUD arena—that of the banking sector. The 1975 passage of the Home Mortgage Disclosure Act (HMDA) and the Community Reinvestment Act (CRA) required banks to track and ultimately report publicly on their mortgage lending prac-tices. In addition, through the CRA, banks were required to document how they were supporting community development in areas they served. These acts reflected concern over ongoing patterns of redlining, and the redirection of deposits out of low-income neighborhoods and into others. The HMDA and CRA gave CDCs power as watchdogs over banking practices. During the 1980s and 1990s, CDCs could engage banks in cre-ating pools of funds for development improvements in urban and low-income areas (Schwartz 2015). Both Acts continue to play a role in keeping banks accountable for their loan patterns and in serving the needs of all depositors.

New Challenges from Recurring Economic Woes

The 1980s were a period with strong anti-government political rhetoric. The Reagan administration and Republican Congresses sought to minimize federal government spending and limit its role in market activities, including housing. There was a severe economic recession, with housing playing a key role. In the first part of the decade, mortgage interest rates peaked at over 16 percent, and the cost of housing skyrocketed. Several initiatives were born of these conditions. One is the introduction of the Low Income Housing Tax Credit (LIHTC). Others include programs to address the homelessness epidemic that emerged in the 1980s (Khadduri 2015).

The U.S. tax code plays an important role in housing policy (Poterba 1994). Its inadvertent but now entrenched, role in subsidizing homeownership is explored in depth in Chapter 6. During the 1980s the federal government created the LIHTC to subsidize the construction of affordable housing units without direct federal expenditures. It has been effective in bringing private investors into partnerships with non-profit housing developers (U.S. Department of Housing and Urban Development, The Low Income Housing Tax Credit 2004). The LIHTC does not show up in the federal budget; rather, the cost of the LIHTC is considered "tax expenditures"—basically, funds not collected due to tax credits and exemptions. Developers of affordable housing units can apply to states for tax credits that they then sell to raise funds for the housing construction. The tax credits are attractive for corporations or individuals with a federal tax liability, as they can use the credit against the liability. The developer uses the cash to lower the cost of construction, and this savings allows for some portion of units to be made available at affordable rents (Schwartz 2015). Those that purchase the tax credit do so at a discounted rate (valuing today cash they will receive in the future) and with an equity interest in the housing development. Today, LIHTC is involved in most new affordable housing production, although often in combination with other subsidies.

The spectacular rise in housing costs of the 1980s and the recession that followed led to a new face for homelessness. In fact, it wasn't until this time that the common use of the word came into being (Hays 1995). While some portion of the population has consistently faced living without permanent shelter, the homelessness that arose in the 1980s was different. Not only was the number of people living on the streets, with other households, or in emergency shelters much larger, the type of households in these positions changed. Rather than the more stereotypical single adult struggling with addiction, mental illness, or trauma, the homeless grew to include families with children, young and old people, employed households, and households that had once been homeowners. After media attention to conditions and pressure from advocates, the federal government passed the Stewart B. McKinney Act in 1987. Various types of assistance were authorized by this legislation, including funds for emergency shelters, supportive transitional housing, and targeted assistance for homeless people with long-term disabilities (Schwartz 2015). These programs have continued to evolve while homelessness, related to a lack of affordable housing, remains a part of the housing landscape in America.

Revisiting the First Wave of Responses

The 1990s became a time of reflection and correction. Deficiencies in earlier programs came to light and corrective actions were taken. There were many legislative initiatives, but we limit our attention here to corrections to what can be thought of as the first wave of housing responses—subsidized affordable units and public housing construction. A commitment to "mixed-income" housing approaches, and a philosophy of the deconcentration of poverty, gained traction.

One major area of correction was in response to what came to be known as the "expiring use crisis." In preceding decades, programs that subsidized housing construction in exchange for affordable units had contractually bound developers to making the units affordable for only 30 years. Looming on the horizon was the end of these contracts and the potential for developers to turn affordable units into market rate units. Affordable units were still very much in demand. If these conversions went forward (and some did), low and moderate income households would be searching for units. Many cities had a staggering number of units eligible for this conversion from affordable units to market-rate units. Ultimately the federal government provided new subsidies and promoted ways to make the maintenance of affordable units attractive to the property owners. This is one of the downsides of having affordable housing managed by the private sector. Today, subsidy programs prefer locking in permanent affordability requirements.

The other correction to prior efforts was in the realm of public housing. High crime rates, staggering vacancies, and a lack of maintenance all contributed to the collapse of public housing highrises serving families. Chapter 9 is devoted to the history of public housing, including the parts that worked and those that did not. It presents the many factors researchers have found that played a role in the ultimate demolition of many of the highrises that served families. What came out of these demolitions was a policy of deconcentrating poverty. One conclusion from the failure of highrises was that families would be better served living in mixed income areas. This became the basis of ongoing efforts to redevelop public housing in new forms. The 1993 HUD programs, HOPE VI and later 2010 Choice Neighborhoods, demolished some public housing developments and replaced them with mixed income, lower density housing expressly integrated into surrounding neighborhoods. The mixed income approach is discussed further in Chapter 6.

Most Recent Crisis

A variety of factors during the 2000s came together to create another major housing crisis marked by an extremely high foreclosure rate and decline in housing values with longer term repercussions for the economy (Schwartz 2015). High housing costs that kept households from homeownership led to new types of mortgages. Among other features, this riskier type of new mortgage, called sub-prime, relaxed standards on income and credit, allowing a greater number of households a way into homeownership. In exchange, these loans came with either higher interest rates or interest rates that changed over time.

An economic slowdown then led to foreclosures for households that had taken out these riskier sub-primes. This term refers to the fact the households did not meet the traditional or "prime" standards for loans due to any number of factors, like low or inconsistent source of income, unverified income amount, high amount of other debt, poor credit rating, or below normal cash down payment. As the economy stalled, however, foreclosures among standard mortgage holders also increased as jobs were lost (Herbert and Apgar 2010). Add to this a precipitous decline in housing values, and many people owed more than their home was worth. This made defaulting on the mortgage (stopping payments) a more palatable choice (Schwartz 2015). According to a report on the crisis prepared for Congress,

> Mortgage industry participants appear to have been drawn to encourage borrowers to take on these riskier loans due to the high profits associated with originating these loans and packaging them for sale to investors. . . . [And] some borrowers did not understand the true costs and risks of these loans while others were willing to take on these risks to tap accumulated home equity or to obtain larger homes.
>
> (Herbert and Apgar 2010)

The federal response to soaring foreclosures included homeowner financial counseling programs and refinancing initiatives to help homeowners stay in their homes. Banks and mortgage companies were encouraged to refinance the loans with terms homeowners could afford.

A part of this crisis was the increase in mortgage-backed securities (MBS) and higher risk private mortgage-backed securities (PMBS). Earlier in this chapter we referenced the 1938 establishment of Fannie Mae as an agency capable of buying mortgages to infuse new capital in loaning institutions. Over the years, Fannie Mae was joined by Freddie Mac (1970), as government sponsored entities (GSE) involved in packaging existing mortgages and selling them to investors. This is known as the secondary mortgage market. Ginnie Mae, created in 1968, also operates in the secondary market, not by issuing MBS but by insuring that MBS were made up of safer loans, all initiated through federal programs.

Private mortgage-backed securities are complex. Banks, or other mortgage companies, make mortgage loans (some riskier than others, as noted above). These loans are sold to the GSE and others, providing the bank with new cash to loan. The mortgages are pooled into PMBS, which investors purchase. What the investor is buying is the stream of dollars that will flow from the many households making the mortgage payments in the package PMBS. Investors discount the future value of receiving this stream of income to a value they are willing to pay today. In valuing these mortgage streams, investors must account for the fact that some of the people paying the mortgages will default, others will prepay early, and some may pay the principal down more aggressively than required. All three of these choices will decrease the income stream. These factors make calculating the actual value of PMBS tricky.

The so-called meltdown of the 2000s is related to PMBS that were rated as safe, but in fact were made up of many high-risk / sub-prime mortgages (Herbert and Apgar

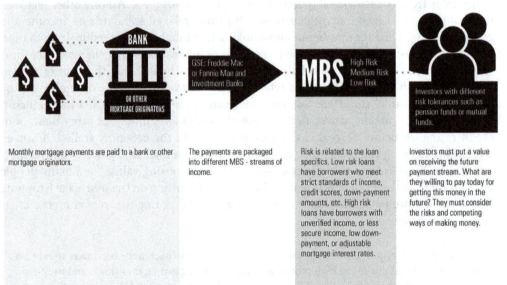

Figure 4.6   Basics of Mortgage Backed Securities

Source: Graphic © Ted Dobek, used with permission

2010). The economic downturn led to the riskier borrowers defaulting and/or walking away, and the investors' return on their PMBS dropped dramatically. Companies that had initiated sub-prime loans went bankrupt. Fannie Mae and Freddie Mac suffered large losses, and ultimately the federal government took them over, even though Fannie Mae and Freddie Mac were not explicitly backed with a federal guarantee (Duca 2013). Subsequently, banks tightened mortgage requirements and the federal government is still determining next steps for Fannie Mae and Freddie Mac. However, since the worst period of this housing and economic tumble, things have become more stable.

GENERALIZED TIMELINE
OF U.S. HOUSING POLICIES

HISTORICAL CONTEXT	ERA	
World War I	1910 to 1920s	United States Housing Corporation
Depression Real Estate Collapse	1930s	Creation of Housing Finance System & Homeownership as Cornerstone Public Housing Beginnings
World War II Baby Boom	1940s	GI Bill/VA Loans Housing Act of 1949/Urban Redevelopment
Suburbanization	1950s	Interstate Highway Act Housing Act of 1954/Urban Renewal
White Flight Urban Riots Civil Rights	1960s	Urban Disinvestment Creation of Department of Housing and Urban Development (HUD) Model Cities Program Fair Housing Laws
Deindustrialization Job Shifts	1970s	Short Term Moratorium on Housing Funds Block Grants: Entitlement and Local Control Rise of the Non-Profit & Community Development Corporation Banking Oversight: Community Reinvestment Act Housing Vouchers Begin
Soaring Inflation/Recession Less Government Movement Privatization Increases	1980s	Private Public Partnerships Mount Laurel, Fair Share, and Inclusionary Practices Rise of Homelessness/McKinney Act Public Housing Distressed Properties
	1990s	Expiring Use Crisis/Mark to Market Hope VI for Public Housing
Housing Bubble Real Estate Collapse	2000s	Foreclosure Crisis Choice Neighborhoods
	2010s	Affirmatively Furthering Fair Housing Rule (AFFH)

Note: This is a generalized timeline and does not include all actions, laws, and events.

Figure 4.7   Generalized Timeline of Federal Housing Policy

Note: This is a generalized timeline and does not include all actions, laws, and events.

Conclusion

This history presents a simplified outline of federal involvement in housing. It is meant to highlight key actions, connecting these actions to precipitating events and motivations. Some main points to take away include:

- Federal government involvement in housing has been motivated by a wide variety of factors: to improve public health; to expand homeownership; to increase jobs and support the economy; to make housing more affordable for low income households; to meet housing needs the market fails to address; to promote income integration and housing choice; to address homelessness; and to protect economic institutions and investors.
- Federal actions have been in response to specific historic events: the depression, wars, the baby boom, the urban crisis, and the foreclosure meltdown. The size of the housing industry means a crisis in housing will have ripple effects for the economy as a whole.
- Federal initiatives vary but have included directly building housing, subsidizing the private construction of affordable housing, supplementing rent payments of tenants in the private market, enforcing fair housing laws, and studying housing conditions.
- Federal housing policy is not limited to direct housing programs—tax policy and banking regulation are also ways the federal government influences housing.
- Federal housing involvement has generally given preference to private sector housing development and management, maintaining a very small amount of publicly owned and managed units.
- Federal programs often leave final decisions in the hands of local political entities. This is true for public housing and block grant programs.
- Federal responses to housing needs generally fall within a comfort zone of dominant political ideologies. Alternative ownership forms have not been supported, and public housing is targeted to a very narrow portion of society. These distinguish American federal housing approaches from those of some European countries.

Questions and Activities

1. Based on your reading, how would you characterize the degree of federal government involvement in housing? Why?
2. What purpose does the preamble of the Housing Act of 1949 serve? Do you see it as relevant today as it was in 1949?
3. Do you see the potential for a shift in the currently dominant preference among Americans for homeownership? What types of alternatives can you imagine? What would have to happen for alternatives to gain popularity?
4. Compare the 1930s Depression era with the post-2007 economic collapse. What similarities and what differences were in play?
5. The federal government has conducted extensive research and even run demonstration projects for housing programs. The research department of HUD, the Office of Policy Development and Research, works with researchers and universities to monitor housing trends and further our understanding of housing. Do some research of your own about any of the federal government's experimental

programs. Some examples of programs you may want to research are: Moving to Opportunity, Experimental Housing Allowance Program, or the Pre-purchase Homeownership Counseling Demonstration. For whatever program you research, be prepared to discuss basic facts about the pilot program (such as when it was implemented, if it is considered successful, and what the major long- and short-term effects of the program were.) Come to class prepared to discuss.

Note

1. Paying a portion of tenant's rents had been tried on a very small scale in prior programs, including in 1937, a program that allowed Public Housing Authorities to pay rent on private units for households, and then through the Experimental Housing Allowance Program (EHAP) in the early 1970s. The so-called Section 8 program represents the most sizeable commitment to this approach.

References

Arnstein, Sherry R. 1969. "A Ladder of Citizen Participation." *JAIP* 35(4): 216–224.

Bedford Stuyvesant Restoration Corporation. 2009. *Bedford Stuveysant Restoration Corporation: History*. Accessed September 16, 2016. www.restorationplaza.org/about/history.

Biles, Roger. 2000. "Pubic Housing and the Postwar Urban Renaissance, 1949–1973." In *From Tenements to the Taylor Homes: In Search of an Urban Housing Policy in Twentieth-Century Housing*, edited by John F. Bauman, Roger Biles, and Kristin M. Szylvian, 143–162. University Park, PA: The Pennsylvania State University Press.

Bureau of Industrial Housing and Transportation. 1918. "Report of the United States Housing Corporation." *Final Report, U. S. Department of Labor*. Washington, DC: Washington Printing Office. https://ia800204.us.archive.org/4/items/cu31924025931084/cu31924025931084.pdf.

Congressional Budget Office. 2015. *Federal Housing Assistance for Low-Income Households*. Washington, DC. www.cbo.gov/publication/50782.

Croce, Brian. n.d. *Builder*. Accessed September 11, 2016. www.builderonline.com/builder-100/builder-100-the-top-25-private-companies_o.

Davis, Kay. 2000. *Documenting the Other Half: The Social Reform Photogrpahy of Jacob Riis and Lewis Hine*. Accessed September 5, 2016. http://xroads.virginia.edu/~ma01/davis/photography/riis/lanternslides.html.

Downs, Anthony. 1974. "The Successes and Failures of Federal Housing Policy." *National Affairs*: 124–145.

Duca, John V. 2013. *Federal Reserve History: Subprime Mortgage Crisis 2007–2010*, November 22. Accessed September 17, 2016. www.federalreservehistory.org/Events/DetailView/55.

Gans, Herbert. 1967. *The Levittowners: Ways of Life and Politics in a New Suburban Community*. New York: Columbia University Press.

Gotham, Kevin Fox. 2000. "Racialization and the State: The Housing Act of 1934 and the Creation of the Federal Housing Administration." *Sociological Perspectives* 43(2): 291–317.

Grunow, Francis. 2003. *thedetroiter*. Retrieved from Paradise Lost: Hastings Street Remembered: www.thedetroiter.com/JUN03/DIGGINGMAY.html

Hanchett, Thomas W. 2000. "The Other 'Subsidized Housing': Federal Aid to Suburbanization 1940s–1960s." In *From Tenements to the Taylor Homes*, edited by John F. Bauman, Roger Biles, and Kristin M. Szylvian, 163–179. University Park, PA: The Pennsylvania State University Press.

Hays, Allen R. 1995. *The Federal Government and Urban Housing: Ideology and Change in Public Policy*. Albany: State University of New York Press.

Herbert, Christopher E., and William C. Apgar Jr. 2010. *Report to Congress on the Root Causes of the Foreclsoure Crisis*. Washington, DC: U.S. Department of Housing and Urban Development.

Jackson, Kenneth T. 1985. *Crabgrass Frontier: The Suburbanization of the United States.* New York: Oxford University Press.

Khadduri, Jill. 2015. "The Founding and Evolution of HUD: 50 Years, 1965–2015." In *HUD at 50: Creating Pathways to Opportunity,* by U.S. Department of Housing and Urban Development, 5–102. Washington D.C.: U.S. Department of Housing and Urban Development. https://huduser.gov/portal/publications/pdf/HUD-at-50-creating-pathways-to-Opportunity.pdf.

Landis, John D., and Kirk McClure. 2010. "Rethinking Federal Housing Policy." *Journal of American Planning Association* 76(3): 319–348.

Lang, Robert, and Rebecca R. Sohmer. 2000. "Legacy of the Housing Act of 1949: Past, Present and Future of Federal Housing and Urban Policy." *Housing Policy Debate* 11(2): 291–299.

Listokin, David. 1991. "Federal Housing Policy and Preservation: Historical Evolution, Patterns, and Implications." *Housing Policy Debate* 2(2): 157–185.

MacDonald, Cathy. 2012. *Walter P. Reuther Library Wayne State University.* Retrieved from Detroit's Black Bottom and Paradise Valley Neighborhoods: http://reuther.wayne.edu/node/8609

Martens, Betsey. 2009. "A Political History of Affordable Housing." *Journal of Housing & Community Development (NAHRO):* 6–12.

Morgenthau, Henry. 1963. *American Experience Citizen King Three Perspectives.* Accessed September 12, 2016. www.pbs.org/wgbh/amex/mlk/sfeature/sf_video_pop_04b_tr_qt.html.

Nenno, Mary K. 1979. "Housing in the Decade of the 1940's—The War and Postwar Periods Leave Their Marks." In *The Story of Housing,* edited by Gertrude Sipperly Fish, 242–267. New York: MacMillan Publishing Co, Inc.

O'Connor, Alice. 2012. "Swimming Against the Tide: A Brief History of Federal Policy in Poor Communities." In *The Community Development Reader,* 2nd Edition, edited by James DeFilippis and Susan Saegert, 11–29. New York: Routledge.

Orlebeke, Charles. 2000. "Evolution of Low Income Housing Policy 1929–1999." *Housing Policy Debate* 11(2): 489–500.

Poterba, James M. 1994. "Public Policy and Housing in the United States." In *Housing Markets in the U.S. and Japan,* edited by Yukio Noguchi and James Poterba, 239–256. Chicago: University of Chicago Press.

Radford, Gail. 2000. "The Federal Government and Housing During the Great Depression." In *From Tenements to the Taylor Homes: In Search of an Urban Housing Policy in Twentieth-Century America,* edited by John F. Bauman, Roger Biles, and Kristin M. Szylvian, 102–120. University Park, PA: The Pennsylvania State University Press.

Ruff, Joshua. 2007. "For Sale: The American Dream." *American History* Dec: 42–49.

Schwartz, Alex F. 2015. *Housing Policy in the United States,* 3rd Edition. New York: Routledge.

Smith, Charles H. and Nancy Schimmel. 2006. *Malvina Reynolds: Song Lyrics and Poems.* Accessed September 18, 2016. http://people.wku.edu/charles.smith/MALVINA/mr094.htm.

Thomas, June Manning. 1997. *Redevelopment and Race: Planning a Finer City in Postwar Detroit.* Detroit: Wayne State University Press.

Thomas, June Manning, & Ritzdorf, Marsha. 1997. Introduction. In June Manning Thomas, & Marsha Ritzdorf, *Urban Planning and the African-American Community: In the Shadows* (pp. 1–22). Thousand Oaks, CA: Sage Publications, Inc.

U.S. Census Bureau. 2013. "C-14A-OO Mortgage Characteristics—Owner-Occupied Units." *American Housing Survey.* Washington, DC. http://factfinder.census.gov/faces/tableservices/jsf/pages/productview.xhtml?pid=AHS_2013_C14AOO&prodType=table.

U.S. Department of Housing and Urban Development. 2004. "The Low Income Housing Tax Credit." *HUD Portal.* January. http://portal.hud.gov/hudportal/documents/huddoc?id=19565_Low IncomeTaxCredit.pdf.

U.S. Department of Housing and Urban Development. 2007. *Title VIII Fair Housing and Equal Opportunity.* September 25. Accessed September 18, 2016. http://portal.hud.gov/hudportal/HUD?src=/program_offices/fair_housing_equal_opp/progdesc/title8.

U.S. Department of Housing and Urban Development. n.d. *HUD Timeline: The 1970s.* Accessed September 16, 2016. www.huduser.gov/hud_timeline/.

U.S. Department of Housing and Urban Development. n.d. *The Community Development Block Grant (CDBG) Program's 40th Anniversary.* Accessed September 16, 2016. http://portal.hud.gov/hudportal/HUD?src=/program_offices/comm_planning/communitydevelopment/CDBG_Turns_40.

Vale, Lawrence J. 2007. *From the Puritans to the Projects: Public Housing and Public Neighbors.* Cambridge, MA: Harvard University Press.

von Hoffman, Alexander. 2012. "History Lessons for Today's Housing Policy the Political Processes of Making Low-Income Housing Policy." *Working Papers*, 321–376. Cambridge MA: Joint Center For Housing Studies Harvard University. www.jchs.harvard.edu/research/publications/history-lessons-today%E2%80%99s-housing-policy-political-processes-making-low-income-0.

5

HOUSING AND DISCRIMINATION

The United States has faced substantial challenges in the quest to provide equal opportunities for all Americans to live in housing of their choice. Bankers, realtors, landlords, and federal agencies have all taken actions in different ways to further segregation and perpetuate prejudice. At times throughout our country's history, discrimination has occurred in explicit and blatant ways, including through state and local laws and private sector practices. In more recent years, we have seen discriminatory practices that take a subtler, less immediately obvious form, but with no less serious consequences for individuals and our society overall.

In this chapter, you will be introduced to historical events and policies associated with housing discrimination that have had a longstanding influence on the evolution of cities and towns. You'll also get an overview of some of the contemporary types of housing discrimination that could be occurring in the cities and towns around you. We will also review the degree to which America is a segregated society, with groups isolated in residential areas in accordance with race, ethnicity, and class. There are communities that are almost all white, and others all black—despite laws against discrimination. Finally, we ask what forces contribute to this pattern, and what the consequences are of living in racial and ethnic enclaves, or areas of extreme wealth or poverty?

As you begin this chapter it might be helpful to reflect on the following questions:

- Is your household paying a fair price for the place where you are living?
- Was the process of securing the financing for your home fair?
- Could your household easily move to another house or apartment if you so desired? In any place you desired?
- Did the color of your skin, your accent, your religion, your clothing, your gender, your physical abilities, your sexual orientation, or your family situation have an influence on your household's ability to secure the housing you occupy?

If you answered "no" to any of these questions, you are not alone. Many households are affected by these issues and face serious challenges in their quest to secure housing in the United States.

If you answered "yes" to these questions, do not rule out their importance. Put yourself in another person's shoes and reconsider the questions above. Think about other members of your extended family, your friends, classmates, acquaintances, and even strangers you see on the street. Could they be answering these questions differently than you did? What is their experience in securing a place to live?

Terminology

To have a shared understanding of housing choice, it is best to clarify certain terms. The terms *prejudice, discrimination,* and *segregation* are intertwined, yet capture distinct aspects of housing choice. *Prejudice* is a negative feeling about a person based on a stereotype related to the person's membership in a certain group (race, ethnicity, sexual orientation, etc.). An example is a false belief that people of Latino heritage are lazy. *Discrimination* is actively acting on such prejudices and treating specific individuals (or groups) differently and unfavorably due to a prejudice. *Segregation* is a pattern of separation or grouping of households according to race, ethnic identity, class, or other characteristics. Many forces contribute to segregation, with discrimination being a major one, but others are economics, government actions (see Chapter 4), and choice (Adelman and Gocker 2007).

Part One

History of Housing Discrimination

The early twentieth century saw the rise of zoning in America, with southern cities choosing to establish districts that restricted blacks to certain areas, and other parts of the United States zoning to limit the mobility of ethnic groups.[1] After the Supreme Court of the United States found racially explicit zoning unconstitutional,[2] such public laws changed into private restrictive covenants (Brown 1972; Hirsch 1992). These covenants appeared on deeds and prohibited sale to certain racial and ethnic groups. Here is an example of the covenant language from a 1911 deed in San Diego, California:

> Provided always that this conveyance is made upon the following express conditions: FIRST: This property shall not be sold, leased, rented to or occupied by any person other than one of the Caucasian race. SECOND: No intoxicating liquors of any kind shall be manufactured or sold upon these premises. THIRD: No dwelling house shall be erected upon said premises which shall cost less than $1000.00.
>
> (Nicolaides and Wiese 2006)

The use of covenants and professional behavior that perpetuated segregation were the social norm embraced by the real estate industry and later integrated into federal government programs. According to historian Arnold R. Hirsch, during the early twentieth century, "local real estate boards and companies acted as so many gatekeepers, steering blacks into all-black areas and preserving the racial homogeneity of white neighborhoods" (Hirsch 1992, 74). In 1924, the Code of Ethics for the National Association of Real Estate Boards (now the National Association of Realtors) was amended to include the prohibition of selling property to those of any race or nationality that would threaten property values. This provision remained through 1950 (Brown 1972). The actions of realtors were supported by local neighborhoods who organized against black households who managed to move in, and by the many incidents of intimidation and violence against households of other races and ethnicities committed by white residents (Hirsch 1992).

Figure 5.1 The Green Book—a travel guide for African Americans published by Victor Hugo Green from 1936–1966. This guidebook listed places black Americans could eat or stay as they traveled the United States, under Jim Crow laws

Source: Schomburg Center for Research in Black Culture, New York Public Library

Box 5.1   Chicago Case Study

As a destination city for the great migration, Chicago has a history of racial discrimination highlighted by the unscrupulous tactics of landlords and real estate brokers, as well as organized intimidation from white neighborhood associations. Drawn from the segregated rural south to jobs in the industrializing north, black workers and their families relocating in the early twentieth century found an unwelcoming Chicago. The places blacks could rent were severely limited, due to racial deed covenants and active discrimination. This map indicates the concentrated area known as the "Black Belt" where these families could find housing. Also indicated are the large portions of the City that were restricted by covenants or were nonresidential.

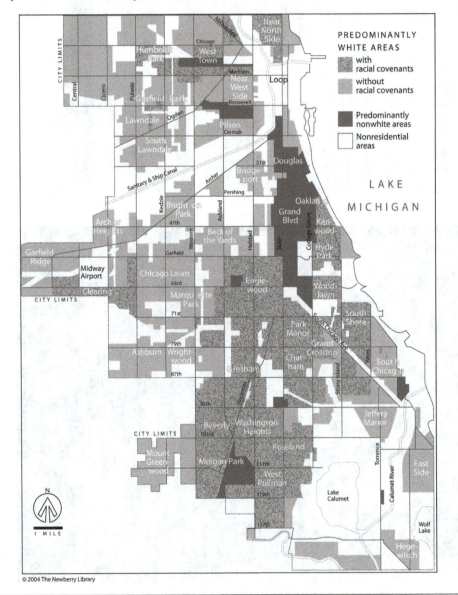

Figure 5.2   Racial Restrictive Covenants on Chicago's South Side in 1947

Source: Image courtesy of Newberry Library Chicago, used with permission

Based on a map compiled for Tovey v. Levy, 401 III. 393(1948)

Large numbers of blacks came to Chicago in search of employment and more freedom, in part fueled by anti-southern articles published in the black newspaper, *The Defender*.[3] In fact, the black population in Chicago increased by 160 percent from 1910–1920. This meant there was a large demand for housing while the supply was unnaturally limited. These conditions allowed real estate brokers to take advantage of black households, routinely charging them more than white households for comparable housing—or even inferior housing. The real estate industry *steered* blacks to the Black Belt. That is, black households were only shown housing in certain neighborhoods.

Another practice called "*blockbusting*" had realtors cause a panic among white renters or homeowners by having one black household take up residence in a white area. This transaction was followed up with a pitch to the rest of the white residents, encouraging them to sell quickly—and often at below top value. Realtors would then turn around and rent or sell the residence at an inflated value to the black householders due to the great pent-up demand. According to Garb, "the brokers and speculators who had provoked the racial transition used white fears and black aspirations to fill their bank accounts."[4]

The combination of strong demand and restricted supply also led to poorer conditions in black neighborhoods as multiple black households shared space, took in lodgers, and taxed the infrastructure. Add to this the tendency of landlords to diminish maintenance of housing once black households moved in, and these areas become marked by poor housing quality.

White residents also actively intimidated and threatened black households that moved into predominantly white areas. Terrorization with words and demonstrations, along with property damage, was not uncommon. Garb notes, "well-to-do white Chicagoans were leading the charge against black residents."[5] The explosive Chicago race riot of 1919 left many dead and 1,000 black families burned out of their homes. Such actions were in part met by black households choosing to avoid the potential for loss of life and/or property by staying within the artificial boundaries drawn by prejudice and discrimination.

Critical to understanding the history of housing discrimination in the United States is the history of *redlining*—the practice of denying or increasing the cost of services such as banking or insurance to residents of certain areas. The history of this practice as it relates to housing discrimination began with the Housing Act of 1934. Recall from Chapter 4 that the Housing Act was part of Franklin D. Roosevelt's New Deal, a set of government programs that were put into place to jump-start the country out of the Great Depression, one of the seminal socioeconomic events in U.S. history.

One of the goals of the Housing Act was to make housing and mortgages more affordable. The Home Owners' Loan Corporation (HOLC) was largely responsible for selecting and providing mortgages to citizens, many of whom would now, under the Housing Act, be able to afford housing when they previously could not. The HOLC created a series of "Residential Security Maps" for prominent United States cities that were the primary tools used for determining the level of security for real estate investments. These maps used a color-coded rating system that indicated which people were desirable home loan candidates based on the part of the city in which they lived. How was this discriminatory? These maps were essentially created based on a racist set of beliefs, assumptions, and generalizations as opposed to an accurate analysis of each household's capability to satisfy lending criteria. The inner parts of cities that contained high concentrations of poor people of color and immigrants were color coded as "undesirable" investment areas on these maps, while areas with high concentrations of white people were shown as highly desirable for real estate investments. The use of these maps when paired with racially based restrictive covenants put on the deeds of houses in white neighborhoods essentially meant that those living in areas defined as "undesirable" were unable to relocate, sell their home, qualify for any type of financing to invest in buying a home, or access loans for improving housing they owned (Hillier 2003, 394).

These maps were also used by the Federal Housing Administration (FHA) as part of its criteria for determining which mortgage loans they would insure. Research indicates the FHA was involved with the majority of mortgage lending activity between 1930 and 1950, yet, largely due to redlining, very few—less than two percent—FHA loans were made to nonwhite home buyers (Seitles 1996).

You can view examples of these maps (in color) at several websites (for instance, go to the Mapping Inequality project housed at the University of Richmond, Digital Scholarship Lab) and see how areas are graded and color coded along a continuum, including:

- A/green = Best. These are newly built neighborhoods on the edge of town and virtually free of African Americans or immigrants (including white immigrants). Lenders were encouraged to offer the maximum loan amount available to people in these areas.
- B/blue= Still Desirable. These areas are not as affluent as A areas and mortgage lenders were advised to make loans at 10 to 15 percent below the maximum available amount.
- C/yellow= Definitely Declining. Older neighborhoods with housing styles that might be outdated, and such areas were subject to "infiltration of a lower grade population."
- D/red = Hazardous. These were areas struggling for survival and characterized by an "undesirable population or an infiltration of it." Mortgage lenders would often refuse to make any loans in these neighborhoods.

(Jackson 1985)

Impacts of Redlining

In addition to blatantly proliferating inequality and racism in the United States, redlining had a number of effects on cities, many of which have had lasting impacts. Such impacts include (but aren't limited to) the following:

- Segregation (particularly because of simultaneous use of restrictive covenants which kept people of color from moving into different neighborhoods)
- Further decay of inner city neighborhoods
- Difficulty attracting and retaining those who could purchase homes without a loan
- Landlord abandonment leading to lower population density
- Other issues such as drugs and crime as a result of the above.

Redlined areas were essentially starved of the funding needed to support housing improvements and sales. This inevitably led to a decline of these neighborhoods—a self-fulfilling prophecy.[6]

Alleviating the Problem

Although housing discrimination undoubtedly remains a problem today, many steps have been taken to alleviate the problem: redlining as it was originally practiced using Residential Security Maps has been ameliorated, racial covenants have been outlawed, and the National Association of Realtors now supports fair housing. While there are many historical and political events that influenced the evolution of housing discrimination in the United States, here we highlight some key events that helped to alleviate this practice.

Shelley v. Kraemer, 1948

This landmark United States Supreme Court case held that racially restrictive covenants could not be held on real estate. The case began with the Shelly family, an African American family, buying a house in St. Louis, Missouri. At the time of purchasing the property, the family was unaware that a restrictive covenant from 1911 barred them from occupying the house. A neighbor, Louis Kraemer, sued the Shellys, attempting to prevent them from taking possession of the property. The case eventually went to the United States Supreme Court, where it was determined that to enforce these restrictive covenants was unconstitutional under the 14th Amendment because the equal protection clause prohibited restrictions on property sales based on race and ethnicity. This decision permitted the private enforcement of such covenants, just not state enforcement.

The Civil Rights Act, 1968

Also known as the Fair Housing Act, the Civil Rights Act of 1968 was signed into law by President Lyndon B. Johnson. The Act prohibited:

- refusal to sell or rent because of race, color, religion or national origin;
- advertising the sale or rental of housing while indicating preference based on race or religion; and
- coercing, threatening, intimidating, or interfering with a person's enjoyment of housing rights based on discriminatory reasons.

The act has also been amended to prohibit discrimination based on gender (in 1974) and to protect the rights of people with disabilities and families with children (in 1988).

Community Reinvestment Act, 1977

This act was passed to reduce discriminatory credit practices (redlining). It was designed to encourage banks and saving associations to meet the needs of people in all segments of communities. The act required banks to offer credit throughout their entire market areas (not just selected portions). It mandated that all banking institutions be evaluated to determine if they had met the credit needs of their entire service area.

Violence and Intimidation

Housing discrimination has been associated with many incidents of violence and intimidation, both before and after federal law made it illegal. While the current climate of discrimination may be arguably less overt, this history includes countless episodes of violence and threatening behaviors towards people of color who were trying to secure housing. Such actions by whites against people of color were not, and are not, an aberration. In Richard Rothstein's (2017) work on race, *The Color Law, A Forgotten History of How Our Government Segregated America*, he discusses the police-tolerated intimidation and violence that took place in the 1950s and 1960s. The context of these actions is the migration of African Americans to centers of employment in the north, after restrictive covenants were outlawed, and during the Civil Rights movement. African Americans who bought houses in all-white neighborhoods were frequently made to feel unwelcome, and intimidated when they attempted to move into such neighborhoods. The acts committed towards these families included mobs of hundreds, or even thousands, of people gathering outside their homes shouting racist epithets; phone threats; vandalism; Ku Klux Klan symbols being painted; the raising of Confederate flags; arson; the throwing of bricks, rocks, or other dangerous objects; or cross-burning. This type of harassment could sometimes continue for weeks on end without local authorities stepping in (Rothstein 2017). In addition, because of the ongoing racism present within law enforcement at that time, if law enforcement officers were dispatched to assist in these situations (which seldom happened) they sometimes refused to perform their duty or stood among the crowd of perpetrators, encouraging them. These types of acts, and their tolerance by law enforcement, helped to maintain racial segregation. White flight to the suburbs in the 1970s led to the tapering off of such threats and force. Violence against African-Americans did not and has not disappeared, however, as increased policing, sometimes as a result of calls from white neighbors, leads to more frequent interactions with law enforcement. Instances of racial epithet graffiti and symbolic threats such as leaving nooses, occur today, aimed at people's homes and African American institutions.

Box 5.2   Dramatizing the Story

Writer Lorraine Hansberry dramatized the reality of discrimination in Chicago— and her own family's lived experience—in her award-winning play *A Raisin in the Sun*. Hansberry was only 29 when the play premiered in 1959—the first Broadway production written by a female African American. The story of the black Younger family conveys the family's longing for a home of their own. The powerful dialogue of the play (and the later movie versions) tells of the universal desire for a home and all it represents in terms of identity, security, and success. The play includes a scene where a white homeowner comes to dissuade the family from moving to their newly purchased home in Clybourne Park, a white neighborhood of Chicago. He offers to buy it from them for more than they paid to maintain the lines of segregation. The play references, but does not show, examples of the violent tactics used by whites against African Americans. Hansberry's play draws from the harassment and violence her family faced when they sued to prevent the enforcement of racial covenants on property they bought on Chicago's south side.[7]

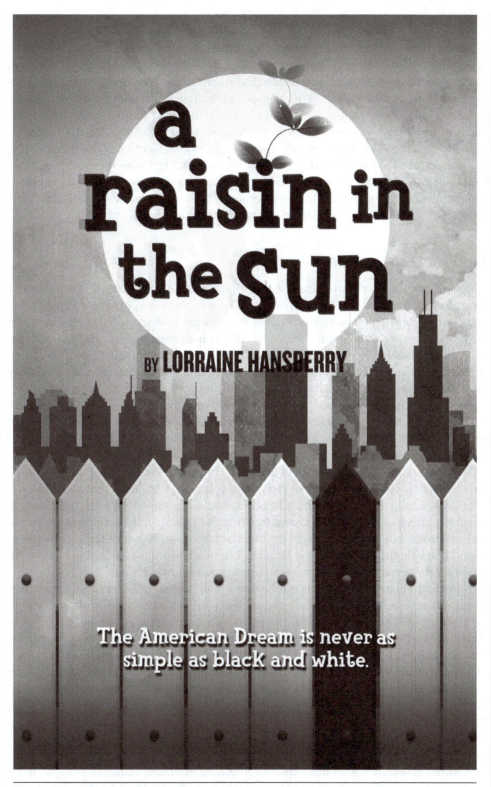

Figure 5.3 *A Raisin in the Sun* production poster

Source: Fred T. Billingsley, Jr., for Springfield Contemporary Theatre, Springfield MO, used with permission

Housing Discrimination in Recent Years

In the past few decades, research has shown that housing discrimination continues to occur not only against people of color, but against other households: same-sex couples, single parents, those with mental or physical disabilities, those using government housing assistance, and other subsets of the population. Researchers have uncovered discrimination through *controlled paired testing*. In these "housing audits," households that are identical in all ways (income, job status, credit scores, etc.) except for the factor being tested (race, ethnicity, sexual orientation, presence of children, physical disability, etc.) are trained and then sent separately to the same rental agencies (or mortgage brokers, banks, etc.). Afterward, each household team independently documents its experience. Such studies have uncovered the persistence of unequal treatment where all relevant economic and reference information on the households is equal.

Ethnic and Racial Discrimination

Linguistic profiling is the practice of discriminating against individuals based on the way they speak. You may be wondering how this type of discrimination would affect where people are living. This practice is a major issue in the housing industry because one of the primary ways people inquire about housing is over the telephone. It has been shown in a variety of different contexts that people who speak Standard English (a traditional, accent-free dialect of English predominantly spoken by white people) are more likely to be called back when they leave a message inquiring about housing. Simply based on the way they speak, they are also less likely to be asked personal questions (for instance, about the number of children in the household or other lifestyle issues), more likely to be quoted lower rental and purchase prices, and have more costs (such as deposits and agency fees) waived during the application process (Massey and Lundy 2001; Baugh 2000).

Researchers such as John Baugh at Stanford University and agencies such as the Massachusetts Fair Housing Center in Holyoke, Massachusetts, have been examining this issue more closely in recent years. Like other methods of discrimination, linguistic profiling can affect a community's characteristics. For example, if landlords who own several apartment buildings in a neighborhood strongly favor Standard English, people who speak "Black English" or "Chicano English" can be discouraged or unable to move to an area, thereby perpetuating ethnic/racial segregation (Baugh 2000).

Following Hurricane Katrina, the National Fair Housing Alliance and John Baugh undertook research to understand how Katrina survivors were being affected by linguistic profiling discrimination as they went about finding housing post-Katrina. During phone tests where participants were identified as Katrina survivors, 66 percent of the time whites were favored over blacks, regardless of similar qualifications. Results showed housing entities were failing to tell African American inquirers about available apartments, failing to return phone messages left by African Americans, failing to provide information to African Americans, quoting higher rent and security deposits to African Americans, and offering special inducements or discounts to white renters (National Fair Housing Alliance 2005). This is particularly significant because Hurricane Katrina disproportionately struck neighborhoods of color.

Another researcher who has explored linguistic profiling issues is Douglas Massey at Stanford University, who used his students to conduct a local housing audit. White and black students were assigned false identities and characteristics. The audit revealed a great deal of phone-based discrimination based on linguistic profiling. Compared to whites, blacks were less likely to get a call back from a rental agent, less likely to be told of a unit's availability, more likely to pay an application fee, and more likely to have credit mentioned as an issue. Those playing the part of lower-class black females were most disadvantaged. Another interesting aspect of this study was the reactions of the student callers who participated. White students reported being shocked at the degree to which blacks were discriminated against, and said that they would not have believed the results prior to the study (Massey and Lundy 2001).

Another form of racial or ethnic housing discrimination that has been shown in more recent years is discrimination based on one's name. For example, Carpusor and Loges conducted a study that examined the responses people received on rental applications based on the ethnicity suggested by the home seeker's name written on the application. The researchers distributed over a thousand inquiries to various landlords advertising apartment vacancies in the Los Angeles area. Of this sample, one of three names that implied Arab, African American, or white ethnicity was assigned randomly to each of the messages. The outcome showed that in general African American and Arab names received far fewer responses than the white names; the African American names received the fewest responses overall (Carpusor and Loges 2006).

Other researchers have examined the marketing techniques used by predatory lenders and characteristics of victims of predatory loans and borrowers of sub-prime loans. Hinnant-Bernard and Crull studied data from the Home Mortgage Disclosure Act, from the Citizens for Community Improvement of Des Moines, Iowa, and from the Iowa Attorney General's office to research such issues and found that African American applicants, low-income applicants, and applicants receiving loans for home refinance had the highest probability of becoming victims of *reverse redlining* (Hinnant-Bernard and Crull 2004). Reverse redlining is defined as the targeted promotion of less favorable loan and insurance terms to specific groups, or in specific neighborhoods.

Zhao's 2005 study examined discriminatory behavior of real estate brokers. Using national audit data from the 1989 and 2000 Housing Discrimination Studies, Zhao found that blacks and Hispanics are shown 30 percent and 10 percent, respectively, fewer units than whites. His results also showed that since 1989, discrimination against blacks increased by 12 percent. Regarding brokers' marketing behaviors, the results pointed to the existence of and an increasing trend of brokers withholding housing in particular neighborhoods from people seeking homes, or, in other words, redlining (Zhao 2005).

Same-Sex Couples and Single Parents

It has been shown that family household structures including same-sex couples and single parents are likely to face discrimination in the housing market. Nathanael Lauster and Adam Easterbrook have shown that these types of household structures are likely to face discrimination. Through inquiries made about one and two bedroom apartments, they analyzed responses to five different two-person household scenarios including one heterosexual couple, two same-sex couples, and two single parents. Their results show that male same-sex couples, single mothers, and single fathers face significant discrimination compared to heterosexual couples. Male same-sex couples, for example, were about 24 percent less likely to receive a positive response from inquiries than heterosexual couples in their studies. They also found that discrimination against same-sex male couples often takes the form of nonresponsiveness, which makes it unlikely such households will recognize the behavior as discrimination (Lauster and Easterbrook 2011).

Women

The experiences of women facing discrimination in the housing market have been explored by researchers in recent years, revealing serious issues in the way that women are treated when trying to secure housing. For example, Paula Barata and Donna Stewart found that landlords were 10 times less likely to report units as available when inquirers identified as coming from a women's shelter and showed that when asked via telephone survey, 23 percent of landlords said they would not rent to a hypothetical battered woman. Their results suggest that this type of discrimination is a serious issue contributing to women finding safe and affordable housing (Barata and Stewart 2010). Other examples are landlords giving eviction notices to victims of domestic violence based on the physical force being a breach of the terms of the lease. In several cases it has been successfully argued that this is discrimination based on sex, and there is a disparate effect on women, who are most often the victims of domestic violence.[8]

Disabled and Elderly Persons

Discrimination against people with disabilities as well as the need for ample housing for the increasing number of elderly and disabled individuals in the U.S. housing market has been explored in a variety of different ways. For example, Smith, Rayer, and Smith examined accessibility for disabled persons in housing, finding it to be a critical issue for city planners and policy makers. Their study projected that 21 percent of households will have at least 1 disabled resident in 2050, pointing out that given the desire for most people to live independently for as long as possible, such numbers reflect a growing need for housing units that are accessible to disabled individuals (2008). That being the case, the need to study, understand, and take measures against disability discrimination in the housing industry will be an accompanying necessity.

The New Discrimination

As shown in these studies, the new discrimination is not easy to detect. No longer are groups directly told their race or ethnicity is problematic, nor are there exclusionary signs posted. Rather, the landlord or real estate agent acts more subtly by rejecting or putting off the potential tenant or buyer with lies and excuses that seem possible. Such discrimination might sound pleasant and apologetic, like:

> "We just rented the last unit."
> "Your son and daughter can't share a bedroom."
> "You can't put a ramp in here."
> "I'd show the place to you but I don't have the key right now."
> "We have a very long waiting list on those apartments."
> "I'm glad to rent to you but your Latino friend can't live here or visit because the neighbors would object."
> "There are a lot of different types living there . . . I'm not supposed to be telling you that, but you have a daughter and I like you." (Mannina, 2008)

Active discrimination in housing through laws, government programs, and the policies and attitudes of banks, realtors, and landlords, have contributed to our highly segregated society. While new protections now allow for litigation against such unequal treatment, research clearly indicates that discriminatory practices based on race, ethnicity, and other characteristics persist. In Chapter 1 (and later in Chapter 7) we explored the very significant role housing plays in life opportunities and identity. Discriminatory practices (and the legacy of past actions) limit the potential of many members of our society and are real barriers to people being able to have equal opportunities in life.

Part Two

Segregation

Many Americans are surprised to learn that today's America is more segregated by race than that of 150 years ago (Desmond and Emirbayer 2016). The urbanization and industrialization of the intervening decades involved the large-scale movement of people, and an influx of immigrants. Where these arrivals settled was shaped by the policies, laws, and behaviors described above, and in Chapter 4. Racialized neighborhoods and ethnic enclaves were formed by deed covenants, real estate practices, federal housing programs, and a preference for co-ethnic living. Much of this pattern, established in the early twentieth century, has persisted across time even after the adoption of Fair Housing laws. While many believed the civil rights era "fixed" the problem of forced segregation, this was not true. Immigrant groups have over time gained social mobility and integrated with increasing class attainment, although black Americans have been uniquely excluded over time. In 1993 Douglas Massey and Nancy Denton published a seminal work on segregation, *American Apartheid: Segregation and the Making of the Underclass*. The word "apartheid" was purposefully chosen to bring segregation out of the shadows and shed light on the individual, institutional, and policy forces that shaped, and were continuing to shape, the residential landscape by race and class.

Segregated living in the United States increased from the Civil War to a peak in the 1960s and 1970s. Since that time, the U.S. Census reveals slow declines in the black-white segregation of America and steady segregation levels between whites and Hispanics (Logan and Stults 2011). Segregation—the degree to which two or more groups live separately—is measured in different ways. A common method is called the Dissimilarity Index, which asks how many people would have to move, for an area to reflect an equal distribution of groups throughout? For instance, if the black population represents 20 percent of the metropolitan region, how many people would have to move for each smaller area (generally census tracts) to be 20 percent black? There are several research groups with websites where you can look up the Dissimilarity Index for the major metropolitan areas of the United States.[9] The general trend shows, nationally from 1980 to 2010, whites' dissimilarity with blacks dropped from 68.4 to 53.5 percent. In other words, to have an even distribution of whites across the country, in 2010, 53.5 percent of white Americans would have to move. The same figures for the white dissimilarity with Hispanics, from 1980–2010 are 40.5 to 42.8 percent. White/black dissimilarity has been the highest, and is only very slowly declining with each decade. A dissimilarity index over 60 is considered very high, and 30–60 moderate. Before 1940, no urban areas in America had a Dissimilarity Index over 60 (Massey 2008). In 2010 the nine major urban areas of Detroit, Milwaukee, New York, Newark, Chicago, Philadelphia, Miami, Cleveland, and St. Louis, with sizeable black populations, all had black/white Dissimilarity Indexes over 70 percent (Logan and Stults 2011).

Another measurement of segregation considers the degree of racial or ethnic isolation that happens in day-to-day living. Figure 5.4 shows the neighborhood composition for average Americans by group. Whites are much more likely to live in neighborhoods that are overwhelmingly single race, that of majority white, than the U.S. Census defined groups of black, Hispanic, and Asian Americans. The neighborhood segregation

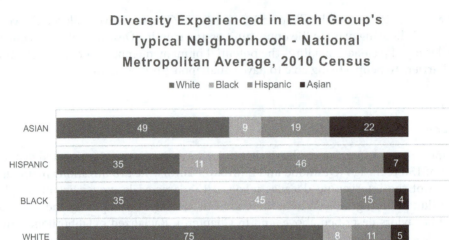

Figure 5.4   Average Neighborhood Composition

Source: John R. Logan and Brian Stults. 2011. "The Persistence of Segregation in the Metropolis: New Findings from the 2010 Census," Census Brief prepared for Project US2010. www.s4.brown.edu/us2010.

patterns are another way of assessing "exposure" to other groups by either attending public school, undertaking routine shopping, or enjoying local entertainment venues.

Causes

Segregation is complex as there are many contributing factors, some historical, some contemporary. The factors can be grouped under the headings of state, market, and social, or race, related actions. Figure 5.5 shows the many contributing factors discussed here. While we will discuss them separately, they act in unison and are often intertwined. Consequently, segregation, drawing from historical roots, has persisted as an American challenge (Adelman and Gocker 2007).

State Actions

By now (see Chapter 4 and part one of Chapter 5) you are familiar with historical state-sponsored actions that segregated black and ethnic minorities into specified residential areas. Deed restrictions, FHA insurance policies, VA programs, public housing (also see Chapter 9), and urban renewal all worked to constrain where black Americans and other groups could live. The legacy of these actions is a racialized America. While some have been able to move to more integrated areas with better services, the unjust state actions have had lasting limiting effects for others. Wealth accumulation for black and minority families has not been the same as for whites, who benefited from the home appreciation financed through FHA and VA programs (Charles 2003; Massey 2008). Furthermore, due to racism, blacks who do become homeowners see in general less appreciation than white households (Carr and Kutty 2008). The implications of this are comparably lower wealth accumulation. Contemporary local zoning practices (see Chapter 10) are additional state actions that uphold segregation. Suburban and rural

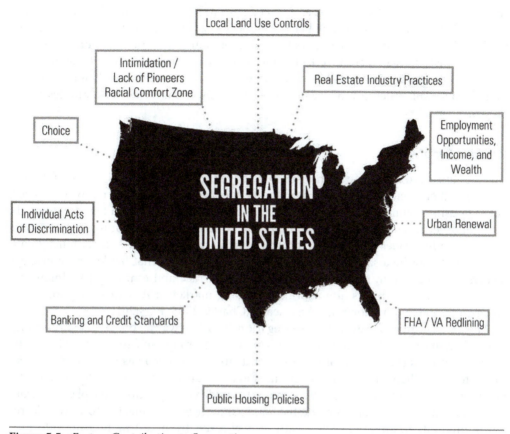

Figure 5.5   Factors Contributing to Segregation
Source: Graphic © Ted Dobek, used with permission

areas have adopted regulations that are exclusionary in effect. While no longer explicitly zoning to deny blacks and others access, communities that do not permit multifamily structures, or require a large minimum lot size, are gatekeeping which groups can live in the community (Briggs 2005).

Market Actions

Market or economic factors contribute to segregation, as nonwhite households (except for Asians) generally have lower incomes than whites (DeNavas-Walt, Proctor, and Smith 2011).[10] Higher unemployment rates and lower wage jobs among blacks and Latinos translate into reduced housing choices. At the same time, these income and wealth factors are both cause and consequence. These economic limitations keep low income households in certain neighborhoods—the very neighborhoods that offer substandard education and a reduced quality of life. (See Chapter 7 for a full discussion of these conditions.) Children raised in areas with poor public education, high crime rates, exposure to environmental toxins, and few jobs, have much to overcome to succeed economically. In this way, the economic segregation of households reinforces inequities and passes on limited options to future generations (Adelman and Gocker 2007).

American society is both racially and economically segregated. The interaction between race and class, however, can make it difficult to determine what drives the segregated pattern of living we see. Are concentrations of wealthy white Americans, and concentrations of low income black Americans, simply a reflection of incomes and wealth? This is a question researchers have been pursuing. The answer is emerging that race does matter—segregation reflects more than disparities in income (Adelman and Gocker 2007; Charles 2003). Whites will actively avoid or leave areas when the population of blacks and other groups reaches a certain level—even if the black families are in the same class.

Race and Social Action

The prejudice and discrimination discussed above play a role in the isolation of groups by race and ethnicity. As we saw, despite having laws on the books, many are locked out of housing and neighborhoods due to active discrimination. Open hostility towards those of other races or ethnicities continues in America, with acts of intimidation and violence sending a clear message that certain groups are unwanted or certain neighborhoods would not be a safe space. Recent studies have found that banks and mortgage lenders discriminate in real estate lending based on race and ethnicity (Adelman and Gocker 2007). This creates almost a dual housing market in America—one for white Americans, and another for black Americans (Charles 2003; Hirsch 1992).

Race, and ethnicity, can affect segregation in other ways, too. A question many researchers have sought to answer is to what degree groups self-segregate. That is, to what extent does the pattern of separate residential areas occur as households choose to locate with others of similar backgrounds and cultures? A preference for living with others in your cultural group can be a choice to reside where institutions, places of worship, and commercial shops provide the goods and services connected to your culture. For immigrants to an area, such a pattern may result from getting housing information through your social network, or a natural tendency to live near extended family members.

As you can imagine, it is not easy to determine to what degree segregation is a choice and to what degree it is about exclusion. In the 1970s researchers Farley and Schumer developed a tool to identify people's preferences for the racial and ethnic makeup of their neighborhood. Figure 5.6 shows a series of cards these researchers used to determine where people said they wanted to live. The cards show differing degrees of integration among racial and ethnic groups. Each card has fifteen houses, with increasing degrees of integration of another group. Participants were asked the following questions: Looking at the makeup of this neighborhood how comfortable would you feel living there? How likely would you be to move if your neighborhood changed to this mix? How likely would you be to move in to this neighborhood? (Farley and Frey 1994).

These neighborhood cards have been used in several studies in the past decades. Reflecting on the results of studies conducted during 1976–2004, lead researcher Reynolds Farley writes that he has "cautious optimism" that attitudes are changing (Farley 2011, 41). As seen in Figure 5.7, over time more whites are willing to live in integrated neighborhoods, although nearly half would still not choose to live in neighborhoods that are one-third black, and this increases to 65 percent when asked about living in a neighborhood that was majority black (Farley 2011). Other studies with these cards have found the preferences of black households are markedly different. The two neighborhoods on the cards that were substantially integrated (8 and 5 black households out of 15) were the preferred options, and black households expressed reluctance to be the only black family in an all-white area (Charles 2003). Expanding this study to include other groups (Hispanics and Asians) Charles found "all groups exhibit preferences for both meaningful

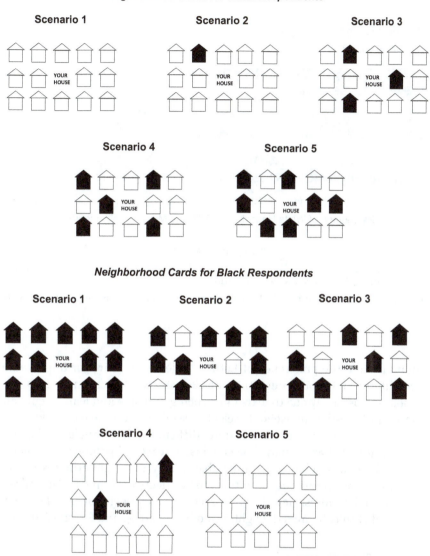

Figure 5.6 Farley-Schuman Neighborhood Cards for Black and White Respondents from the 1992–1994 Multi-City Study of Urban Inequality, used with permission by Farley and Schumann.

integration and a substantial presence of same-race neighbors, although preferences for same-race neighbors are not uniform across groups: whites exhibit the strongest preference for same-race neighbors and blacks the weakest" (Charles 2003, 185).

Others studying segregation have sought to better understand these preferences, investigating if whites rated neighborhoods with black or Latino Americans less desirable as they associated such areas with social problems such as crime, vacant property, and unemployment, rather than rejecting the areas based on the race of residents alone. Researchers have found whites reject these areas not solely based on a perception of inferior conditions. For whites, part of the rejection of certain areas is related to the race of residents—not household income or neighborhood conditions (Swaroop and Krysan 2011). Blacks in this study preferred more integrated areas largely due to the improved

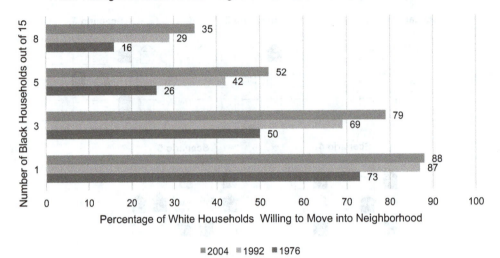

Figure 5.7   Measuring Attitudes toward Integration

Source: Data from Farley, Reynolds. 2011. "The Waning of American Apartheid?" in *Contexts* 10 (3): 38–42.

living conditions, and the preference of Latinos reflected a desire for improved neighborhood conditions and more integration. Blacks were unlikely to move into all-white neighborhoods—most likely due to fears of not being welcome and fear of reprisal.

The question of whether households reject areas due to the race of residents or the social conditions is far from settled. It is quite difficult to disentangle the factors, attitudes, and behaviors that are in play. The conclusion reached by these researchers, however, is that "efforts to build and sustain stable integrated neighborhoods cannot rely solely on improving neighborhood conditions to be effective, but must also address how individuals, especially whites, view different-race/ethnicity neighbors and how they perceive racially and ethnically mixed neighborhoods" (Swaroop and Krysan 2011, 1227).

Consequences of Segregation

Under segregation some groups enjoy great advantage; others are greatly disadvantaged. The study of segregation rests on the realization that this pattern of residential living is inequitable, and comes at a cost for American society. The following drawbacks are associated with segregation:

- Stereotypes and racism are fortified. Neighborhoods are a primary place for social interactions. If one does not encounter and interact with those of other classes, races, or ethnicities in one's routine life, then one relies on stereotypes, and other false accounts, to understand the other groups and their life experiences (Charles 2003).
- Inequality and disadvantage are produced and reproduced. Residential areas with concentrated poverty suffer from disinvestment, and services are poor. Those that live there experience substandard conditions and those raised there are less likely to be able to succeed. In this way, there is a "self-reinforcing cycle where income

inequalities cause segregation and segregation furthers income inequality" (Metropolitan Planning Council 2017, 5).

- Schools, generally a locally based service, are segregated and unequal. Schools in white communities prepare students for a system and institutions designed by the white middle class. The formal education, and the informal networks and assumptions about college, support this type of success and mobility. Schools in areas of concentrated poverty have fewer resources. Integrated schools are needed to prepare students to live and work together, and to sustain a future non–white majority society (Orfield, Ee, Frankenberg, and Siegel-Hawley 2016).
- Many never reach their potential. Those who are unable to move to areas of opportunity may not achieve academic success or full employment. While it is not possible to calculate what is lost in terms of creativity and productivity, it is clear our segregated living squanders the resource of the potential contributions of many individuals (Adelman and Gocker 2007) and can emotionally scar those isolated in declining areas (Desmond and Emirbayer 2016).
- American democratic values go unrealized. The complexity and covert nature of the forces furthering segregation make it difficult to pinpoint and address the causes. Given this, America has not focused on altering this reality. The current pattern of segregation, however, is not inevitable. Its continued existence conflicts with our shared cultural value of equal opportunity for all, and yet its stark reality gives symbolic validity to the false belief in differences between groups (Desmond and Emirbayer 2016).

Conclusion

To examine the pattern of residential areas in America is to see segregation along the lines of race, ethnicity, and class. One cannot consider the state of housing in America without facing the issues of discrimination and segregation, which work against decent housing for all. Outlawing discrimination in housing did not eliminate the practice; it only made it less blatant, and enforcement efforts are not robust. Continued instances of discrimination bolster our segregated patterns of living. Whites benefit economically from segregation, while blacks, the group most highly segregated, are dealt unequal schools, inaccessibility of employment, and lower public safety. Our future is one of diversity; our present segregated living does not bode well for an America embodying its values and reaching its full potential.

Questions and Activities

1. This chapter began with a series of questions meant to get you thinking about your own personal experience with housing discrimination (or lack thereof) and the experience of those around you. Now that you have learned a bit more about different types of housing discrimination, take some time to reconsider the questions at the beginning of the chapter. In small focus group of three or four people, review these questions together. Do others in your group have answers that differ from your own? If you are comfortable sharing your experiences, open up to your fellow group members and reflect on these questions together.

2. You are on a team of professionals that are working to alleviate a supermarket-redlining problem occurring in the region (the practice of major chains not locating in or leaving specific low-income neighborhoods). You need to determine the extent of the problem and what steps should be taken to alleviate it.

To do this, you must collect appropriate data to understand the problem and its impacts on the region. Please determine eight types of data that you would collect for this purpose. Your data can be quantitative (numbers-based) or qualitative (description-based). Be sure to explain your choices.

3. Use of Primary Documents: Review the four copies of actual FHA neighborhood analysis sheets (Figures 5.8–5.11). For each, note what comments there are on economic conditions, as well as comments on the racial and ethnic makeup of residents. Review each form and: (1) Note how the Section 1. Population classifies people, including the notes in 1.e. (2) Read through the description and characteristics of the area in Section 8. (3) What surprises or disturbs you about these documents? What racial prejudicial terms are used? What characteristics of the area that the forms reflect were considered in the evaluation? Considering these are official documents, what can you conclude about the federal government's role in determining what areas received housing funding? Discuss how stereotypes and norms on prejudice have changed since this time.

4. There is little question that we have ample evidence that housing discrimination occurs today in a variety of different formats. However, there is also little question that reporting and getting solid documentation of housing discrimination presents many challenges, particularly depending on the nature of the discrimination at hand. Given this, consider the following questions:

   a. What type of discriminatory housing offense might be straightforward to report to local authorities? Explain your answer and provide examples.
   b. What type of housing discrimination might be more of a challenge to report? Explain your answer and provide examples.

5. Earlier in this chapter you were introduced to a study completed by the National Fair Housing Alliance investigating post-Katrina housing discrimination against African Americans. Based on the results that were previously discussed in this chapter, the report produced a list of nine recommendations to deal with this type of housing discrimination. These recommendations, along with the entire report, can be found at the National Fair Housing website.

   As your assignment, review this ten-page report including these recommendations (found on page 8) and offer your analysis. What are your impressions? Do you think these recommendations will help alleviate the problem? Which ones will be more effective than others? Are there any you feel will be ineffective?

6. To prepare for Part 2 (Segregation) of this chapter, choose the urban area closest to where you live and collect the census data on the racial breakdown of the city and its surrounding suburban communities. List each community and the percent of its population the U.S. Census reports as white, black, and Hispanic. (These figures are easy to get through the U.S. Census American Fact Finder website.) Compare these figures. Write down what you think contributes to the pattern you see in terms of where racial groups live. Bring your reasons to the class, and working in a team, group your answers into categories (e.g., economic factors, discriminatory actions, etc.).

7. Go back and review Figure 5.6 that shows the neighborhood survey cards for black and white respondents from the 1992–1994 Multi-City Study of Urban Inequality conducted by Farley-Schuman. Examine these cards and consider what your answers would be to these questions: Would you be comfortable in this neighborhood? Would you move from this neighborhood? And would you move into this neighborhood? Write down your thoughts on what is behind your choices.

AREA DESCRIPTIONS - SECURITY MAP OF <u>LOS ANGELES COUNTY</u>

1. POPULATION: a. Increasing <u>Slowly</u>   Decreasing _____   Static _____

  .b. Class and Occupation <u>Business & professional men, skilled artisans, & white</u>
                <u>collar workers. Income $1800 to $3600 & up</u>

  c. Foreign Families <u>Few</u> % Nationalities <u>None subversive</u>   d. Negro <u>None</u> %

  e. Shifting or Infiltration <u>None apparent</u>

2. BUILDINGS:

	PREDOMINATING 85%	OTHER TYPE %
a. Type and Size	5, 6 & 7 rooms	Large outmoded types 5%
b. Construction	Frame, stucco & masonry	8, 9 & 10 rooms 10%
c. Average Age	16 years	
d. Repair	Good	
e. Occupancy	98%	
f. Owner-occupied	75%	
g. 1935 Price Bracket	$ 3250-5000 % chge	$ % chge
h. 1937 Price Bracket	$ 3500-5500 %	$ %
i. 1939 Price Bracket	$ 3500-5500 %	$ %
j. Sales Demand	Good	
k. Predicted Price Trend (next 6-12 months)	Static	
l. 1935 Rent Bracket	$ 25-50 % chge	$ % chge
m. 1937 Rent Bracket	$ 30-60 %	$ %
n. 1939 Rent Bracket	$ 30-60 %	$ %
o. Rental Demand	Good	
p. Predicted Rent Trend (next 6-12 months)	Static	

                               $4500 to $7500
3. NEW CONSTRCTN (past yr) No <u>35</u> Type & Price <u>5 & 6 rooms</u> How selling <u>Moderately</u>

4. OVERHANG OF HOME PROPERTIES: a. HOLC <u>1 ?</u>   b. Institutions <u>Few</u>

5. SALE OF HOME PROPERTIES (<u>3</u> yr) a. HOLC <u>None</u> ?   b. Institutions <u>Few</u>

6. MORTGAGE FUNDS: <u>Ample</u>   7. Total Tax Rate per $1000 (193<u>7/8</u> $49.54
                                       Co. $37.54 Cy. $11.90

8. DESCRIPTION AND CHARACTERISTICS OF AREA: Terrain: level with favorable grades.
No construction hazards. Land improved 85%. Deed restrictions have expired
but movement is on foot to cover area with protective racial restrictions.
Zoning is single family residential. Conveniences are all readily available.
This area has been developing steadily for more than 25 years and is still
comparatively active. Construction is of standard quality or better and maintenance indicates a high pride of occupancy. Population is homogeneous, the
district being particularly favored by the business men of the community.
Variance in size and types of improvements gives a heterogeneous aspect to
parts of area. Convenience of location and stability are outstanding
characteristics. Proximity to Pasadena Golf Club and Altadena Recreational
Center are favorable influences. Prevalence of age and obsolescence are
derogatory factors. Indications are that the area will remain desirable for
a number of years to come and it is accorded a "medial blue" grade.

9. LOCATION <u>North Pasadena</u>   SECURITY GRADE Med. B AREA NO. <u>B-29</u>   DATE <u>4-14-39</u>

Figure 5.8   HOLC Appraisal Sheets from the National Archives

1. **POPULATION:** a. *Increasing* _____ *Decreasing* _____ *State* Yes

   b. *Class and Occupation* Skilled artisans, letter carriers, laborers, & WPA workers

                                      Income $700-$1800

   c. *Foreign Families* Few% *Nationalities* Mexicans & Italians   d. *Negro* 5 %

   e. *Shifting or Infiltration* Indications of increasing subversive racial influences

2. **BUILDINGS:**   PREDOMINATING 90 %   OTHER TYPE   %

	PREDOMINATING 90%		OTHER TYPE %	
a. Type and Size	5 & 6 room			
b. Construction	Frame & stucco			
c. Average Age	18 years			
d. Repair	Fair			
e. Occupancy	96%			
f. Owner-occupied	80%			
g. 1935 Price Bracket	$ 3000-4000	% change	$	% change
h. 1937 Price Bracket	$ 2750-3750	%	$	%
i. 1939 Price Bracket	$ 2750-3750	%	$	%
j. Sales Demand	Poor			
k. Predicted Price Trend (next 6-12 months)	Downward			
l. 1935 Rent Bracket	$ 25-35	% change	$	% change
m. 1937 Rent Bracket	$ 25-35	%	$	%
n. 1939 Rent Bracket	$ 25-35	%	$	%
o. Rental Demand	Fair			
p. Predicted Rent Trend (next 6-12 months)	Static			

3. **NEW CONSTRUCTION** (*past yr.*) No. 0 *Type & Price* -- *How Selling* --

4. **OVERHANG OF HOME PROPERTIES:** a. HOLC 0   b. *Institutions* Few

5. **SALE OF HOME PROPERTIES** (3 *yr.*) a. HOLC 1   b. *Institutions* Few

6. **MORTGAGE FUNDS:** Limited   7. TOTAL TAX RATE PER $1000 (1937-) $ 50.27
                                 County $11.90-City $38.37   1938

8. **DESCRIPTION AND CHARACTERISTICS OF AREA:**

Terrain: Level with favorable grades. No construction hazards or flood threats. Land improved 85%. Zoned single family residential. All conveniences. This area is favorably located but is detrimentally affected by 10 owner occupant Negro families located in center of area north and south of Ball St. between Marvista and Catalina Aves. Although the Negroes are said to be of the better class their presence has caused a wave of selling in the area and it seems inevitable that ownership and property values will drift to lower levels. Construction, maintenance and architectural designs while not of the highest type are generally of good quality. The area is accorded a "high red" solely on account of racial hazards. Otherwise a medial yellow grade would have been assigned.

Figure 5.9 HOLC Appraisal Sheets from the National Archives

AREA DESCRIPTIONS - SECURITY MAP OF __LOS ANGELES COUNTY__

1. POPULATION: a. Increasing __Rapidly__ Decreasing _____ Static _____

   b. Class and Occupation __Business & professional men, retired people, Jr. executives,__
   __public officials, etc.__ Income $2400 to $5000 and up.

   c. Foreign Families __None__ % Nationalities _____ — _____ d. Negro __None__ %

   e. Shifting or Infiltration __None apparent__

2. BUILDINGS:

	PREDOMINATING 85 %	OTHER TYPE %
a. Type and Size	6, 7 & 8 rooms	5 rooms 5%
b. Construction	Frame, stucco & masonry	
c. Average Age	3 years	
d. Repair	Good	
e. Occupancy	99%	
f. Owner-occupied	95%	
g. 1935 Price Bracket	$ Very few % chge	$ % chge
	constructed	
h. 1937 Price Bracket	$ 6000-10000 %	$ %
i. 1939 Price Bracket	$ 6000-10000 %	$ %
j. Sales Demand	Good	
k. Predicted Price Trend (next 6-12 months)	Static	
l. 1935 Rent Bracket	$ Not a % chge	$ % chge
m. 1937 Rent Bracket	$ rental %	$ %
n. 1939 Rent Bracket	$ district %	$ %
o. Rental Demand	—	
p. Predicted Rent Trend (next 6-12 months)	—	

3. NEW CONSTRCTN (past yr) No __125__ Type & Price __$6500-$10000 6, 7 & 8 rooms__ How selling __Readily__

4. OVERHANG OF HOME PROPERTIES: a. HOLC __None__ b. Institutions __Few__

5. SALE OF HOME PROPERTIES (_3_yr) a. HOLC __None__ b. Institutions __Few__

6. MORTGAGE FUNDS: __Ample (FHA)__ 7. Total Tax Rate per $1000 (193_7/8_) $ 48.80

8. DESCRIPTION AND CHARACTERISTICS OF AREA:
   Terrain: Level with favorable grades. No construction hazards. Land improved 60%.
   Deed restrictions provide for architectural supervision and protect against subversive racial hazards. Conveniences are all readily available. This is a recent subdivision which has grown very rapidly in the past few years under the stimulus of
   promotional effort and FHA Title II financing. While owner occupancy is very high,
   indications are that in most cases equities are low, which has a decided bearing
   upon the economic stability of the area. Construction and maintenance are of
   excellent character. Architectural designs are attractive and population is homogeneous. Improvements are noticeably larger and more imposing on Orange Grove Ave. and
   Mountain St. This, however, does not affect the harmonious appearance of the area.
   Indications are that development of the area will progress along the established
   pattern and it is therefore accorded a "low green" grade.

9. LOCATION __Pasadena__ SECURITY GRADE __Low A__ AREA NO. __A-11__ DATE __4-14-39__

Figure 5.10 HOLC Appraisal Sheets from the National Archives

Security Map of __LOS ANGELES COUNTY__

1. **POPULATION:** *a. Increasing* _____ *Decreasing* _____ *Static* Yes

   b. Class and Occupation Laborers, farm and WPA workers. Income $700-$1000

   c. Foreign Families 100 % *Nationalities* __Mexicans__ *d. Negro* 0 %
   Many American born - impossible to differentiate

   e. Shifting or Infiltration of goats, rabbits and dark skinned babies indicated.

2. **BUILDINGS:**

	PREDOMINATING 100 %		OTHER TYPE	%
a. Type and Size	2 to 5 rooms			
b. Construction	Shacks and hovels			
c. Average Age	50 or more years			
d. Repair	Terrible			
e. Occupancy	98%			
f. Owner-occupied	50% (formerly homesteads)			
g. 1935 Price Bracket	$ Up to $1000	% change	$	% change
h. 1937 Price Bracket	$ Up to $1000	%	$	%
i. 1939 Price Bracket	$ Up to $1000	%	$	%
j. Sales Demand	Poor			
k. Predicted Price Trend (next 6-12 months)	Static			
l. 1935 Rent Bracket	$ Up to $10	% change	$	% change
m. 1937 Rent Bracket	$ Up to $10	%	$	%
n. 1939 Rent Bracket	$ Up to $10	%	$	%
o. Rental Demand	Good			
p. Predicted Rent Trend (next 6-12 months)	Static			

3. **NEW CONSTRUCTION** (past yr.) No. None Type & Price — How Selling —

4. **OVERHANG OF HOME PROPERTIES:** a. HOLC 0 b. Institutions 0

5. **SALE OF HOME PROPERTIES** (3 yr.) a. HOLC 0 b. Institutions 0

6. **MORTGAGE FUNDS:** None 7. **TOTAL TAX RATE PER $1000** (1937-8) $ 47.58

8. **DESCRIPTION AND CHARACTERISTICS OF AREA:**
   Terrain: Low lying level. Some adobe soil. Land improved 90%. Many dwellings
   have small acreage adjoining. Deed restrictions and zoning are lacking. Conveniences are all readily available, including bus line on Whittier Blvd. This
   is an extremely old Mexican shack district, which has been "as is" for many
   generations. Like the "Army mule" it has no pride of ancestry nor hope of pos-
   terity. It is a typical semi tropical countryside "slum".
   The area is generously accorded a "low red" grade.

Figure 5.11 HOLC Appraisal Sheets from the National Archives

Notes

1. An example is regulating the location of laundries in San Francisco as a means of restricting the movement of Chinese immigrants. See Christopher Silva, 1997, "The Racial Origin of Zoning in American Cities," in *Urban Planning and the African American Community: In the Shadows*, edited by June Manning Thomas and Marsha Ritzdorf, 23–42. Thousand Oaks, CA: Sage Publications.
2. See the 1917 case of Buchanan v. Warley.
3. See Alan D. DeSantis, Fall 1998, "Selling the American Dream Myth to Black Southerners: The Chicago Defender and the Great Migration of 1915–1919," *Western Journal of Communication* 62(4): 474–511.
4. Margaret Garb, "Drawing the 'Color Line': Race and Real Estate in Early Twentieth Century Chicago," *Journal of Urban History* 32(2006): 778.
5. Ibid., p. 780.
6. Jane Jacobs is quoted as referring to redlining as a self-fulfilling prophecy in Kenneth T. Jackson, 1985, *Crabgrass Frontier: The Suburbanization of the United States*, 216.
7. Judith Smith, 2004, *Visions of Belonging: Family Stories, Popular Culture and Post War Democracy 1940–1960*. New York: Columbia University Press, and Kristin L. Matthews, 2008, "The Politics of 'Home' in Lorraine Hansberry's A Raisin in the Sun," *Winter Modern Drama* 51(4): 556–578.
8. See http://nhlp.org/files/NHLP%20DV%20Fair%20Housing%20Toolkit%20FINAL.pdf, Domestic Violence and the Fair Housing Act: A Toolkit for Grantees, 2008, National Housing Law Project.
9. See the American Communities Project, *Diversity and Disparities Data Sets*, available at: https://s4.ad.brown.edu/Projects/Diversity/Data/Data.htm and the University of Michigan's Population Studies Center, *New Racial Segregation Measures for Large Metropolitan Areas: Analysis of the 1990-2010 Decennial Censuses*, available at: www.psc.isr.umich.edu/dis/census/segregation2010.html.
10. The U.S. Census figures on median household income for 2010 by household type are as follows: White-$51,846; Black-$32,068; Asian- $64,308; and Hispanic Origin- $37,759.

References

Adelman, Robert M., and James Clark Gocker. 2007. "Racial Residential Segregation in Urban America." *Sociology Compass* 1(1): 404–423, p. 407.

Barata, Paula C., and Donna E. Stewart. 2010. "Searching for Housing as a Battered Woman: Does Discrimination Affect Reported Availability of a Rental Unit." *Psychology of Women Quarterly* 34(1): 43–55.

Baugh, John. 2000. "Racial Identification by Speech." *American Speech* 75(4): 362–364.

Briggs, Xavier de Souza. 2005. "Introduction." In *The Geography of Opportunity*, edited by Xavier de Souza Briggs, 1–16. Washington, DC: Brookings Institution Press.

Brown, Jr., William H. 1972. "Access to Housing: The Role of the Real Estate Industry." *Economic Geography* 48(1): 66–78, p. 68.

Carpusor, Adrian G., and William E. Loges. 2006. "Rental Discrimination and Ethnicity in Names." *Journal of Applied Social Psychology* 36(4): 934–952.

Carr, James H., and Nandinee K. Kutty. 2008. "The New Imperative for Equality." In *Segregation: The Rising Costs for America*, edited by James H. Carr and Nandinee K. Kutty, 1–38. New York: Routledge.

Charles, Camille Zubrinski. 2003. "The Dynamics of Racial Residential Segregation." *Annual Review of Sociology*: 167–207.

DeNavas-Walt, Carmen, Bernadette D. Proctor, and Jessica C. Smith. 2011. "Income, Poverty, and Health Insurance Coverage in the United States: 2010." *Current Population Reports*. Washington, DC: U.S. Government Printing Office.

Desmond, Matthew, and Mustafa Emirbayer. 2016. *Race in America*. New York: W.W. Norton & Company, Inc.

Farley, Reynolds. 2011. "The Waning of American Apartheid?" *Contexts*: 36–43.

Farley, Reynolds, and William H. Frey. 1994. "Changes in the Segregation of Whites From Blacks During the 1980s: Small Steps Toward a More Integrated Society." *American Sociological Review*: 23–45.

Hillier, A. 2003. "Redlining and the Home Owners' Loan Corporation." *Journal of Urban History* 29(4): 394.

Hinnant-Bernard, Thessalenuere, and Sue R. Crull. 2004. "Subprime Lending and Reverse Redlining." *Housing and Society* 31(2).

Hirsch, Arnold R. 1992. "With or With-out Jim Crow: Black Residential Segregation in the United States." In *Urban Policy in Twentieth Century America*, edited by Arnold R. Hirsch and Raymond A. Mohl, 65–95, p. 73. New Brunswick: Rutgers University Press.

Jackson, Kenneth T. 1985. *Crabgrass Frontier: The Suburbanization of the United States*. New York: Oxford University Press.

Lauster, Nathanael, and Adam Easterbrook. 2011. "No Room for New Families? A Field Experiment Measuring Rental Discrimination Against Same-Sex Couples and Single Parents." *Social Problems* 58(3): 389–409.

Logan, John R., and Brian Stults. 2011. "The Persistence of Segregation in the Metropolis: New Findings From the 2010 Census." *Census Brief Prepared for Project US2010*.

Mannina, Jonathan. 2008. *What is Illegal Discrimination?* July. http:// masslegalhelp.org/housing/private-housing/ch7/what-is-illegal-discrimination.

Massey, Douglas S. 2008. "Origins of Economic Disparities: The Historical Role of Housing Segregation." In *Segregation: The Rising Costs for America*, edited by James H. Carr and Nandinee K. Kutty, 39–80. New York: Routledge.

Massey, Douglas S., and Garvey Lundy. 2001. "Use of Black English and Racial Discrimination in Urban Housing Markets: New Methods and Findings." *Urban Affairs Review* 36(4): 452–469.

Metropolitan Planning Council. 2017. *The Cost of Segregation: Lost Income, Lost Lives, Lost Potential*. Chicago. metroplanning.org/costofsegregation.

National Fair Housing Alliance. 2005. *No Home for the Holidays: Report on Housing Discrimination Against Hurricane Katrina Survivors*. Washington, DC.

Nicolaides, Becky M., and Andrew Wiese, eds. 2006. *The Suburb Reader*. New York: Routledge.

Orfield, Gary, Jongyeon Ee, Erica Frankenberg, and Genevieve Siegel-Hawley. 2016. "Brown at 62: School Segregation by Race, Poverty and State." *Research Brief*. Los Angeles, CA: Civil Rights Project, UCLA. www.civilrightsproject.ucla.edu/research/k-12-education/integration-and-diversity/brown-at-62-school-segregation-by-race-poverty-and-state.

Rothstein, Richard. 2017. *The Color of Law: A Forgotten History of How Our Government Segregated America*. New York: Liveright Publishing Corporation.

Seitles, Marc. 1996. "The Perpetuation of Residential Racial Segregation in America: Historical Discrimination, Modern Forms of Exclusion, and Inclusionary Remedies." *Journal of Land Use & Environmental Law*: 89–192, p. 90.

Smith, Stanley K., Stefan Rayer, and Eleanor A. Smith. 2008. "Aging and Disability: Implications for the Housing Industry and Housing Policy in the United States." *Journal of the American Planning Association* 74(3): 289–306.

Swaroop, Sapna, and Maria Krysan. 2011. "The Determinants of Neighborhood Satisfaction: Racial Proxy Revisited." *Demography* 48(3): 1203–1229.

Zhao, Bo. 2005. "Racial and Ethnic Discrimination in Urban Housing Markets: Evidence From Audit Studies." https://surface.syr.edu/ecn_etd/23/ Syracuse University.

6

HOUSING NEEDS, AFFORDABILITY, AND FEDERAL RESPONSES

In this chapter, we examine the nature and extent of housing needs American households face. Housing conditions today are very different from what they were 100 years ago. Regulations and code enforcement, technological and material improvements, and economic transformations have all played a part in the evolution of the quality and cost of housing. We will start by defining housing needs and then turn to a deeper exploration of the mechanics of housing programs designed to meet these needs. Defining housing needs is a very important and highly debated topic, but if we are to move toward decent housing for all people, we must first grasp the extent of housing needs in this country. In addition to understanding this "total need" figure, understanding how these needs are distributed among household types and geographies will help to target policies and programs (Stone 2013). It is good to remember that this information describes how we have set up technical definitions to measure and respond to housing needs, and that beyond this data-heavy narrative are households struggling to establish stable homes.

We will consider several questions on housing needs in this chapter, including: How are housing needs defined? What types of needs are there? Who are the households with these needs? How do government programs determine who is in need? What government programs have been developed to meet the various types of housing needs? And how well are housing needs being met? This chapter will consider these questions from the perspective of homeowners and renters, as well as considering the dimensions that race, ethnicity, and special needs add to the overview.

Defining Housing Needs

Coming to a common understanding on the definition of housing need is fundamental to developing a consistent housing approach. A common way of classifying the needs that households face when seeking housing is to consider the following characteristics of the housing:[1]

1. **Adequacy**: the physical condition of the housing. Are the major systems (electrical, plumbing, heating/cooling) in good working order? Is it structurally sound (foundation, roof)? Is it safe for occupation (no mold, lead paint, etc.)? Is the square footage and arrangement appropriate for the household (that is, are the number of bedrooms right for the makeup of the household or is there overcrowding)?
2. **Accessibility**: the physical, social, and geographical accessibility of the housing. This considers not only accessibility in the literal sense (for those that may require adaptation of entryways and interior spaces), but also accessibility in terms of discriminatory barriers. Accessibility also is a characteristic of the housing as

it relates to other household requirements—does the housing provide access to needed transportation options, employment centers, daycare centers, and health-care facilities?

3. **Affordability**: the cost of purchasing or renting the housing. The right house or apartment in the perfect location may be priced out of range for a household. When households spend a large portion of their income on housing, it puts them at risk for not having enough money to cover other living expenses, including groceries, medical bills, or unexpected emergencies. Affordability is a concern for both renters and homeowners.

These characteristics are distinct but not mutually exclusive. Households may face one or more needs from these characteristics. For example, a housing unit may be affordable but be a poor-quality housing unit, or be in a location that is both expensive and isolated from jobs.

Adequacy of Housing

In Franklin D. Roosevelt's 1937 State of the Union address, he said:

> many millions of Americans still live in habitations which not only fail to provide the physical benefits of modern civilization but breed disease and impair the health of future generations. The menace exists not only in the slum areas of the very large cities, but in many smaller cities as well. It exists on tens of thousands of farms, in varying degrees, in every part of the country.
>
> (Franklin D. Roosevelt Library & Museum 2016)

Since that dark declaration in 1937, the physical condition of the American housing stock has greatly improved. A summary of the major shift in American housing characteristics is represented in Figure 6.1. Adequacy of the housing stock is no longer a major concern; we are now a country of majority owners living in suburban locations, struggling to have the purchasing power to afford housing.

Chapter 2, Housing and Culture, described the upgrades to the physical condition and average size of the American housing stock that took place during the twentieth century, as our cultural norms evolved. These changes in housing norms contributed

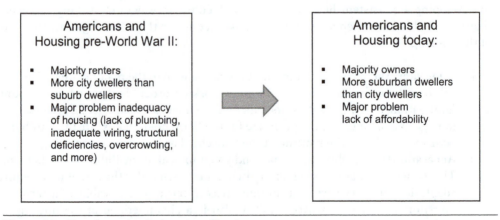

Figure 6.1   Transformation in American Housing

Source: Information from Housing Policy in the United States, Third Edition by Alex F. Schwartz 2015

to the improvement in the physical condition of the housing stock, along with effective building codes, improved building technologies, and newer construction. According to the U.S. Census Bureau, 45 percent of our current housing stock has been constructed since 1980—meaning this portion of housing meets modern standards (U.S. Census Bureau n.d.).

A 2013 U.S. Department of Housing and Urban Development report states, "inadequate housing is very rare and . . . most inadequate units do not remain in that condition for very long" (Eggers and Moumen 2013). This report goes on to compare results from the American Housing Surveys (AHS) completed in 2005, 2007, and 2009. For all three years, less than 2 percent of all housing units in America were found to be severely inadequate. This compares with 1940 data indicating that 45 percent of households lacked plumbing (directly comparable inadequacy data is not available) (Schwartz 2015, 28). Of the 2009 total of 1.8 million units cited in the report as severely inadequate, more than 90 percent had only one deficiency from the list of 14 possible deficiencies that fall into the major categories of plumbing (e.g., no running water, lack of a bathroom), heating, electrical (e.g., wiring), and upkeep (e.g., water leaks or cracks to the outside) (Eggers and Moumen 2013, 3; Steffen et al. 2015).

Inadequacy is less of a concern today than in past decades, even when the data is reviewed within subgroups of the population (see Table 6.1 with data from the 2013 AHS). Renters are more likely to have severe housing inadequacy problems than homeowners, but the level is still quite small at just under 3 percent. In fact, comparing all households with renters alone, black households alone (renters and homeowners), Hispanic households (renters and homeowners), and households of very low income (renters and homeowners making below the poverty line), the highest percentage of severe physical housing problems among these groups is just more than 3 percent. More households face moderate housing inadequacies, but these are still relatively low, ranging from 3.4 percent of all households to 6.7 percent of households with incomes below

Table 6.1 Housing Inadequacy Problems from the 2013 American Housing Survey (in thousands)

HOUSEHOLD TYPE	TOTAL	SEVERE PROBLEM/ % OF TOTAL	MODERATE PROBLEM/ % OF TOTAL	COMBINED PROBLEM TOTAL/ % OF TOTAL
All Occupied Housing Units	115,852	1,942 (1.7)	3,946 (3.4)	5,888 (5.1)
Homeowners	75,650	783 (1)	1,432 (1.9)	2,215 (2.9)
Renters	40,201	1,159 (2.9)	2,514 (6.2)	3,673 (9.1)
Black Alone	15,015	428 (2.8)	959 (6.4)	1,387 (9.2)
Hispanic	14,675	367 (2.5)	687 (4.7)	1,054 (7.2)
Below Poverty Line	18,457	595 (3.2)	1,237 (6.7)	1,832 (9.9)

Source: U.S. Census Bureau American Housing Survey (AHS), Available at: www.census.gov/programs-surveys/ahs/data/2013/ahs-2013-summary-tables/national-summary-report-and-tables—-ahs-2013.html

the poverty line. A recent study also found that households in the U.S. Census–defined group of American Indians and Alaska Natives (AIAN) experience much greater degrees of poor housing conditions. While the national household average for plumbing deficiencies was 1 percent, for AIAN households it was 6 percent; heating deficiencies was 2 percent nationally but 12 percent for AIANs in tribal areas; and overcrowding was 2 percent nationally but 16 percent for AIANs in tribal areas (Pindus et al. 2017).

Some researchers caution that the national or regional level aggregated data indicating a small number of substandard units can fail to detect hot spots of poor conditions at the local or neighborhood level. These researchers point out that poor quality housing may be a trade-off some people make to get more affordable housing. One 2003 study indicated the 3.1 percent of the overall New York City housing stock with severe maintenance deficiencies had hot spots at the borough or neighborhood level of up to 13 percent (O'Dell, Smith, and White 2004, 36).

Accessibility of Housing

Accessibility of housing includes an evaluation of a variety of factors, some more easy to quantify than others. One factor that is easier to evaluate is whether the housing includes features that allow persons with physical disabilities to inhabit it. These features, such as accessible parking spaces, laundry rooms, trash facilities, entryways, and public spaces, are legal requirements for new multifamily buildings under the Fair Housing Act, and for federally assisted housing under the Uniform Federal Accessibility Standards (UFAS). Within the housing unit interior, features such as lowered kitchen cabinets, grab bars in bathrooms, roll-in showers, appropriate hardware on doors and drawers, and more, must also be present so those with a physical disability could live in the unit with a high degree of functionality and independence. Recently, the American Housing Survey (AHS) added questions about accessibility features. Using the results of the 2011 AHS, a HUD sponsored examination reported the following:

> our analysis of United States (US) housing data suggests that although around a third of housing in the US is potentially modifiable for a person with a mobility disability, currently less than five percent is accessible for individuals with moderate mobility difficulties and less than one percent of housing is accessible for wheelchair users.
>
> (Bo'sher et al. 2015)

By comparison, recent figures from the American Community Survey report 7.1 percent of persons in the United States have a mobility disability, indicating a shortfall of accessible units for these Americans (Erickson, Lee, and von Schrader 2016). Also, relevant here is the aging of the American population. In the coming years there will be a greater demand for housing designed for those with limited mobility.

As mentioned in other chapters of this book, access to housing can also be limited by discriminatory practices. Chapter 5, Housing and Discrimination, includes data on recent studies indicating the persistence of discriminatory behaviors. Many households of color will be unable to occupy housing units that are otherwise adequate and affordable, but due to discriminatory behaviors access will be denied. Efforts against discriminatory practices are still needed to remove accessibility barriers for some households.

Other aspects of accessibility of housing are assessed on a geographically specific basis. Housing that is physically adequate and affordable may not provide access to required services such as public transit, jobs, healthcare facilities, childcare centers, and more. Where affordable and physically prime housing is in locations that lack these essentials, the housing may not meet the actual needs of households. The accessibility aspect of housing highlights how decisions on the location of new (or rehabilitated) affordable units should consider the relative location of these other site characteristics.

A specific group that faces accessibility barriers to housing are returning citizens. The Department of Justice estimates nationally the number of prisoners being released at 10,000 per week, or 650,000 per year (Office of Justice Programs 2016). These ex-offenders, coming home to their communities after completing their sentences, face enormous challenges. Finding housing is just one of them. Depending on the criminal charges, public housing agencies may disqualify convicted felons or ex-drug dealers from living in public housing—either in their own unit or with a family member. The same is true for private subsidized and nonsubsidized housing. Fair Housing laws do not protect the class of returning citizens from tenant screenings by landlords. Such practices are part of what is termed the "collateral consequences" of arrests and convictions (Washington Lawyers' Committee for Civil Rights & Urban Affairs 2014). Despite having completed the penalty time for their crimes, returning citizens find their criminal record continues to reverberate, making it difficult if not impossible for them to find housing and to get a job. Given how fundamental housing is to stability, safety, and personal identity, the successful reentry of these returning citizens must include the provision of housing. Returning citizens need a place to sleep the first day out. Most spend time with relatives or friends, others go to shelters, but permanent housing is required. If recidivism is to be reduced, more transitional and supportive housing is needed to meet the outstanding needs (Fontaine and Biess 2012).

Affordability

Today, as in many recent decades, finding affordable housing is the single largest housing need among households (O'Dell et al. 2004). In the words of one blogger from Minneapolis, "Searching for 'affordable' housing seem[s] like searching for a myth" (McDaniel 2016). Affordable housing means households don't have to make choices between necessities—going without food, childcare, medicine, transportation, or other necessities—just to pay rent. Because shelter is a necessity, households end up in housing they cannot afford, and an extremely large portion of their income is spent on housing. This leaves them vulnerable to unexpected expenses, and with a budget spread so thin it is difficult to cover other routine and required expenses. The lack of affordable housing among renters has even been shown to decrease overall spending on food, healthcare, and retirement by low-income households. A recent report, by the Joint Center for Housing Studies of Harvard University, found that those "who paid more than half their incomes for housing spent 38 percent less on food and 55 percent less on healthcare. . . . and put 42 percent less toward retirement savings than otherwise similar renters living in affordable housing" (Fernald 2013).

What qualifies as affordable housing? The operational definition the Department of Housing and Urban Development (HUD) uses to assess eligibility for housing assistance, and to set the level of such assistance, is that low and moderate income households should not pay more than 30 percent of their gross income (before taxes) on housing (Jewkes and Delgadillo 2010). For renters, the 30 percent should cover rent and any utility costs that are not included in the rent. For homeowners, this 30 percent includes the mortgage payment, homeowner insurance payment, utilities, and property taxes. For potential homeowners, the 30 percent standard (sometimes ranging from 28–32 percent of gross income) is used by the mortgage industry as a guide for approving loans to purchase a home. Lending institutions also consider your overall level of debt and how large a down payment you make toward the purchase of the home. To be eligible for a mortgage loan, your total debt—home, car, education, medical, credit cards, and other loans—should not exceed 43 percent of your income.

HUD programs set eligibility for assistance based on household income limits. For some programs, that limit is an income that does not exceed 80 percent of the HUD-defined "area median income" (AMI), and for other programs it's an income that does not exceed 60 or 50 percent of the AMI. The area median income represents the income value where half of households in the area make more income, and half of the households make less income (see Table 6.2). AMI is calculated annually by HUD based on the U.S. Census Bureau's statistics for geographically defined metropolitan regions and counties, and adjusted for the number of family members in a household.[2]

Such eligibility for HUD programs should not be confused with a *guarantee* of assistance—many income-qualified households must wait years for openings. Unlike other federal assistance programs, housing assistance is not operated as an entitlement program; assistance is limited by the funding allocated by Congress, which results in many eligible households going without. However, some programs prioritize openings for those households with the most need. HUD has created classifications for households in need that include "cost burdened," a low-income household paying 30–49 percent of their income toward their housing, and "severely cost burdened," a low-income household where costs exceed 50 percent of their income (U.S. Department of Housing and Urban Development n.d.).

Critiques of the Legislated Housing Need Measure

While the 30 percent of gross income for housing figure is widely used by government and the private sector and is easy to calculate, it has been criticized as inaccurately portraying housing needs (Stone 2013). Some contend it is somewhat arbitrary and point out that the value has crept up over time from 20 percent to 25 to 30 percent—an indicator of its imprecise nature (PD & R Edge 2014; Hulchanski 2013). Concerns are that this gross measurement is not sensitive enough to "differences that may exist across age groups, family types and sizes, income levels, and location" (O'Dell et al. 2004, 31;

Table 6.2   HUD Classifications and Terms on Housing Needs

Household income	To be eligible for housing assistance household income must be at or below 80% of the Area Median Income (AMI) adjusted for family size, with some programs setting the limit at 60% AMI or 50% AMI.			
	81–120% of AMI is considered: *moderate income*	50–80% of AMI is considered: *low income*	30–49% of AMI is considered: *very low income*	below 30% of AMI is considered: *extremely low income*
Housing costs	Some HUD programs prioritize income eligible households by the degree to which their non-subsidized housing cost is a burden. Programs define such cost burdens by the percent of income they represent.			
	Housing cost is 30–49% of income: *cost burdened*		Housing cost is 50% or more of income: *severely cost burdened*	

Source: U.S. Department of Housing and Urban Development. Available at: http://portal.hud.gov/hudportal/
HUD?src=/program_offices/comm_planning/affordablehousing

Jewkes and Delgadillo 2010). Others contend that the figure may capture too large of a group and dilute targeting of the most vulnerable when it comes to housing need (O'Dell et al. 2004).

Two of the most well-known proposed alternative measures to the 30 percent rule of thumb are those of residual income and the combined Housing and Transportation Affordability Index. Michael Stone's 1993 book *Shelter Poverty* presents his argument for using a residual income approach to determine housing needs. For Stone, the specific cost of household necessities must be calculated and compared to household income. The funds left over after paying for housing are what is available to go toward other household expenditures. This approach looks at the actual values (using available measures) and takes into consideration the different life-stage demands a household may face (childcare for those parenting or increased medicine for the elderly) and the regional variation of costs (heating in New England or high living costs in San Francisco) are

Figure 6.2 Housing Affordability

Source: Cartoon © Roger K. Lewis, used by permission

determined and applied. Stone argues the simplistic 30 percent of gross income measure fails to uncover the extent of need among large low-income families (Stone 2013). He suggests those paying too much of their income for housing are "shelter poor"—they have housing but cannot afford other needed goods and services.

The Housing and Transportation Affordability Index (HTA), developed by the Center for Neighborhood Technology, seeks to address the increasingly large impact transportation costs can have on household budgets (Tegeler and Berstein 2013). Today, transportation is often the second largest cost of a household budget and, in some cases, can exceed housing costs (U.S. Housing and Urban Development 2016). The HTA Index considers the reality that housing is fixed in place. In some regions, households have had to move further and further away from job centers to find affordable housing. Naturally this leads to a significant increase in the household's transportation expenditures. The HTA Index recommends household need for assistance be measured by allowing 45 percent of income toward housing and transportation costs combined (Center for Neighborhood Technology 2016). Factoring in the transportation costs is a way to ensure the household budget can cover other nondiscretionary expenses. Under this index, households exceeding this measure (even if the housing itself is less than 30 percent of income) should be considered for assistance.

Application of HUD Measure: Who Has Affordability Needs?

Applying HUD's income cap and 30 percent housing cost ratio, we can determine the extent and nature of housing needs in the United States that are based on affordability. Table 6.3 presents data from a 2015 *Report to Congress on the Worst Housing Needs*, prepared for HUD (Steffen et al. 2015). From this figure, we see that of all U.S. households in America, only 4.7 percent receive some form of direct housing assistance. This includes those living in public housing (1 percent), using a housing voucher (1.9 percent), or living in a unit that has some other housing subsidy (1.8 percent). In terms of affordability, the number of combined homeowner and renter households with cost burdens are approximately one-third of all U.S. households. Since this may include those with higher incomes for whom the 30 percent standard is less applicable, looking more closely at lower income households is appropriate. Combining renters and homeowners that are low income (make less than 80 percent of the AMI) we find 75 percent of these households fall into the category of housing cost burdened. Of all the renter households that make less than 80 percent of the AMI, 65.6 percent receive no housing assistance but are housing cost burdened. Within this group, 9.5 million low-income renter households have a severe housing cost burden and yet receive no housing assistance. A 2015 report prepared by the Congressional Budget Office states:

> Moreover, in 2013, 7.7 million households had what HUD describes as "worst-case housing needs," meaning that they had income of no more than 50 percent of AMI, were eligible for but did not receive federal housing assistance, *and* were paying more than half of their income in rent (or living in severely substandard conditions). That number was nearly 50 percent higher than a decade earlier.
>
> (Congressional Budget Office, Federal Housing Assistance for
> Low-Income Households, 2015; italics added)

The HUD website illustrates affordability needs in another way, noting that a family with one full-time worker earning the minimum wage cannot afford the going market rent[3] for a two-bedroom apartment anywhere in the United States (U.S. Department of Housing and Urban Development n.d.). The inescapable conclusion from these figures is there is a vast unmet need for affordable housing. Families are stretching budgets and making trade-off decisions among necessities just to maintain a roof over their heads.

Table 6.3 Affordability Housing Needs in America 2013

HOUSEHOLDS AND HOUSING NEEDS (IN THOUSANDS)	2013
Total Households	**116,032**
Owners	75, 750
(Percent of total)	(65.0%)
Renters	40,273
(Percent of total)	(34.7%)
With Housing Assistance*	5,530
(Percent of total)	(4.7%)
Total Renters	**40,273**
With Housing Assistance	5,530
(Percent of total)	(13.7%)
Housing Cost Burdened/No Assistance	19,036
(Percent of total)	(47.3 %)
Severely Burdened/No Assistance	9,744
(Percent of total)	(24.1%)
Renters Making Less than 80% of AMI	**26,316**
With Housing Assistance	5,216
(Percent of total)	(19.8%)
Housing Cost Burdened/No Assistance	7,761
(Percent of total)	(29.5%)
Severely Burdened/No Assistance	9,511
(Percent of total)	(36.1%)
Total Owners	**75,759**
Housing Cost Burdened/No Assistance*	20,658
(Percent of Total)	(27.2%)
Severely Burdened/No Assistance	9,066
(Percent of total)	(11.9%)
Owners Making Less than 80% of AMI	**27,225**
Housing Cost Burdened/No Assistance	14,565
(Percent of Total)	(53.4%)
Severely Burdened/No Assistance	8,025
(Percent of total)	(29.5%)

Source: "Worst Case Housing Needs 2015 Report to Congress," by Barry L. Steffen, et al. Data from Appendix A; Note: Severely burdened is not included in cost burdened.

Note: Housing Assistance includes housing units receiving a subsidy as defined by the American Housing Survey: "a housing unit is classified as having a subsidy if the household pays a lower rent because a federal, state, or local government program pays part of the cost of construction, mortgage, or operating expenses. These programs include rental assistance programs where part of the rent for low-income families is paid by HUD, and direct loan programs of HUD and the Department of Agriculture for reduced cost housing. These do not include households receiving tax exemptions associated with homeownership. See p.A-24 of Appendix A. Definitions, at www2.census.gov/programs-surveys/ahs/2003/2003%20AHS%20National%20 Definitions.pdf.

Federal Responses to Housing Needs

The federal response to housing needs includes programs to support homeownership, subsidize the financing and construction of new affordable units, fund a portion of tenant's rent payments in existing private units, and support publicly owned and managed affordable units (public housing). Federal initiatives are funded through *tax expenditures* and *direct expenditures* (Schwartz 2015). Tax expenditures are made up of deductions, credits, and preferential tax rates that are part of the federal tax laws.[4] These provisions lower the federal tax liability of households and corporations, and result in less taxes collected by the government. The amount of taxes forgone is not subject to Congressional appropriation, although the Treasury Department is required to estimate its worth (Schwartz 2015). Direct expenditures are dollars that show up in the federal budget as program line items. These are the direct expenditures approved by Congress for specific programs.

Tax expenditures related to housing (funds not collected) far exceed the number of dollars spent directly on housing programs. The Joint Committee on Taxation estimated the value of 2014 tax expenditures that support homeowners (mortgage interest deductions, property tax deductions, and capital gains exclusions on home sales) at $127.5 billion (Joint Committee on Taxation 2014). This contrasts with the HUD budgeted program expenditures for 2014 of $45 billion on direct programs (Congressional Budget Office 2015). This difference in magnitude has been consistent for many years. Of interest when considering affordability is who is being served by each of the expenditure types. First, we turn our attention to whom tax expenditures serve, and then consider those served by the housing programs funded through the national budget.

Tax Expenditures

Homeowners are the major beneficiaries of housing related tax expenditures. The tax benefits include being able to deduct the interest paid on mortgage loans, deduct the property taxes paid on housing, and to exclude from taxes capital gains made on selling a primary residence. The deduction of mortgage interest was not adopted as an intentional housing subsidy for homeowners, but rather was part of the exemption of all interest when income taxes were first instituted in 1913 (Carliner 1998). However, this deduction (which includes mortgage interest for a primary and second home), survived the elimination of other interest deductions under the Reagan administration in 1986. Interest groups including the National Association of Realtors, and the National Association of Homebuilders, actively advocate for the maintenance of the mortgage interest deduction (MID).

Recently, the nonpartisan Center on Budget and Policy Priorities prepared an analysis indicating higher-income homeowners are the largest beneficiaries of housing tax expenditures. The report, "Chart Book: Federal Housing Spending Is Poorly Matched to Need," concludes,

> Most homeownership expenditures go to the top fifth of households by income. More than four-fifths of the value of the mortgage-interest and property tax deductions goes to households with incomes of more than $100,000 and more than two fifths goes to families with incomes above $200,000.
>
> (Fischer and Sard 2016, 1)

Low-income homeowners may struggle to cover housing costs, but they benefit much less from the homeownership-related tax deductions because in order to use the deduction you must itemize your deductions, and most low-income households do not meet the minimum expenditure threshold to itemize. Also, the interest and property tax amounts for these households are lower as generally their homes are valued for less. Finally, incomes at lower levels are subject to lower tax rates which makes the effective value of the deduction worth less to these households than to higher income households.

Eliminating these deductions has been routinely considered by administrations of both major parties, as it is contended that these subsidies do not greatly impact home-ownership rates (Turner, Toder, Pendall, and Sharygin 2013). Since the bulk of the bene-fits accrue to those most able to afford homeownership, elimination of these provisions would not change the affordability of homeownership for those of low and moderate incomes (Schwartz 2015).

Figure 6.3 indicates rates of homeownership for the United States as calculated from the 2013 American Housing Survey. Overall, 65.3 percent of American households are homeowners. This compares to 70 percent of white households, 43 percent of black households, 49 percent for American Indian and Alaskan Native households, and 48 per-cent for households that self-identified as of two or more races. These discrepancies are in part a legacy of the discriminatory practices of the FHA/VA loan program, and are also reflect persistent gaps in income. Just as the tax expenditures for homeownership skew in favor of those with higher incomes, racial and ethnic groups with lower home-ownership rates participate less in the benefits of the tax expenditures. In the interest

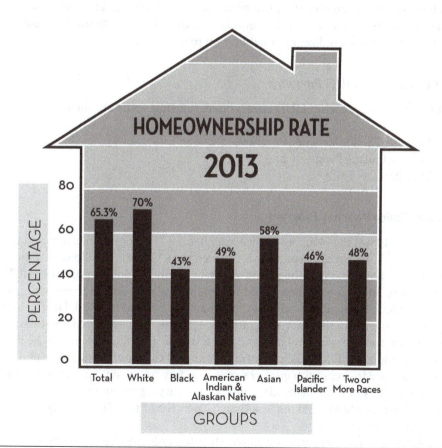

Figure 6.3   Homeownership by Household Types 2013. Graphic © Allison Terkelsen, used with permission

Source: U.S. Census, American Housing Survey, 2013

of equity, some have advocated for a renter income tax break (Sard and Fischer 2013). At least eight states currently offer partial state income tax relief to renting households based on rent payments. No such provision exists at the federal level, but if it did, renters would be better able to afford monthly payments.

A non-homeowner tax expenditure that has taken on a significant role for expanding low income housing is that of the Low Income Housing Tax Credit (LIHTC). This credit allows investors to provide cash payments toward the development of privately owned housing, and in return to receive credits to use against outstanding federal tax liability. LIHTCs are structured through brokers who match people in need of tax credits with developers of mixed income housing developments. The investors receive the tax credit and may also take an ownership interest in the project. The developer receives a cash subsidy that is used to offset the costs of maintaining some of the units of the development as affordable for households making 50 to 60 percent of the AMI. Currently the LIHTC is one of the key funding sources supporting the development of new affordable housing units. While its estimated tax expenditure value is relatively small ($7 billion for 2014) there are few other sources to play the role it does (Joint Committee on Taxation 2014). The LIHTC is a key subsidy type for current affordable housing projects, although many projects must combine a variety of subsidies to make projects financially viable (Schwartz 2015; Stoutland 1999).

There are a variety of other tax expenditure provisions that support affordable housing, all of which are smaller than the homeowner deductions. These include investors deducting interest on state housing bonds and owners of multifamily housing using depreciation schedules to lower tax liability on rental housing.

Direct Expenditures HUD Programs

The three major approaches HUD uses to meet housing needs are the following:

1. Housing Choice Voucher Program,
2. Public Housing Program, and
3. Unit-based Subsidies.

Housing Choice Voucher Program

Since the late 1980s, the Housing Choice Voucher (HCV) program has received the most funding. The HCV program, commonly referred to as "Section 8," allows income eligible renters to take a voucher into the private market and find an appropriate unit. HCV holders contribute 30 percent of household income to the rent and the voucher covers the rest (or, in effect, the landlord collects the remaining amount from HUD). To ensure the adequacy of housing in the HCV program, the apartment to be rented must pass a quality inspection and the rent level must not exceed what HUD determines to be sufficient or "fair" for the area. The HCV program is intended to give the renter the ability to be mobile and move to areas with quality services, safety, and stability. It is consistent with HUD's philosophy of deconcentrating poverty and mixing income groups. This program is targeted to households making less than 50 percent of the HUD family size adjusted regional area median income.

The HCV program represents a major shift toward subsidizing the demand side of housing (subsidizing households) rather than the supply side (subsidizing the production of units). In some cases, voucher holders may improve, but not expand, the housing stock by causing landlords to upgrade substandard units to meet the program requirements (Winnick 1995).

Vouchers now represent 50 percent of all household subsidies HUD funds with direct expenditures (Office of Policy Development and Research 2014). Support for HCV grew as the cost of production increased, and the demand side approach found favor with those looking to have the private sector play the largest role in the provision of housing. Republican administrations enlarged the HCV program, as it was recognized that low incomes were the major obstacle to decent housing (Winnick 1995).

For many people, the voucher approach works very well (Turner 2013). Yet in some regions, voucher holders can have great difficulty finding apartments that meet the quality standards and fall within the fair rent limits.[5] As the program also involves a landlord, it can be a challenge for tenants to find landlords willing to participate in the HCV program.[6] The lack of affordable rental units in areas of job opportunity or in locations served by mass transit can also frustrate a renter's pursuit of housing that fits the household's needs. The searching household has a limited amount of time to find a suitable unit, which adds pressure to the process.

Research has found that a significant portion (20 percent) of voucher holders with children live in areas of low poverty (places where less than 10 percent of households have incomes below the poverty line) and another 10 percent live in extremely high poverty areas (places where more than 40 percent of households have incomes below the poverty line) (Sard and Rice 2014). While these figures are somewhat disappointing, HCV performs better than public housing programs in achieving mobility for households and deconcentrating poverty (Turner 2013). Despite the promise of HCV, funding for the program has consistently been at low levels compared to the demand. Most local housing authorities, and others administrating HCV programs, have waiting lists of eligible households running into hundreds or even thousands of names. This can easily translate into waiting 2–5 years or more for a voucher (Collinson, Kearney, and Rennane 2016). For 2014, HUD reported a national average wait time of 30 months (Office of Policy Development and Research 2014). During this period, households may be stretching their budgets to cover housing, doubling up with family or friends, or residing in shelters. A profile of the households in the HCV program is presented in Table 6.4.

Table 6.4   Profile of Households in Housing Choice Voucher Program (2015)

Total served:	2,447,016 households
Household income:	$ 13,821 average
	80% of households make less than $ 20,000
Rent payment:	$ 364 average household contribution
	$ 775 average HCV/HUD contribution
Major source of income:	30% Wages 4% Welfare 62% Other
	(Other may include: Social Security, Social Security Disability, Alimony, Pension, etc.)
Race and ethnicity:	47% Black 32% White 17% Hispanic 3% Asian/Pacific 1% Native American
Disability:	23% of households have a member with a disability
One-person Household:	34% of all households have only one person

Source: Picture of Subsidized Households available at: www.huduser.gov/portal/datasets/picture/year lydata.html#data-display-tab

Public Housing

The Public Housing program is covered in detail in Chapter 9, including information on its history, evolution, and the households served. Public Housing has remained a small part of the country's approach to meeting housing needs. HUD reports that 1,141,596 households were served by Public Housing in 2014—merely 1 percent of all American households, and representing 22.7 percent of all households benefiting from a direct housing subsidy (Office of Policy Development and Research 2014).

Other Unit-Based Subsidies

HUD has a large variety of other programs that provide subsidies for the development of affordable units—far too many to recite here. These programs are grouped together as unit-based assistance because a subsidy is attached to the housing unit—not the household. If a household moves out, the unit must be rented to another income-qualified household. The household leaving the affordable unit does not take the subsidy but must find another subsidized unit, pursue a Housing Choice Voucher, or enter the private market. Depending on the program, the developer of these units may be a nonprofit entity or a private corporation.

Unit-based assistance programs focus on a variety of low income household types including the elderly, disabled, persons with AIDS, tenants in distressed public housing, and households facing homelessness. A wide range of approaches are used in the creation of unit-based affordable housing. HUD funding may be used to rehabilitate units of housing into affordable units or lower some aspect of the cost for the new construction of units. These varied subsidies reflect the diversity of ways to affect the cost of housing as illustrated in Figure 6.4. The units created must be rented to households falling within the specific AMI limits of the program involved, but all are below 80 percent of AMI.

While the HCV achieves affordable housing by increasing the tenants' ability to pay for housing, and public housing provides government owned and managed housing, unit-based assistance to secure affordable units can take many forms. The land the housing sits on can be subsidized (or donated; see Chapter 10), the cost of site improvements can be offset, contributions can go to the direct construction costs, some aspect of financing (interest rates on loans, insurance costs) can be reduced, or some portion of operation costs (rent supplement commitments for certain units) can be covered. HUD provides data to indicate 1,474,486 households were in such housing in 2014. While consisting of only 1.3 percent of all American households, this group represents 29.3 percent of all of HUD's subsidized housing units (Office of Policy Development and Research 2014).

HUD program choices for meeting housing needs strongly favor approaches that are consistent with the philosophy of deconcentrating poverty, or promoting mixed-income development. This underlying principle is not without its critics. Many advocate for investing in neighborhoods showing signs of decline, rather than promoting the out-migration of residents. Reinvestment is encouraged over mobility (Polikoff, Goetz, Goering, and Olsen 2014). One advocate testifying to Congress made this observation:

> On the issue of deconcentrating poverty, my experience has been that, even though a neighborhood's physical experience may not look so good from the outside, there still exists a community. In my neighborhood, people would gather to talk, watch one another's children, and form strong bonds. Although it might have looked to some as not such a good neighborhood, there was good neighboring.
>
> (George Moses quoted in House of Representatives Hearing, 109th Congress- Poverty, Public Housing and the CRA, 2006)

WAYS TO SUBSIDIZE HOUSING

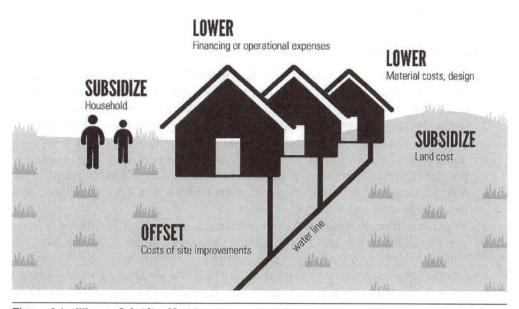

Figure 6.4   Ways to Subsidize Housing
Source: Graphic ©Ted Dobek, used by permission

Residents who relocate often leave behind support systems. While there is evidence of success in income and education for those that move to areas of greater opportunity, many advocates suggest HUD would do best to support choices in housing—both improving neighborhoods in decline for those who wish to stay, and providing mechanisms for those who wish to relocate.

Conclusion

The nature of housing needs has changed during the past 100 years. Today the major obstacle standing in the way of decent housing for all is a crisis of affordability. Many working households, elderly households, and disabled households do not have sufficient income to cover the cost of private sector housing. The standard developed to assess a low-income household's ability to pay is if housing requires more than 30 percent of a household's income the household is cost-burdened and at risk of not being able to cover other basic needs. Both low-income homeowners and renters face steep housing costs. Tax policy provides some favorable treatment for homeowners but the clear majority of these benefits go to high income households.

The federal government has established a variety of programs to meet the need for affordable housing among low income renters, but the amount of funding provided has consistently fallen well below the need for such assistance. Income eligible housing assistance does not function as an entitlement program—most eligible households must wait several years before getting assistance. HUD's major programs for meeting housing needs are the Housing Voucher Program, Public Housing, and Unit-Based Assistance.

These programs are restricted to households making less than 80 percent of the AMI, and many are targeted to those with incomes that are less than 50 percent of the AMI.

While much has been studied and learned about designing effective housing initiatives, without a commitment of an adequate level of funding, decent housing for all will remain an unfulfilled goal.

Questions and Activities

1. Consider the main housing need facing Americans—the lack of affordable housing. Is this a problem in all parts of America? Can you think of specific areas you know where housing prices are extremely high? What makes them that way?
2. Apply the housing burden standard to the following situation: A household with two working adults—one a teacher making $35,000, the other a bank teller making $26,000—and two children. What is the most money they should spend on housing? Can you find them an affordable 3-bedroom apartment in your housing market? Look for places on Craigslist, realty sites such as Trulia or Zillow, or in local newspapers and websites.
3. Take some time to understand how mortgages work. Start by finding a house you would like to buy and then finding a mortgage rate for a 30-year fixed-rate mortgage. Use a web based mortgage calculator (there are many) to compute the monthly mortgage payment needed to purchase the home you choose. Research the area's property taxes (which can be found on Zillow or Trulia) and add to the monthly payment an amount to cover your property taxes. Also add to the monthly payment $300 for homeowner's insurance. What would your household income need to be to afford the home? You will need to solve the simple algebraic equation: .30 x (monthly gross income) = monthly mortgage payment + monthly property taxes + monthly homeowner's insurance.
4. Think about why a landlord may not want to participate in the Housing Choice Voucher program. What program requirements would affect the landlord? What other perceptions might the landlord bring to this decision? What advantages does participation it the HCV program provide landlords?
5. Many United States Presidents (of both major parties) have suggested the elimination of the mortgage interest deduction. Given economists view of its effectiveness, why do you think it has been so difficult to achieve this? For background and discussion purposes listen to and watch the video produced by the NPR show Planet Money in 2012, www.npr.org/sections/money/2012/10/18/163106924/a-tax-plan-that-economists-love-and-politicians-hate.
6. Compare and contrast the two approaches of improving living conditions: investing in neighborhoods or investing in households (supporting households moving to other areas). Consider the full range of impacts (social, personal, economic, etc.) on the households involved.

Notes

1. These are common categories of housing needs, although the categories are presented in different ways in different literature/research. Some researchers present them as affordability, adequacy, and availability (see for example *National Analysis of Housing Affordability, Adequacy, and Availability: A Framework for Local Housing Strategies*, 1993, prepared by the Urban Institute for HUD), or, more recently, when considering the disabled, the groupings

have been affordability, accessibility, and appropriateness (see for example *The State of Housing in America in the 21st Century: A Disability Perspective*, 2010, prepared by the National Council on Disability). The broader meaning of accessibility, as used here, captures concerns about the mismatch between housing and jobs, and other shortcomings in neighborhoods where the housing may otherwise be affordable and adequate. It is more consistent with a Housing as a Human Right Framework (see for example, *Encyclopedia of Human Rights*, 2nd edition, edited by Edward Larson, 1996. Washington, DC: Taylor and Francis).

2. This is also known as HAMF-HUD-adjusted area median family income.
3. This is based on the HUD established Fair Market Rent (FMR) levels.
4. There are tax deductions, credits, and preferential tax rates for a wide variety of good and services—not just for housing. Agriculture, Commerce, and Energy are some of the other areas where tax expenditures exist.
5. A criticism of the HCV has been that the area fair market rents are set for too large an area and mask differences at lower levels. HUD has been experimenting with a smaller Fair Market Rent program to see if this flexibility can improve the performance of the HCV program. See: www.huduser.gov/portal/datasets/fmr/smallarea/index.html.
6. As of 2016, twelve states and many cities have passed regulations extending fair housing practices making it illegal to discriminate based on "source of income." Elsewhere it is legal to discriminate on this basis, including turning down applicants because they would use a Housing Voucher to cover the total rent costs. See a Summary report by the Poverty & Race Research Action Council, available at: www.prrac.org/pdf/AppendixB.pdf.

References

Bo'sher, Luke, Sewin Chan, Ingrid Gould Ellen, Brian Karfunkel, and Hsi-Ling Liao. 2015. *Accessibility of America's Housing Stock: Analysis of the 2011 American Housing Survey (AHS)*. Washington D.C.: U. S. Department of Housing and Urban Development.

Carliner, Michael S. 1998. "Development of Federal Homeownership 'Policy." *Housing Policy Debate* 9(2): 299–321.

Center for Neighborhood Technology. 2016. "About the Index." *H & T Index*, October 29: http://htaindex.cnt.org/about/.

Collinson, Robert, Melissa S. Kearney, and Stephanie Rennane. 2016. "Low Income Housing Policy." In *Economics of Means-Tested Transfer Programs in the United States*, Volume 2, edited by Robert Moffitt, 59–126. Chicago: University of Chicago Press.

Congressional Budget Office. 2015. *Federal Housing Assistance for Low-Income Households*. Washington, DC. www.cbo.gov/publication/50782.

Eggers, Frederick J., and Fouad Moumen. 2013. *American Housing Survey: Housing Adequacy and Quality as Measured by the AHS*. Washington DC: U.S. Department of Housing and Urban Development.

Erickson, W., C. Lee, and S von Schrader. 2016. *2014 Disability Status Report United States*. Ithaca, NY: Cornell University.

Fernald, Marcia ed. 2013. *America's Rental Housing: Evolving Markets and Need*. Cambridge, MA: Joint Center for Housing Studies of Harvard University.

Fischer, Will, and Barbara Sard. 2016. *Chart Book: Federal Housing Spending is Poorly Matched to Need*. Washington DC: Center on Budget and Policy Priorities. http://www.cbpp.org/research/housing/chart-book-federal-housing-spending-is-poorly-matched-to-need.

Fontaine, Jocelyn, and Jennifer Biess. 2012. *Housing as a Platform for Formerly Incarcerated Persons*. Washington DC: Urban Institute.

Franklin D. Roosevelt Library & Museum. 2016. "FDR and Housing Legislation." *FDR Presidential Library and Museum*. Accessed October 2016. https://fdrlibrary.org/housing.

Hulchanski, David J. 2013. "The Concept of Housing Affordability: Six Contemporary Uses of the Housing Expenditure-to-Income Ratio." In *The Affordable Housing Reader*, edited by J. Rosie Tighe and Elizabeth J. Mueller, 79–94. New York: Routledge.

Jewkes, Melanie D., and Lucy M. Delgadillo. 2010. "Weaknesses of Housing Affordability Indices Used by Practitioners." *Journal of Financial Counseling and Planning* 21(1): 43–52.

Joint Committee on Taxation. 2014. *Estimate of Federal Tax Expenditures for Fiscal Years 2014–2018*. Washington, DC: Congress of the United States. www.jct.gov/publications.html?func=startdown&id=4857.

McDaniel, Benjamin. 2016. *The Affordable Housing Income Conundrum in the Twin Cities*. March 3. Accessed October 23, 2016. http://streets.mn/2016/03/03/the-affordable-housing-income-conundrum-in-the-twin-cities/.

O'Dell, William, Marc T. Smith, and Douglas White. 2004. "Weaknesses in Current Measures of Housing Needs." *Housing and Society* 31(1): 29–40.

Office of Justice Programs. 2016. "Prisoners and Prisoner Reentry." *United States Department of Justice*, November 20. www.justice.gov/archive/fbci/progmenu_reentry.html.

Office of Policy Development and Research, U. D. 2014. "Picture of Subsidized Housing." *HUD User*. www.huduser.gov/portal/datasets/picture/yearlydata.html#download-tab.

PD & R Edge. 2014. "Rental Burdens: Rethinking Affordability Measures." *HUD User*, September 22. www.huduser.gov/portal/pdredge/pdr_edge_featd_article_092214.html.

Pindus, Nancy, G. Thomas Kingsley, Jennifer Biess, Diane Levy, Jasmine Simington, Christopher Hayes, and Urban Institute. 2017. *Housing Needs of American Indians and Alaskan Natives in Tribal Areas: A Report from the Assessment of American Indian, Alaskan Native, and Native Hawaiian Housing Needs*. Washington DC: U.S. Department of Housing.

Polikoff, Alexander, Edward G. Goetz, John Goering, and Edgar O. Olsen. 2014. "Point of Contention: Poverty Deconcentration." *Cityscape: A Journal of Policy Development and Research (U.S. Department of Housing and Urban Development Office of Policy Development and Research)* 16(2).

Representatives, H. of. 2006. *House Hearing, 109th Congress-Poverty, Public Housing and the CRA: Have Housing and Community Investment Incentives Helped Public Housing Families Achieve the American Dream?* Washington, DC: U.S. Government Printing Office.

Sard, Barbara, and Douglas Rice. 2014. *Creating Opportunity for Children: How Housing Location Can Make a Difference*. Washington DC: Center on Budget and Policy Priorities.

Sard, Barbara, and Will Fischer. 2013. *Renters' Tax Credit Would Promote Equity and Advance Balanced Housing Policy*. Washington DC: Center on Budget and Policy Priorities. http://cbpp.org/sites/default/files/atoms/files/7-13-12hous.pdf.

Schwartz, Alex F. 2015. *Housing Policy in the United States Third Ed.* New York: Routledge.

Steffen, Barry L., George R. Carter, Marge Martin, Danilo Pelletiere, David A. Vandenbroucke, and Yunn-Gann David Yao. 2015. *Worst Case Housing Needs 2015 Report to Congress*. Washington, DC: U.S. Housing and Urban Development.

Stone, Michael E. 2013. "What is Housing Affordability? The Case for the Residual Income Approach." In *The Affordable Housing Reader*, edited by J. Rosie Tighe and Elizabeth J. Mueller, 95–110. New York: Routledge.

Stoutland, Sara E. 1999. "Community Development Corporations: Mission, Strategy and Accomplishments." In *Urban Problems and Community Development*, edited by Ronald F. Ferguson and William T. Dickens, 193–240. Washington D.C.: Brookings Institution.

Tegeler, Philip, and Scott Berstein. 2013. "Counterpoint: The Housing + Affordability Index and Fair Housing." In *The Affordable Housing Reader*, edited by J. Rosie Tighe and Elizabeth J. Mueller, 116–121. New York: Routledge.

Turner, Margery Austin. 2013. "Strengths and Weaknesses of the Housing Voucher Program." In *The Affordable Housing Reader*, edited by Rosie J. Tighe and Elizabeth J. Mueller, 288–294. New York: Routledge.

Turner, Margery Austin, Eric Toder, Rolf Pendall, and Claudia Sharygin. 2013. *How Would reforming the Mortgage Interest Deducation Affect the Housing Market?* Washington DC: Urban Institute. http://webarchive.urban.org/UploadedPDF/412776-How-Would-Reforming-the-Mortgage-Interest-Deduction-Affect-the-Housing-Market.pdf.

U.S. Census Bureau, U. D. n.d. "Selected Housing Characteristics 2010–2014 American Community Survey 5-Year Estimates." *Amercian FactFinder*. Accessed October 23, 2016. http://

factfinder.census.gov/faces/tableservices/jsf/pages/productview.xhtml?pid=ACS_14_
5YR_DP04&src=pt.

U.S. Department of Housing and Urban Development. n.d. "Affordable Housing." *HUD.gov*. http://
portal.hud.gov/hudportal/HUD?src=/program_offices/comm_planning/affordablehousing.

U.S. Housing and Urban Development. 2016. "About the Portal." *Location Affordability Portal Version 2*, October 29. www.locationaffordability.info/about.aspx.

Washington Lawyers' Committee for Civil Rights & Urban Affairs. 2014. *The Collateral Consequences of Arrests and Convictions Under D.C., Maryland, and Virginia Law*. Washington, DC: Washington Lawyers' Committee for Civil Rights & Urban Affairs. www.washlaw.org/pdf/wlc_collateral_consequences_report.pdf.

Winnick, L. 1995. "The Triumph of Housing Allowance Programs: How a Fundamental Policy Conflict Was Resolved." *Cityscape: A Journal of Policy Development and Research* 1(3): 95–121.

7

HOUSING AND OPPORTUNITY

Earlier we talked about housing being unique, as it sits in a specific location. One way to identify the location of a house is by its postal zip code. In popular culture, zip codes can be a stand-in for affluence (think of the "90210" television show that aired on the CW Television Network) or a way to claim neighborhood space (rap music often invokes zip codes to mark a connection with a specific neighborhood (Forman 2002)). Beyond providing place identity, where we live is so intertwined with our health that research has shown your zip code has a correlation with your lifespan—some people living up to 25 years less or being three times more likely to have a heart attack corresponding to where they live (Robert Wood Johnson Foundation 2014). These spatial inequities have been a persistent fact of American life creating a pattern of "geographic 'hot-spots'" (Sampson 2012, 13).

While our housing provides physical shelter, it is also a large determinant of our quality of life because it establishes our access to opportunities or nearness to risks, affecting our lives in both positive and negative ways. Elements of the physical, social, and service qualities of neighborhoods influence our health and behaviors (Braveman, Cubbin, Egerter, and Pedregon 2011). Positive neighborhood features include good schools, steady places of employment, affordable nutritious food, safe parks and recreational areas, health care facilities, and effective transportation systems. On the other hand, neighborhoods with crime, toxic waste and other environmental hazards, and concentrations of liquor stores and fast food restaurants can negatively affect people's lives. This chapter will examine how where we live shapes our quality of life, with emphasis on the links between housing and health, and housing and education.

Housing and Public Health

The opportunities for good health—both physical and mental—begin in our homes and neighborhoods, yet access to those opportunities remains unequal in America for many reasons. Policies governing land use, housing, and transportation all have an impact on health factors, as they shape access and exposure. Market decisions (where to invest or disinvest) can also contribute to environmental conditions and land uses in a neighborhood. (Of course, policies and market decisions can influence each other.) In addition, as discussed in Chapter 5, racism and segregation (by race and class) in America have contributed to a landscape of inequities.

The location and the cost of our housing can have a profound impact on our health. Exposure to poor air quality, excessive noise, lead paint, and toxins can undermine our physical health. Additionally, the lack of access to nutritional resources, health care facilities, and safe recreational space can limit our ability to easily care for ourselves and our families. Stress due to housing costs exceeding our budget, fear of crime, and worry for

Figure 7.1 Poster from Fair Housing Month

Source: National Fair Housing Training Academy, U.S. Department of Housing and Urban Development

our children's future can take a toll on our bodies and our minds. In the following sections we will explore the ways in which housing can support or undermine physical and mental health and the connection between housing and public health.

Nutritional Opportunities

> Food is life. It is necessity and pleasure, family and community, culture and power. When plentiful and freely shared, food creates healthy communities and strong societies; when scarce or unfairly distributed, it damages and, in time kills, spirit, body, family, community.
> (American Civil Liberties Union, New York Law School Racial Justice Project 2012)

At the most basic level, having the ability to be healthy includes access to nutritious food. Increasingly in the United States we are finding that opportunities to access healthy foods are not equal for members of the population, and often those who live in the poorest areas have the greatest challenges in accessing healthy foods.

While many people living in the United States are a five-minute car ride from a grocery store or even multiple grocery stores that have a wide array of fresh fruits, vegetables, and other healthy foods, many poor people living in urban areas do not have access to supermarkets where they can purchase healthy foods at reasonable prices. Those that need affordable groceries the most are faced with having to pay higher prices for food of lesser quality and lesser nutritional value, and go further to get it.

With an increasing number of grocery stores moving to the suburbs and closing in urban locations, this problem has affected many people throughout the last several decades. Urban planners, public health professionals, public policy experts, geographers and those in other related fields, are turning their attention toward this critical issue, known as *supermarket redlining*. Another term associated with this problem is *food desert*, a large geographic area with no grocery stores or very distant access to grocery stores (Mari Gallagher Research & Consulting Group 2006).

Studies show that those living in food deserts face more health issues related to their diet than those who do not live in these areas. Such problems are worsened by the presence of more fast food stores in these areas (Mari Gallagher Research & Consulting Group 2006), as well as an increased number of convenience stores, corner stores, and liquor stores that increase people's access to unhealthy, processed products including tobacco, alcohol, canned goods, candy, soft drinks, and other foods that are not good to consume regularly in a healthy diet.

One of the first major studies to underscore the significance of food deserts focused on Chicago, showing that African American communities in Chicago were less likely to have access to large grocery stores, travel the furthest distance for access to any type of grocery store, and most likely to be living in a food deserts (Mari Gallagher Research & Consulting Group 2006). Another city where access to food has been a challenge for poor people of color is Detroit, with research showing that within the most impoverished neighborhoods in the city, the neighborhoods in which African Americans resided were on average over a mile further away from the nearest supermarket (Zenk et al. 2005).

As food deserts are further studied, we are learning that solutions may not be simple. In some areas, political, investment, and infrastructure challenges make large grocery chains hesitant to open in inner city areas. However, other initiatives to help bring fresher foods to inner city areas are being explored and, in many cases, have been successful. These initiatives include supporting owners of small- or medium-size stores in increasing their stocks of fresh foods, urban farming, and community gardens in at-risk neighborhoods (Ghosh 2016).

Figure 7.2   A customer purchasing fruit through the Food Trust's Healthy Corner Store initiative
Source: The Food Trust of Philadelphia, used with permission

Box 7.1   The Food Trust of Philadelphia: The Healthy Corner Store Initiative

The Food Trust of Philadelphia, PA has been working on solutions to the problem of food deserts in Philadelphia and piloted the Healthy Corner Store Initiative in 2004. By working directly with owners of small corner stores, conducting consumer education, providing recipe cards to customers featuring healthy ingredients, and loaning out refrigerators to enable stores to sell fresh fruits and vegetables, this initiative has helped provide healthier food options for neighborhoods that otherwise would have very limited access to such choices (Charles 2012). The Food Trust is active in over 600 corner stores in the Philadelphia area focusing on increasing stores capacity to sell and market healthy foods for local communities, working with storeowners to make these changes to their inventory profitable, and marketing healthy message to customers to encourage healthier food selections. The organization also works with stores to host nutrition education, and links stores to community partners, local farmers and fresh food suppliers (The Food Trust 2012).

Access to Open Space

Another very basic component of being able to make healthy choices is the ability to do physical activity. Safe open spaces available to enjoy fresh air and participate in recreational activities are unequally distributed in the United States. Researchers have shown time and time again that poor people, and disproportionately people of color, have less access to secure, green outdoor areas and this is a contributor to obesity and other serious health problems. One study looking at public park provision in the greater Los Angeles metropolitan region demonstrated that low-density, affluent white neighborhoods are substantially more likely to be closer to large expanses of open spaces and have higher park acreage compared to older inner city neighborhoods that are typically low-income communities of color—going so far as to show that Hispanics and African Americans have up to six times less park acreage per capita compared to whites (Sister 2007). In a related study examining the provision of urban public recreational programs in Southern California, research showed that cities marked by such characteristics as low household income, minority populations, and multifamily housing are disadvantaged when it comes to recreation provisions and such disparities could increase the public health risk in these areas (Dahmann, et al. 2010).

Health and Development Patterns

Urban form and the pattern of development in our communities also influence our health. One of the most profound changes in geography that we have seen in the most recent half of the twentieth century is a significantly increased amount of *sprawl*—expansion of cities away from central urban areas into expansive, low-density, car-dependent suburbs. We can see that this heavier reliance on cars to get from place to place has significantly impacted the geography that surrounds us, and has also had a severe impact on the natural environment, creating pollution, increased impermeable surfaces, destruction of natural habitats, and other environmental degradation. Researchers have also shown that this reliance on cars is contributing to the American obesity epidemic (Lopez-Zetinaa, Leeb, and Friisa 2006; Jacobson, King, and Yuan 2011) and other health problems. For example, as children's homes have become further from schools, there has been an increasing need for children to be driven or bused to school, as opposed to walking or biking, which results in significantly less daily exercise and adds to the childhood obesity epidemic (Ewing 2003). In 1969, 48 percent of children between 5 and 14 years of age usually walked or biked to school; in 2009, this number was only 13 percent (National Center for Safe Routes to School 2011). In addition to the greater distances that must be driven overall when living in these suburbs, the choice to drive has become a self-perpetuating cycle: as overall motor vehicle traffic increases, parents become increasingly convinced that it is unsafe for their children to walk or bike to school, so they drive them there, thereby adding more traffic to the road and continuing the cycle (National Center for Safe Routes to School 2011).

Decisions about the design of urban areas have also led to negative health impacts. Children in urban areas of concentrated disadvantage have elevated rates of asthma and other respiratory ailments (Gern 2010). Studies have shown this can be correlated to living near a major highway or living in a neighborhood with businesses and industries served by diesel trucks (Hood 2005). Asthma attacks are also known to be associated with dust and mold in homes, and stress. So, for children living in an environment where violence is not uncommon or financial pressures hang like a cloud, a predilection for asthma may be triggered by these physical and social factors. Add to this the challenge of maintaining regular access to preventive medicine and treatment, and you can see neighborhoods where children's hospitalization for asthma is much higher than other areas—resulting in a greater number of school absences (Gern 2010).

Yet another condition of the built environment documented to have serious health implications is that of exposure to lead paint. Given that the age of housing stock is directly related to the presence of lead-tainted dust, children living in urban areas with older housing stock are at serious risk. Studies have documented a much higher incidence of lead poisoning among African American children than white or Hispanic children. Lead poisoning has irreversible effects on the brain associated with lifelong behavioral and learning difficulties (Gaitens et al. 2009).

Researcher Robert Bullard launched and has pioneered actions toward "environmental justice." Beginning with his book *Dumping in Dixie*, Bullard has been able to bring attention to the land use decision-making process that favors the location of toxic and waste recycling facilities in the neighborhoods of the poor and people of color (1990). His work was successful in translating this issue into the realm of policy. The Environmental Protection Agency has integrated environmental justice into its programs, defining it as

> the fair treatment and meaningful involvement of all people regardless of race, color, national origin, or income, with respect to the development, implementation, and enforcement of environmental laws, regulations, and policies.
>
> (United States Environmental Protection Agency n.d.)

At the heart of the matter is that some are disproportionately exposed to environmental pollution through the siting of hazardous industries, and there is a nexus between the location of affordable housing and heavy industrial and waste recycling facilities. This can include scrap metal recycling, landfills, and Superfund sites. Much of the exposure takes the form of polluted air and more study is needed to understand the implications of exposure to the full range of toxins—particularly for children who, due to biological development, are the most vulnerable (Brulle and Pellow 2006; Landrigan et al. 2015).

Crime Victimization and Exposure

Physical and mental well-being are directly linked to one's exposure to crime. For victims of crime there is risk of injury, hospitalization, and death. But there is also a negative effect on one's mental health (and associated physical symptoms) by directly witnessing and having family members experience threatening acts and violent crime. Not surprisingly, those that reside in low-opportunity areas are at greater risk from these crime-related effects (Gibson, Morris, and Beaver 2009). It has been reported that in 2008 those with family incomes of less than $15,000 were more than three times as likely to be victims of personal crimes than those with family incomes of $75,000 or more (Kearney, Harris, and Parker 2014).

Cost of Housing and Health

Organizations such as the Center for Housing Policy have explored the link between housing and health outcomes. In Chapter 6 you learned about housing costs and the great need for more affordable housing in the United States. Tied to the basic need for housing itself are numerous health outcomes that result from having access to quality, affordable housing. One of the most basic and important health outcomes that affordable housing has been shown to provide is freeing up household funds to pay for health care and healthy food. In addition, families who have access to affordable, quality housing experience a greater feeling of stability, less stress, and fewer stress-related health issues (Desmond 2016). Another health outcome that well-constructed affordable housing provides is that it can significantly reduce the health problems associated with poor-quality housing. Also important to mention is that access to affordable housing allows survivors of abuse to escape abusive situations, improving mental and physical health (Maqbool, Viveiros, and Ault 2015)

Access to Reproductive Health Facilities

In addition to the important connection between housing and health issues already discussed, it is important to point out the connection between housing and access to women's reproductive health. As with other public health issues, poorer people, and in this case poorer women, are disproportionately faced with reproductive healthcare limitations related to where they live. For example, recent studies (Texas Health and Human Service Commission 2015, Texas Women's Healthcare Coalition 2013) have examined the effects of the closing of numerous reproductive health clinics in the state of Texas. With the closing of these clinics, many women located in rural Texas have to travel significantly further for their reproductive healthcare and are losing their access to routine care, contraception consultation, cancer screenings, preventative exams, and other important services. The lack of clinics in rural areas has particularly negative consequences because women can't afford the loss of pay due to missed work or do not have transportation to travel longer distances for a health exam. National Public Radio's show *All Things Considered* covered this issue in a 2016 episode, outlining the experience of a college-aged woman living in rural Texas, who, because of the impediments to accessing local reproductive health care, had to travel more than four hours away for an appointment (Goodwyn 2016). This makes it increasingly unlikely that poor women will regularly see doctors, which leads to an increase in pregnancy and adverse health effects from conditions that could be treated if preventative care was readily available.

Housing and Education

Most children in the United States—about 73 percent—attend the public school assigned to them based on geographical boundaries within their school district (United States Department of Education 2009). In other words, for most families, where they live determines where their children go to school. The majority of the money for public elementary and secondary schools in America—about 93 percent—comes from state and local government (United States Department of Education 2009), but this funding is not equal for every public school. In most states, the local funds for public schools come from property taxes set by the school board, citizens, or local officials. This means that places that have higher property values generally have more money going into their public schools. Such a system causes dramatic differences in schools between states and within districts. Depending on the property wealth of a municipality, the schools within it could have beautiful buildings and state-of-the-art equipment or be completely dilapidated and outdated. Municipalities that are within a mere few miles of each other could have wildly different resources for their public schools (The Education Trust 2015; Woodruff 2008):

> some [students] stand in state-of-the-art classrooms with brand new smartboards and bookshelves stuffed to the brim. Others, however, gaze at peeling paint and water stains on the ceiling, at empty shelves and blackboards with no chalk. Some see before them a fully equipped laboratory; others, a tattered textbook they aren't allowed to take home. And right now, which of those classrooms a child stands in has a lot to do with his family's wealth or the color of her skin.
> (The Education Trust 2015, 1)

Many states provide the least amount of funding to schools and districts serving students with the greatest needs. While money is not the sole factor for a student's academic success, districts with more resources can pay teachers more, making it easier for them to attract strong educators, as well as more support and enrichment, which is particularly important for students who do not have such opportunities outside of school (The Education Trust 2015).

Education and Affordable Housing

Beyond the geographic definition of school districts, a family's access to stable, affordable housing has been linked to children's academic success. Research has found that the lack of access to safe and affordable housing in a stable environment keeps children from achieving academic success. Such issues include frequent disruptive moves, housing-related stress, health hazards in their neighborhood, and of course, homelessness. These issues and their impact on a child's achievement make it all the clearer that the development of ample safe, quality, affordable housing is critical to families (Brennan, Reed, and Sturtevant 2014).

Questions on the Geography of Opportunity

Some researchers ask about the roots of the findings of studies documented within this chapter. Are these findings a representation of a place, or a reflection of individual choices made by a group of people? That is, could it be that some of these findings reflect a self-selection of people with some common characteristics and behaviors, rather than the effect of deprivation? Does the lack of a grocery store lead to obesity or is it the result of an individual choice to purchase fast food?

The work of sociologist Robert Sampson includes a review of much of the literature on neighborhood effects. His book is positioned to advance our understanding of the causal relationship among individuals, neighborhood effects, and larger forces. Writing with others, Sampson contends the breadth of research on neighborhood effects provides convincing evidence that they exist and matter—these realities are not simply a product of individual choices (Sampson, Morenoff, and Gannon-Rowley 2002). Sampson does not deny that individual choice can play a role, yet he suggests those choices themselves are shaped by the neighborhood context people encounter in daily life. Noting, "neighborhood is consequence and cause, outcome and producer," he suggests people make choices that are shaped both by the reality of conditions in an area and their perception (even if not based in fact) of the neighborhood, which is shaped by reputation and common portrayals (Sampson 2012, 358).

A related policy question follows from this debate: is it more effective, then, to invest in places, making them better, or to invest in people, facilitating the movement of households from areas of low opportunity to areas of strong opportunity? This policy question also connects to how to weigh the connection people have to their homes and neighborhoods when considering relocation.

One well-known, large study undertaken by the federal government during 1994–1998 sought to get at the question of whether people would benefit from moving to places that had better opportunities. The study, Moving to Opportunity (MTO), followed three groups of low income households chosen from a neighborhood considered to offer limited life chances. While there has been much discussion and critique of the methods of the study, in general the findings are accepted—although researchers are still working to fully understand the dynamics behind the outcomes.

In MTO, one group of households was given housing vouchers that could be used *only* if they moved to places of opportunity; another group of households stayed in place in subsidized housing; and the third group of households were given vouchers to move to any location (National Bureau of Economic Research n.d.). In general, 4 to 7 years after the program started, MTO showed that adults who moved to places of opportunity felt safer and more content and their health outcomes were better, and girls in these households reported less stress. Educational outcomes and employment, however, were not improved. Recent analysis, benefiting from a longer study horizon, has analyzed the adult circumstances of those who moved to opportunity as young children. This research has found a correlation between the ages the individuals moved, and their college attendance and incomes. That is, those who moved to a safer place with better schools before they were 12 years old ended up doing better in life as adults (Chety, Hendren, and Katz 2015).

Conclusions

This chapter has presented many ways that our housing opportunities connect with other critical forces in our lives that impact our health and wellbeing. Our housing is more than just a roof over our heads because it serves as a connector between where we live and the resources we have to address critical aspects of our lives, including health, education, career, and others. While inequities of place have long been part of American society, in recent years researchers have started to make connections across disciplines, such as urban planning and public health, to unravel the interconnections among life disparities. The link between transportation options and childhood obesity is one example. The link between transportation access, affordable housing locations, and jobs is another. Among researchers, there are several essential debates that are part of the continued search to understand why American neighborhoods look and operate as spaces of inequity. Certainly the way features are interconnected makes it difficult, and perhaps meaningless, to study one aspect of the quality of life in isolation. Continued research to further our understanding, however, can only improve the design and implementation of policies to equalize opportunities for all Americans.

Question and Activities

1. To what degree are individuals in charge of their own food and exercise choices and the health outcomes that follow? Would the presence of facilities guarantee changes (farmer's markets, parks, etc.)? Split the class and debate.
2. Think about the phrase *transportation policy is health policy*. What does this mean?
3. Watch Mari Gallagher's TED[X] talk on food deserts, available online. What are some important points that you take away from her talk?
4. The *New York Times* featured an op-ed piece by David L. Kirp entitled "Here Comes the Neighborhood". This article comments on results of a study about affordable housing in an affluent suburban community, with Kirk arguing that having the opportunity to live in a peaceful neighborhood with good schools can transform lives (Kirp 2013). Read this article and reflect on the digital story you created at the beginning of the class. How does what Kirp writes connect (or not connect) to what you talked about in your housing biography? (Gonchar 2013).
5. Have students compare two or more indices that have been created to categorize areas in terms of opportunities and resources. Have them look at the categories of criteria selected, the scale of measurement used (neighborhood, municipality, region), and the sources of data used. Possible choices include: Opportunity Map

by National Center for Smart Growth Research and Education and the Austin Opportunity mapping report completed by the Green Doors and The Kirwan Institute for the Study of Race and Ethnicity.
6. Refer students to one of many municipal or regional equity plans completed in the past 10 years. Have them summarize the goals and action items of one of the areas addressed (e.g., education, transportation, food, etc.). (Policylink is a leading firm in conducting such analyses; they have an extensive list of reports available at their website (www.policylink.org/) under the "Find Resources" tab.)
7. Take a walking tour of local neighborhoods and think about the various concepts that we discussed in this chapter related to opportunities based on housing. You can use the Robert Woods Johnson calculator for local lifespans versus U.S. averages here: https://www.rwjf.org/en/library/interactives/whereyouliveaffectshowlongyoulive.html. Try to take notice of neighborhood attributes and resources, as well as small details about local quality and conditions. What do the people in each neighborhood have access to? What is further away or out of reach without transportation? Take notice of the following and consider how they could affect adults and children:

- Location of schools
- Condition of (or existence of) sidewalks
- Amount of traffic
- Access to local hospital/clinic
- Local parks and their condition
- Bus/mass transit access
- Condition of buildings and local properties
- Access to food and the type of food retailers—grocery stores, farmers markets, corner stores, restaurants, fast food, etc.
- Exposure to pollution from highways, businesses, or industry
- What else do you notice about opportunities that this neighborhood can or cannot access?

References

American Civil Liberties Union, New York Law School Racial Justice Project. 2012. *Unshared Bounty: How Structural Racism Contributes to the Creation and Persistence of Food Deserts.* New York: American Civil Liberties Union, New York Law School Racial Justice Project.

Braveman, Paula, Catherine Cubbin, Susan Egerter, and Veronica Pedregon. 2011. "Neighborhoods and Health." *Issue Brief 8: Exploring the Social Determinants of Health Series.* Robert Wood Johnson Foundation. www.rwjf.org/content/dam/farm/reports/issue_briefs/2011/rwjf70450.

Brennan, Maya, Patrick Reed, and Lisa A. Sturtevant. 2014. *The Impacts of Affordable Housing on Education: A Research Summary.* Center for Housing Policy. Washington, DC: National Housing Conference.

Brulle, Robert J., and David N. Pellow. 2006. "Environmental Justice: Human Health and Environmental Inequalities." *Annual Review of Public Health* 27: 103–124.

Bullard, Robert. 1990. *Dumping in Dixie.* Boulder, CO: Westview.

Charles, Dan. 2012. "What Will Make the Food Desert Bloom?" *All Things Considered.* National Public Radio.

Chety, Raj, Nathaniel Hendren, and Lawrence F. Katz. 2015. "The Effects of Exposure to Better Neighborhoods on Children: New Evidence from the Moving to Opportunity Experiment." *Working Paper Number 21156.* Cambridge: National Bureau of Economic Research. www.nber.org/papers/w21156.

Dahmann, Nicholas, Jennifer Wolch, Pascale Joassart-Marcelli, Kim Reynolds, and Michael Jerrett. 2010. "The Active City? Disparities in Provision of Urban Public Recreation Resources." *Health & Place* 16(3): 431–445.

Desmond, Matthew. 2016. *Evicted: Poverty and Profit in the American City*. New York: Crown Publisher.

The Education Trust. 2015. "Funding Gaps 2015: Too Many States Still Spend Less on Educating Students Who Need the Most." https://edtrust.org/wp-content/uploads/2014/09/Funding-Gaps2015_TheEducationTrust1.pdf.

Ewing, Barbara A., and McCann Reid. 2003. *Measuring the Health Effects of Sprawl: A National Analysis of Physical Activity, Obesity and Chronic Disease*. Surface Transportation Policy Project. Washington, DC: Smart Growth America.

The Food Trust. 2012. *What We Do: In Corner Stores, Working With Students and Communities to Teach Healthy Snacking and Improve Fresh Food Access*. Accessed June 28, 2016. http://thefoodtrust.org/what-we-do/corner-store.

Forman, Murray. 2002. *The 'Hood Comes First: Race, Space, and Place in Rap and Hip-Hop*. Middletown, CT: Wesleyan University Press.

Gaitens, Joanna M., Sherry L. Dixon, David E. Jacobs, Jyothi Nagaraja, Warren Strauss, and Jonathan W. Wilson. 2009. "Exposure of U.S. Children to Residential Dust Lead, 1999–2004: I. Housing and Demographic Factors." *Environmental Health Perspectives* 117: 461–467.

Gern, James E. 2010. "The Urban Environment and Childhood Asthma Study." *The Journal of Allergy and Clinical Immunology* 3: 545–549.

Ghosh, Debarchana, and Mengyao Zhang. 2016. "Spatial Supermarket Redlining and Neighborhood Vulnerability: A Case Study of Hartford, Connecticut." *Transactions in GIS* (John Wiley & Sons Ltd) 20(1): 79–100.

Gibson, Chris L., Sara Z. Morris, and Kevin M. Beaver. 2009. "Secondary Exposure to Violence During Childhood and Adolescence: Does Neighborhood Context Matter?" *Justice Quarterly* 26(1): 30–57.

Gonchar, Michael. 2013. "How Much Does Your Neighborhood Define Who You Are?" *The New York Times*, October 22.

Goodwyn, Wade. 2016. "Texans Try to Repair Damage Wreaked Upon Family Planning Clinics." *All Things Considered*. National Public Radio. https:// npr.org/2016/01/28/464728393/texas-tries-to-repair-damage-wrought-upon-family-planning-clinics.

Hood, Ernie. 2005. "Dwelling Disparities: How Poor Housing Leads to Poor Health." *Environmental Health Perspectives* 113(5): A310–A317.

Jacobson, Sheldon H., Douglas M. King, and Rong Yuan. 2011. "A Note on the Relationship Between Obesity and Driving." *Transport Policy* 18(5): 772–776.

Kearney, Melissa S., Benjamin H. Jacome, Elisa Harris, and Lucie Parker. 2014. "Ten Economic Facts About Crime and Incarceration in the United States." *Policy Memo*. The Hamilton Project. www.hamiltonproject.org/assets/legacy/files/downloads_and_links/v8_THP_10Crime Facts.pdf.

Kirp, David L. 2013. "Here Comes the Neighborhood." *The New York Times*, October 19.

Landrigan, Philip J., Robert O. Wright, Jose F. Cordero, David L. Eaton, Bernard D. Hennig, Bernhard Goldstein, Raina M. Maier, David M. Ozonoff, Martyn T. Smith, and Robert H. Tukey. 2015. "The NIEHS Superfund Research Program: 25 Years of Translational Research for Public Health." *Environmental Health Perspectives* 123(10): 909–918.

Lopez-Zetinaa, Javier, Howard Leeb, and Robert Friisa. 2006. "The Link Between Obesity and the Built Environment. Evidence from an Ecological Analysis of Obesity and Vehicle Miles of Travel in California." *Health & Place* 12(4): 656–664.

Maqbool, Nabihah, Janet Viveiros, and Mindy Ault. 2015. *The Impacts of Affordable Housing on Health: A Research Summary*. Center for Housing Policy, National Housing Conference. Washington, DC: Center for Housing Policy.

Mari Gallagher Research & Consulting Group. 2006. *Examining the Impact of Food Deserts on Public Health in Chicago*. Chicago: LaSalle Bank.

National Bureau of Economic Research. n.d. *A Summary Overview of Moving to Opportunity: A Random Assignment Housing Mobility Study in Five U.S. Cities.* Cambridge, MA. www.nber. org/mtopublic/MTO%20Overview%20Summary.pdf.

National Center for Safe Routes to School. 2011. "How Children Get To School: School Travel Patterns From 1969 to 2009." http://archive.saferoutesinfo.org//sites/default/files/resources/ NHTS_school_travel_report_2011_0.pdf.

Robert Wood Johnson Foundation. 2017. "Does Where You Live Affect How Long You Live?" Accessed June 3, 2017. https:// rwjf.org/en/library/interactives/whereyouliveaffectshow longyoulive.html.

Sampson, Robert J. 2012. *Great American City: Chicago and the Enduring Neighborhood Effect.* Chicago: University of Chicago Press.

Sampson, Robert J., Jeffrey D. Morenoff, and Thomas Gannon-Rowley. 2002. "Assessing 'Neighborhood Effects': Social Processes and New Directions in Research." *Annual Review of Sociology* 28: 443–478.

Sister, Maria Chona E. 2007. "Do Blacks and Browns Have Less Green? Examining the Distribution of Park and Open Space Resources in the Greater Los Angeles Metropolitan Region." *University of California Dissertation*, August. Los Angeles, CA: University of Southern California.

Texas Health and Human Service Commission. 2015. "Texas Women's Health Program: Savings and Performance Reporting." *Financial Services Division, Strategic Decision Support, Texas Health and Human Service Commission.* https://hhs.texas.gov/reports/2015/03/ texas-womens-health-program-savings-and-performance-reporting.

Texas Women's Healthcare Coalition. 2013. "Texas Women's Healthcare in Crisis." *Texas Women's Healthcare Coalition.* http://texaswhc.org/wp-content/uploads/2017/04/Texas-Womens-Healthcare-in-Crisis.pdf.

United States Department of Education. 2009. "The Condition of Education 2009." *National Center for Education Statistics, Institute of Education Sciences.* https://nces.ed.gov/pubs2009/ 2009081.pdf.

United States Environmental Protection Agency. n.d. *Environmental Justice.* www.epa.gov/ environmentaljustice.

Woodruff, Judy. 2008. "Where We Stand: America's Schools in the 21st Century." *Public Broadbasting Service.* Accessed June 20, 2016. www.pbs.org/wnet/wherewestand/reports/finance/ how-do-we-fund-our-schools/?p=197.

Zenk, Shannon N., Amy J. Schulz, Barbara A. Israel, Sherman A. James, Shuming Bao, and Mark L. Wilson. 2005. "Neighborhood Racial Composition, Neighborhood Poverty, and the Spatial Accessibility of Supermarkets in Metropolitan Detroit." *American Journal of Public Health* 95(4): 660–667.

8

HOUSING AND THE ECONOMY

One of the important things we have reflected upon so far is how, for residents, the value of housing is much more than simply the shelter it provides—it is a foundation for life's opportunities. However, the value of housing for nonresidents depends on one's position. For builders, housing is a product to manufacture for profit, for developers an investment to generate income, or for financiers an asset to trade. The pursuit by some of housing as a home coexists with the objectives of others to make profits—often this is a conflicted coexistence as profit maximization controls outcomes. Homeowners themselves may act both to secure their connection to a special place and to maximize their main investment.

In this chapter, we explore the cost of housing by considering the components of the housing market, using neoclassical economics to shed light on the aspects of housing supply and demand. But housing is a multifaceted product and it is also greatly shaped by social and political choices. We will focus on market characteristics as well as significant trends. For Americans, the housing market is essential, as most Americans receive housing through the private sector. Topics concerning the private market and housing costs covered here include the relationship between regulations and housing costs, the premise of housing filtering, and the phenomenon of gentrification.

The Housing Market

It is important to realize that housing markets function at a local level. Housing characteristics, costs, and trends vary greatly among cities, metropolitan regions, and rural localities. In some areas, housing costs are reasonable, in others exorbitant. Markets can be hot, weak, or mixed. Housing is often conceived of as having distinct, price-driven submarkets within regional markets. This is why the federal Department of Housing and Urban Development sets programmatic rent levels by metropolitan area (see Chapter 6). The housing market should not, however, be conceived of as an entity independent of government. In fact, the market very much relies on government and would not exist without the rule of law and societal institutions and controls (Oxley 2004). There is no pure, natural market; seeing the market as a natural process denies the many social and political choices that underlie its function. The neoclassical economic models present useful simplifications, but the true complexity of the housing market and the ability to control and affect it discussed in other chapters (tax policies, mortgage systems, racism and discriminatory practices, etc.) is also significant in comprehending how housing is produced and delivered.

To an extent, the fundamental laws of supply and demand can be used to review housing dynamics and the cost of housing. The basic idea is that demand for a good product drives suppliers to meet the demand. Decreases in demand lead to decreases in supply. Price is a function of demand and supply. Low supply and high demand translates to higher prices for consumers; high supply and low demand translates to lower prices for consumers. But the unique characteristics of housing introduced in Chapter 1 are relevant to a discussion on market forces. These characteristics are repeated here:

1. Housing is more than just a product—there are strong emotional and psychosocial components to housing.
2. Housing is heterogeneous—each dwelling unit is unique.
3. Housing is generally the largest purchase a household makes.
4. Housing choices can change but the financial and emotional costs of moving can be high.
5. Housing is durable and typically appreciates over time.
6. Housing is shaped by cultural norms *and* institutional practices.

Our examination of demand and supply will reference these characteristics, noting how housing may not always follow the economic rules of a typical good.

Housing Demand

When it comes to demand, all households seek shelter. This includes households of all economic classes and each of the two tenure types—homeowners and renters. The nature of the demand in a local market is a function of the area's demographics (number and type of households) and incomes of households. Other elements that affect financial access to housing such as interest rates and credit availability are also related to the level of demand: lower interest rates and less restrictive credit standards can extend housing demand.

The cultural norms described in Chapter 2 play a role, as they can establish basic preferences that add cost, such as an attached garage or air conditioning (according to the U.S. Census, in 2011 89 percent of American households reported having central air or an air conditioning unit (U.S. Census Bureau 2011)). This has led housing expert Peter Salins to write, "By many objective standards Americans are the best-housed people in the world" (1993). While generally we are well-housed, the United States housing market does not equally serve all parts of the population.

Neoclassical economics assumes households act rationally to maximize their utility or well-being as they consider housing purchases (including rentals) within their incomes (Oxley 2004). Most researchers have found that increasing incomes are *eventually* associated with allocating more toward housing costs—that is, as housing becomes more affordable to households, they will in turn buy more or exchange what they have for higher quality housing (Bier 2001). Changing housing is not simple, so the consumption of additional housing is not necessarily an immediate response to a rise in income or drop in financing costs. In the terminology of economics, this makes short-term housing demand relatively *inelastic*. Households make choices that may include staying put and accepting some dissatisfaction over taking on the disruption associated with moving (A. O'Sullivan 1993).

Recall that we have often characterized housing as a heterogeneous product. Each housing unit is unique and households are deciding among the bundle of trade-offs associated with each housing unit. For instance, one apartment may be close to mass transit while another has slightly more square footage; one single family home may have a large yard while another is in a desirable school district. Some studies have found households are more likely to change housing to obtain a different neighborhood or higher quality construction rather than move simply for additional square footage (A. O'Sullivan 1993). This bundle of characteristics and housing's connection to identity sets housing apart from other goods. It can also make it more difficult for economic models to capture the decision-making process of housing consumers.

Where people are in their lifecycle plays a role in the type of housing they seek. Retirees may seek one style, while young families look for other housing features. The formation of new households, be it through marriages, divorces, or new adulthood, translates into an increase in the demand for housing. Demand may also be affected by the location decision of employers. New businesses may draw additional households to an area, reflecting interdependency between the locational decisions of households and those of firms (Straszheim 1975). The loss of an industry, for example the decline of automobile manufacturing in Michigan, will in turn decrease the demand for housing.

Housing Supply

The supply of housing through the private market[1] involves a variety of actors including land owners, the construction industry and tradespeople, developers, bankers/mortgage originators, real estate agents, and landlords. Supply is driven by an ability to profit from housing production and management. Demand must be there, and the costs of inputs—land, labor, materials, financing (construction and mortgage loans), operating—must be such that pricing produces a profit. Each of these inputs can also become the focus of a government program seeking to reduce the cost of housing (see Chapters 6 and 10).

Supply responds to demand. Falling demand, in the form of increasing vacancies, will decrease prices and eventually lead to decreased supply. This can take the form of decisions to divest in an area by minimizing the maintenance of, or even abandoning, property. Growing demand may lead to an increase in supply, within the constraints of local conditions, such as land availability, density regulations, permitting processes, and financing. Barriers in these characteristics can slow or limit the construction of additional housing (this is discussed more below).

Demand also responds to supply. Oversupply in an area can lead to declining property values and housing costs. This has been a concern for neighborhoods that experienced high levels of foreclosures during the 2008–2010 crisis (Levitin and Wachter 2013). Such declining property values and disinvestment can feed a decreased demand in an area, furthering the area's decline.

Given housing's durability, housing supply is met largely through the existing—i.e., used—housing stock. This stock deteriorates slowly over time, and the degree of maintenance put into these housing units will determine their quality. In addition to the existing housing stock, a decision to invest in major renovations can add to the stock, as can the adaptive reuse of non-residential buildings (e.g. schools, churches, etc.) into housing units. In contrast, new construction adds housing—typically of a higher quality—but represents only a small percentage (2–3 percent) of the overall housing choices available annually (A. O'Sullivan 1993). This new housing is more likely than older housing to meet current regulatory standards for construction. In general, local regulators do a better job of ensuring new construction meets codes than they do of monitoring and enforcing code violations against the older housing stock of a community (Downs 1974).

The supply side of housing is also considered inelastic in the short term—that is, a change in the price of housing, such as an increase, will not yield an immediate response

Figure 8.1   New Construction on an Infill Site in Rhode Island
Source: Image © M.Bull, used with permission

in the form of new units. Housing supply has been called "sluggish" (A. O'Sullivan 1993, 444). Typically, an increase in demand for a product will raise prices and draw in more suppliers. However, for housing, the response "add more product" can take several years, as new construction and remodeling are both processes requiring permitting and the coordination of tradespersons (Sternlieb and Listokin 1987). Some have noted this slow response in supply makes policies to increase affordable housing that rely on *demand* more attractive. Programs such as Housing Vouchers (see Chapter 6) that fund households—not programs subsidizing housing production—are more effective in the short term (Galster 1997). Moreover, the construction industry tends to be conservative—that is, innovation in the types of products produced happens very slowly (Coiacetto 2006). Developers tend to build proven housing types due to the high costs and long timeline of real estate construction. For instance, the standard single-family suburban style home has proven to be a winner, and thus fewer developers consider mixed-use buildings, or different styles of multi-unit buildings, even when local controls try to promote housing diversity and affordability.

A real question is whether the affordable housing crisis is a function of the cost of the housing (as set by the suppliers) or the income of the households. This has implications for how best to intervene to achieve affordable housing for all. Should incomes be increased or can the cost of housing be lowered? A report by the Joint Center for Housing sums it up this way:

Given the costs of land, building materials, labor, and capital, market forces face a fundamental challenge in supplying housing that is within reach of the lowest-income segments of society—the elderly, the disabled, the working poor, and those underemployed and unemployed workers seeking full-time jobs.

(Fernald 2013, 39)

Economists Edward Glaeser and Joseph Gyourko have calculated that "the majority of homes in this country are priced close to construction costs" (June 2003, 22). They suggest that this means affordable housing is not a matter of housing being overpriced but incomes being too low.[2] In an analysis of housing costs in different markets, they found that in most of the United States, production costs are in line with the pricing of the area, but in some submarkets, production costs exceed the pricing of the area, and in some areas (where demand is high due to employment and amenities) housing costs are excessive. They conclude these high costs are the result of local barriers that restrict the supply. Other economists argue it would be wrong to blame high land prices for housing costs. Instead, they contend, expensive land is a result of unmet demand and reflects a tight supply (A. O'Sullivan 1993).

Housing and Regulations

The inputs into the construction of housing play a role in the cost of housing. The price of direct inputs such as plywood, concrete, and roofing materials, fluctuate with the market. However, regulations on the development of housing can also affect cost by dictating the materials used, the amount of land required, and the necessary infrastructure to support the housing. Such regulations are an example of the exercise of *police power* by states and municipalities. Police power is the ability to regulate private property to further public health, safety, and welfare. Building codes that some states adopt for electrical, structural, and plumbing systems are an example of this. In other states, building codes are handled at the municipal level. These codes are intended to ensure that buildings are safe—for example, they will not catch fire, and the roof and walls will withstand normal strains and conditions.

Other regulations controlled at the local level that may set minimum housing conditions—and thus influence the cost of housing units—include the following:

- *Subdivision Regulations* specify standards for the construction of new roads sidewalks, street trees, and other supporting infrastructure such as stormwater facilities. These costs are paid by the developer and passed on to homebuyers.
- *Zoning Regulations* establish districts mapping the land where housing can be located and other specifics such as the lot size per house, building heights, and parking needed for new houses and apartment buildings.
- *Environmental Laws* set construction rules relative to setting aside land to protect wetlands, floodplains, endangered species habitats, and more.
- *Health Regulations* govern the sewer/septic and water systems necessary for housing.
- *Growth Management* directs the building rate (e.g., number of new units per year) and location of new housing.
- *Impact Fees* assess a fee towards infrastructure needed to service new housing units, such as schools, additional water supply, or traffic improvements.
- *Historic Preservation/Aesthetic Design* rules define construction specifics for new (or renovated) housing to maintain character.

Not all these controls are present in every community, but studies of local regulation have established that such standards and requirements add to the cost of housing. In

general, regulations also tend to be slow to approve new technologies that could poten-
tially decrease costs. Given that these regulations are meant to protect health, safety,
and welfare, balance is required between how stringent the standards should be and
the expense involved. All regulations adopted by government involve a determination of
how much health and safety we can afford. Consider this example: earthquake-resistant
design will add expense but could save lives. Which homes should be required to build
to this strict standard? All homes? Only homes in areas where the risk of earthquakes is
determined to be great? How great a risk? This is essentially a rough calculation of the
benefits to be gained (lives saved, property protected) versus the costs required.

Researchers have attempted to quantify how much regulations increase costs, and these
results have varied, with ranges from 20–30 percent—although this does not indicate how
much of such an increase is for "excessive" regulations (Salins 1993). A national study
completed for HUD in 2007 reported that 91 percent of the 497 communities surveyed
had one or more regulatory standards that exceeded what was classified as a basic health
and safety benchmark. This report estimated that the cost of housing was increased 5
percent due to "excessive" subdivision regulations alone (NAHB Research Center 2007).
Rolling back regulation is a strategy for reducing housing costs that many people promote.
However, given the profit motivation, it is not guaranteed that such reduced costs would
be passed on to consumers versus absorbed as increased profits by developers.

Studies have shown that these regulations can be a type of artificial barrier to the
"natural" expansion of the housing supply. A contained supply, where demand is strong,
may lead to rising housing costs. Critique of regulations involves determining which
rules may be unnecessary or excessive and adopted to deliberately inflate costs or reduce
housing expansion. Some question if all these regulations are necessary to protect health
and safety, or if the regulations fall into the category of promoting the general "welfare"
of the community.

Often, existing property owners seek to limit further construction and prevent additional residents from moving to the community. The power for making such decisions
rests with these homeowners or elected officials who are responsive to these homeowners. The motivation given is to protect property values and to maintain the existing character of an area. Multiple studies have, in fact, failed to document a negative
effect on property values from the construction of affordable housing (Bratt, Degenova,
Goodwin, Moriarity, and Robitaille 2012). For some communities, these regulations act
to keep housing expensive to prevent low-income households and households of color
from moving to the community. Such *exclusionary zoning*, zoning that requires large lots
or denies multi-family buildings, has been challenged in the courts with mixed results
(see Chapter 10 for more discussion). Communities can also deliberately adopt what is
known as *fiscal zoning*—zoning that favors uses that typically generate more revenue
than they require in services. Since residential uses can bring school children and public
education is the most expensive service communities provide, communities often seek to
cap residential expansion. These types of regulations are not necessary for public health
and safety, and only serve the welfare of those already owning homes in the area.

Some studies have found a correlation between areas that are desirable due to jobs
and quality of life with a high degree of regulations. Restrictions through regulations
can limit access to areas of greater opportunities (see Chapter 7), and the artificially
increased housing costs hurt our low-income households the most. Covering high housing costs means a greater percentage of the income of poor households must be used for
housing than the percentage allocated by moderate and high-income households (Ikeda
and Washington 2015).

In addition to the direct material costs, the administration of these regulatory systems adds expense to housing construction. To get permits approved, developers must submit plans, pay application, review, and inspection fees, hire professionals to present their plans at hearings, and wait for boards to make decisions. These processes add costs that the developer ultimately passes through in the housing cost. As there can be multiple local boards making determinations on the same project, the approval and review process can be time consuming and complex. Developers often borrow funds to buy the land or pay construction costs, so they are paying interest on these loans throughout the lengthy permitting process. Finally, developers also complain that the many different boards and reviewers involved in the process can lead to different interpretations of regulations or conflicts between boards—another contributing factor to a lengthy, and thus costlier, permitting process (Ben-Joseph and Phelan 2005).

Housing Filtering

One way the private housing market is said to provide housing for lower income households is through a market process known as "filtering." According to the *Encyclopedia of Housing*, filtering can be described this way: "as houses become old and obsolete, they decline in value and rent, and trickle down from richer to poorer families. The upper level of the housing market is replenished by new construction, creating new units that will filter down in turn" (Carswell 2012). Filtering then is about the lifecycle of both housing units and of households. It is a result of the mobility of households (on average Americans move thirteen times in a lifetime), the new construction of housing, and the aging of existing housing (Bier 2001). As households move up the economic ladder, they leave housing for newer, more up-to-date options. Others move into the vacated housing which, due to wear and tear and age, is a less expensive option. It has been estimated that one new housing unit will lead to a chain of 3.5 moves in other units (Powell and Stringham 2008). Filtering can also mean the abandonment of some housing that households leave for a step-up, as it can no longer be profitable and is severely deteriorated.

In a recent analysis, an economist calculated rates of filtering, noting that such rates differ by markets (they are lower in markets with high housing costs) and by tenure, although it was pointed out that a form of filtering is for housing units to switch from homeownership to be rental units (Rosenthal 2014). The study quantified local filtering documenting an increase in the availability of lower cost housing, and filtration by rental units more quickly than ownership units. However, it was not established that the profile of this supply matches the profile of affordable housing needs. The filtered price may still be too great for many households, and the number of units opened up may fall short of the existing need for affordable units. This empirical work makes the additional point that in tight housing markets, filtering cannot be relied upon to create affordable housing. Where prices are high, older housing is invested in and does not filter down.

Some have argued that as filtering provides for more affordable housing, promoting new high-end or moderate housing construction has the "trickle-down" effect of freeing up housing for poorer households. It is also pointed out that excessive regulations slow down filtering by constraining new construction. Most housing advocates reject a policy approach that promotes filtering over more direct ways of meeting the need for affordable housing, such as the construction of affordable housing or housing vouchers. They point out filtering is an extremely slow and uneven process. Not all aging housing declines in value—some places see reinvestment due to an historic character, a desirable location, or a restricted supply (Somerville and Mayer 2003). Many urban neighborhoods have seen a form of "reverse" filtering known as *gentrification*.

Gentrification

The term "gentrification" was coined by sociologist Ruth Glass in 1964 when she was studying changes in a London neighborhood (Lees, Slater, and Wyly 2008). At its root is the word "gentry," a term used in the United Kingdom to describe people that are "well-bred" or members of the aristocracy. This word root clearly connects the phenomenon Glass documented to socioeconomic class. While there are various definitions, one in a publication by the Urban Institute captures the elements widely agreed upon: "gentrification is the process whereby higher-income households move into low income neighborhoods, escalating the area's property values to the point that displacement occurs" (Levy, Comey, and Padilla 2006). Often the displacement is not only one of higher income replacing lower income households, but also one of white households replacing households of color and other ethnicities. The displacement of residents has made gentrification a highly politicized term, as the source of such displacement is related to how societal systems skew power to some groups over others, such as the haves and have-nots. Anti-gentrification has become a rallying point for many who would like to see improvements in low opportunity areas, but not at the cost of current residents having to leave. Given the strong connections between people and their homes noted in earlier chapters (see Chapter 1), gentrification can be distressing for many.

Concerns around gentrification focus on urban neighborhoods where the poor are pushed out as higher-income groups begin to buy up and invest in properties. Existing landlords act to maximize rents—positioning themselves to get the most out of their investment. This can mean ending leases to some, or even harassing tenants to encourage their leaving prior to the leases end (Madden and Marcuse 2016). New investments occur in neighborhoods suffering from decades of disinvestment and the effects of past white flight to suburban areas. One study notes that in 1970, only about one quarter of our large cities had one gentrifying neighborhood, but by 2010, one half of large cities and even 15 percent of small cities had at least one gentrifying area (Hwang and Lin 2016). Central city neighborhoods can become attractive to higher income groups due to proximity to new jobs, historic character of buildings, or access to mass transit. A preference for city living with its walking access to shops, museums, and other cultural attractions, over the limitations of suburban lifestyles, can also be a driver of gentrification.

Gentrification is related to filtering in that some claim it is a natural market process. This is refuted by others who document how government investments and actions can reinforce (or modify) neighborhood changes (Lees et al. 2008). As a higher economic class moves into an area, the existing housing stock is upgraded—new roofs, new windows, additions, and interior upgrades occur. Government investments in infrastructure can encourage such property investments. Decisions by public agencies to construct new mass transit stops, bicycle facilities, parks, street landscaping, and more, can facilitate gentrification by increasing property values and catering to the preferences of specific households. These decisions can be the source of resentment on the part of existing residents, if they perceive the improvement (needed all along) is only happening to serve the new residents. It can be difficult to determine cause and effect between public investments and neighborhood change, and certainly public investment does not always lead to gentrification. Municipalities often seek private investment as a match to such public investments, as this development activity can bring new jobs and additional tax revenues.

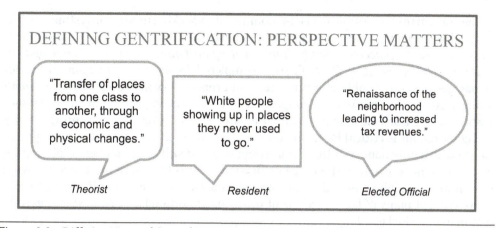

Figure 8.2 Differing Views of Gentrification
Source: Graphic by M. Bull, used with permission

In gentrifying neighborhoods, changes in residential properties are accompanied by commercial and street activity transitions. Commercial enterprises, such as high-end coffee shops, boutique grocery stores, yoga studios, and expensive restaurants, open in the area to serve the new higher income residents. The low-income residents of the area may experience a variety of losses—a loss of affordable retail outlets, a loss of neighbors, a loss of culture, a loss of neighborhood identity, and even a loss of some types of political power.

Involuntary displacement from a neighborhood—having to relocate even when you would prefer to stay—can occur in a variety of ways. Rents can rise, making apartments unaffordable; evictions can come as buildings change from rental to ownership status or owners renovate for higher rents; landlords can stop taking housing vouchers to get higher rents; or property taxes may increase beyond the affordability of homeowners with low or fixed incomes. Gentrification can also mean housing costs keep low and middle-income households from moving into an area, as vacancies occur.

Professor and researcher Lance Freeman has studied gentrification extensively, and he suggests it is a complicated topic. In some cases, existing residents benefit from the changes in the area. From interviews he conducted in three neighborhoods of New York City, he found existing residents were able to stay in place and even welcomed some of the reinvestment as crime declined, job opportunities increased, and aesthetics improved (2006). He suggests gentrification is highly varied—in some cases it can take decades, in others it happens more quickly. While neighborhoods are in flux—only a portion of the housing stock has changed from low to middle or higher income residents—the original residents may be able to benefit from the changes. In fact, some researchers distinguish urban investment or urban renaissance from gentrification based on whether involuntary displacement occurs (Bates 2013). Derek Hyra, professor at American University, puts it this way: "gentrification as a means to poverty displacement, instead of poverty relief, is destructive" (Reese 2017). Others suggest that the mixed-income areas sought by HUD programs such as HOPE VI and Choice Neighborhoods (see Chapters 4 and 9) are a type of gentrification, but meant to achieve economic diversity. Also it is important to consider during gentrification where the displaced households are likely to relocate. In search of affordable options, they may be limited to the types of areas discussed in greater detail in Chapter 7, as places of low opportunity (Bates 2013).

There are many tool kits designed for communities seeking urban reinvestment, without the displacement of existing residents and businesses. For an example, read the *Gentrification and Displacement Study: Implementing an Equitable Inclusive Development Strategy in the Context of Gentrification* completed for Portland, Oregon. Strategies include getting control of land, setting caps on property tax increases, providing small business assistance, and funding nonprofit affordable housing development. To be successful, these actions must be taken before an area has gentrified, so monitoring activity in neighborhoods is critical for timely intervention (Bates 2013). Ultimately, such proactive steps will only happen if there is a strong political will to act on behalf of existing residents. Some researchers submit gentrification today is less about the gradual moving in, building by building, of higher income individuals, than it is major investments and redevelopment plans of large sections of urban neighborhoods, by real estate interests (Adelman and Gocker 2007).

Box 8.1   Case Study in Gentrification: Philadelphia Neighborhoods Undergo Change

Figure 8.3   Gentrifying Neighborhood of Philadelphia
Source: Image © The Pew Charitable Trusts, used with permission

In the second half of the twentieth century, Philadelphia went through the same urban decline as most U.S. cities. But today it is on a rebound with a growing population and some hot real estate markets. Interest in property renovations and new construction is strong. Some of this development pressure can be characterized as gentrification as residents of lower income areas see investments on their block and encounter new younger, wealthier, and whiter residents. Lots of these long-term residents are people of color who moved into these neighborhoods as children, and others are second generation natives. They have stayed committed to the area through the dark times of vacant houses, high crime rates, and deficient public services.

Now, however, there is strong interest in city living and young people looking to move in. "They are always knocking on my door telling me they want to buy my house," said one elderly resident. "Well, I am not selling."

Another old-timer adds to the feeling of a community being invaded, "In many cases, these newcomers assume they are better because they may earn more money than we do and have rooftop decks and things that are not a part of our community."

These residents have strong ties to their homes and neighborhoods and the rising property values are a challenge. In the neighborhood with the most dramatic property value increase, median sales prices went from $11,250 in 2000–01 to $140,000 in 2013–14 (Pew Charitable Trust, 2016). For elderly homeowners on fixed incomes the associated higher property taxes are a shock.

The City is working on tax abatements, new affordable housing, and land banking lots as ways to maintain existing residents, while reaping the benefits of new investment.

Source: Adapted from www.philly.com/philly/news/Gentrification_in_Philadelphia.html

Figure 8.4 Point Breeze Neighborhood of Philadelphia 2004

Source: Image © Bradley Maule, used with permission

Figure 8.5 Point Breeze in 2016

Source: Image © The Pew Charitable Trusts, used with permission

Conclusion

Different parts of the United States are experiencing different housing conditions. People live in urban, suburban, and rural situations. To assess the most pressing concerns, local conditions must be considered. In doing so, economics alone will not explain the dynamics of the local housing market, but neoclassical economics is helpful to understanding the supply and demand. On its own the housing market is not always efficient or equitable (T. O'Sullivan 2003). The behavior of consumers is influenced by cultural dictates and tax policies (e.g., subsidizing homeownership), while the supply is shaped by local zoning and other land use regulations. To further our national objective of adequate housing for all, we must track factors that influence housing costs, and transitions due to filtering or gentrification, that may close or open affordable opportunities for quality living. Another persistent theme is raised in this discussion: the price of housing does not indicate all that people value about housing. Memories, connections, community also matter.

Questions and Activities

1. Consider the cities in the United States said to have "hot" housing markets (San Francisco, Boston, Seattle, etc.). What forces do you think drive the high cost of housing in these areas?
2. Summarize the ways that housing supply can be constrained. For each, note what could be done and by whom to reduce the limitations on supply.
3. Review Figure 8.2 that presents gentrification from the perspectives of different actors in a neighborhood. Add quotes from a local builder, an existing store owner, and a nonprofit housing developer.

4. Attend a meeting of a local board overseeing the regulation of development—e.g., a planning board, site plan review authority, conservation commission, etc. Write up a short description of the meeting, including who was in attendance, what types of information was presented, and how the decision on the application was made. Was it a smooth process? Can you determine how long the decision-making process will take (from date application is filed to when decision is made)?

5. See if your local community (or one nearby) has a guide to permitting reviews meant to assist applicants. Review the guide and write about what you learned—is the process well-coordinated and clear? How many approvals might a proposal require? Can you suggest ways to "streamline" the permitting process?

6. Prepare for a class debate on gentrification. Consider the costs and benefits of urban reinvestment and the nature of housing. Roles to take may include: existing low-income resident; elected official; new resident; existing homeowner; new store owner; and local contractor.

7. View one of the many documentaries on gentrification, such as: *My Brooklyn* (2013), *Flag Wars* (2003), or *Battle for Brooklyn* (2011). Use the film as a vehicle for exploring the experiences of those involved, from new residents to old residents, trades people, business owners, those in the real estate industry, and elected officials. The first two movies also have study guides with questions.

Notes

1. In Chapters 6 and 10 we discuss how not-for-profit groups are also involved in producing housing. These organizations are not organized to make money but motivated to meet the need for affordable housing.

2. These economists argue there is not an affordable housing crisis but a low-income crisis. For the most part housing is priced at what it costs to produce it. Households that cannot afford this cost should be subsidized with more income. The exception is areas where the housing cost far exceeds the actual production cost. For these areas, Glaeser and Gyourko argue regulations and administrative processes artificially inflated the costs and should be revised.

References

Adelman, Robert M., and James Clarke Gocker. 2007. "Racial Residential Segregation in Urban America." *Sociology Compass* 1(1): 404–423.

Bates, Lisa K. 2013. *Gentrification and Displacement Study: Implementing an Equitable Inclusive Development Strategy in the Context of Gentrification*. Portland, OR: Bureau of Planning and Sustainability City of Portland.

Ben-Joseph, Eran, and Kath Phelan. 2005. "Regulating Subdivisions in Massachusetts Practices and Outlooks." *Working Paper*. Cambridge, MA: Lincoln Land Policy.

Bier, Thomas. 2001. "Moving Up, Filtering Down: Metropolitan Housing Dynamics and Public Policy." *Discussion Paper*. Washington, DC: Brookings Institute.

Bratt, Rachel G., Alexandra Degenova, Brendan Goodwin, Shannon Moriarity, and Jeremy Robitaille. 2012. "Fear of Affordable Housing: Perception vs. Reality." *Shelterforce*, Summer.

Carswell, Andrew. 2012. *The Encyclopedia of Housing*, 2nd Edition. Washington, DC: Sage Publications.

Coiacetto, Eddo. 2006. "Real Estate Development Industry Structure: Consequences for Urban Planning and Development." *Planning, Practice & Research* 21(4): 423–441.

Downs, Anthony. 1974. "The Successes and Failures of Federal Housing Policy." *National Affairs*: 124–145.

Fernald, Marcia, ed. 2013. *America's Rental Housing: Evolving Markets and Needs*. Cambridge, MA: Joint Center for Housing Studies of Harvard University.

Freeman, Lance. 2006. *There Goes the 'Hood: Views of Gentrification From the Ground Up*. Philadelphia: Temple University Press.

Galster, George. 1997. "Comparing Demand-Side and Supply-Side Housing Policies: Sub-Market and Spatial Perspectives." *Housing Studies* 12(4): 561–577.

Glaeser, Edward L., and Joseph Gyourk. June 2003. "The Impact of Building Restrictions on Housing Affordability." *FRBNY Economic Policy Review*: 21–39.

Hwang, Jakelyn, and Jeffrey Lin. 2016. "What Have We Learned About the Causes of Recent Gentrification?" *Cityscape* (U.S. Department of Housing and Urban Development) 18(3): 9–26.

Ikeda, Sanford, and Emily Washington. 2015. *How Land-Use Regulation Undermines Affordable Housing*. Arlington, VA: Mercatus Research, Mercatus Center George Mason University.

Lees, Loretta, Tom Slater, and Elvin Wyly. 2008. *Gentrification*. New York: Routledge.

Levitin, Adam J., and Susan Wachter. 2013. "Why Housing?" *Housing Policy Debate*: 5–27.

Levy, Diane K., Jennifer Comey, and Sandra Padilla. 2006. *In the Face of Gentrification: Case Studies of Local Efforts to Mitigate Displacement*. Washington, DC: The Urban Institute.

Madden, David, and Peter Marcuse. 2016. *In Defense of Housing*. Brooklyn, NY: Verso.

NAHB Research Center. 2007. *Study of Subdivision Requirements as a Regulatory Barrier*. Upper Marlboro, MD: National Association of Home Builders. Accessed January 27, 2017. www.huduser.gov/portal/publications/subdiv_report.pdf.

O'Sullivan, Arthur. 1993. *Urban Economics*, 5th Edition. Boston: McGraw Hill.

O'Sullivan, Tony. 2003. "Economics and Housing Planning." In *Housing Economics and Public Policy*, edited by Tony O'Sullivan and Kenneth Gibb, 218–234. Malden, MA: Blackwell Science Ltd.

Oxley, Michael. 2004. *Economics, Planning and Housing*. New York: Palgrave MacMillan.

Pew Charitable Trust. 2016. "Philadelphia's Changing Neighborhoods." Accessed February 7, 2018. www.pewtrusts.org/en/research-and-analysis/reports/2016/05/philadelphias-changing-neighborhoods.

Philly.com. 2018. "The Problems and the Promise: Gentrification in Philadelphia." Accessed 7 February, 2018. http://www.philly.com/philly/news/Gentrification_in_Philadelphia.html.

Powell, Benjamin, and Edward Stringham. 2008. "Housing." In *The Concise Encyclopedia of Economics*, edited by David A. Henderson. Library of Economics and Liberty. Accessed January 27, 2017. www.econlib.org/library/Enc/Housing.html.

Reese, Frederick. 2017. "How Gentrification Is Undermining the Notion of Black Community and Destroying Black Businesses." *Atlantic Black Star*, June 20. http://atlantablackstar.com/2017/06/20/how-gentrification-is-undermining-the-notion-of-black-community-and-destroying-black-businesses/.

Rosenthal, Stuart. 2014. "Are Private Markets and Filtering a Viable Source of Low Income Housing?" *American Economic Review* 104(2): 687–706.

Salins, Peter D. 1993. "Housing." In *The Concise Encyclopedia of Economics*, edited by David R. Henderson. Library of Economics and Liberty. Accessed January 20, 2017. www.econlib.org/library/Enc1/Housing.html.

Somerville, Tsuriel C., and Christopher J. Mayer. 2003. "Government Regulation and Changes in the Affordable Housing Stock." *FRBNY Economic Policy Review* (FRBNY Economic Policy Review): 45–62.

Sternlieb, George, and David Listokin. 1987. "A Review of National Housing Policy." In *Housing America's Poor*, edited by Peter D. Salins, 14–44. Chapel Hill: University of North Carolina Press.

Straszheim, Mahlon R. 1975. "The Role of the Housing Market." In *An Economic Analysis of the Urban Housing Market*, edited by Mahlon R. Straszheim. Cambridge, MA: The National Bureau of Economic Research. Accessed January 11, 2017. http://papers.nber.org/books/stra75-1.

U.S. Census Bureau. 2011. "Extended Measures of Well-being: Living Conditions in the United States, 2011." *U.S. Department of Commerce*. Accessed January 15, 2017. www.census.gov/hhes/well-being/publications/extended-11.html.

9

Public Housing

Public housing is the oldest form of government assisted housing in the United States. Yet, since its beginnings in the 1930s, America's relationship with public housing has been rife with tension. A preference for the market to meet needs combined with a reluctance for the government to compete with the private sector and a cultural elevation of "independence," has made direct government provision of housing a least-favored option. This valuation is clear when the figures on public housing are examined. Unlike other industrialized countries, America has a very small percentage of publicly owned and managed housing units—1 percent of America's housing stock versus up to 20 percent for other countries (Vale 2007)—and in past decades there has been a trend of a steady decline in the overall stock of publicly owned housing units. This is a significant loss as, unlike other privately developed subsidized units, these are homes that are permanently affordable and controlled by publicly accountable government agencies.

Public housing was at one point considered some of the nation's best housing, but several challenges have subsequently stigmatized the program (Broadman 1982). Unfortunately, many of the physically and functionally effective public housing units that provide what people need seem to escape the public eye, while those that have not been as successful have been the focus of media scrutiny, with criticisms of residents and government management. Public housing has been labeled as the "housing of last resort," meaning it is not a place that is chosen, but the default option when no other choice is available. Yet the full story of public housing is much more complex. For many, public housing has provided a decent and stable living space, and its shelter and refuge has supported some—including current Supreme Court Justice Sonia Sotomayor—in achieving better life outcomes (Andersson et al. 2013).

This chapter profiles public housing today, describing the physical dimensions of this part of America's housing stock, and considering whom it serves. Then a short history of public housing lays out its path, before the chapter explores the factors researchers have held responsible for the failures of parts of public housing. It concludes by assessing the tactical responses to the malfunctions and current thinking about public housing.

It is important to understand that the terms *public housing* and *affordable housing* are not interchangeable. Public housing is affordable, but not all affordable housing is public housing (Lotzar 2015). There are many other differences in terms of ownership, financing, and tenants served (Table 9.1). Public housing describes housing that has been developed entirely with public funds, and which is owned and managed by a local government agency. Tenants of public housing contribute no more than 30 percent of their income toward their rent. Other affordable housing includes housing developed by private or nonprofit groups with a federal subsidy program (see Chapter 6) that offers some affordable units, and typically the developer is bound to keeping them affordable only for a limited period of time, typically 30 years. This housing can be called subsidized housing.

Table 9.1   Terminology Matters: Public Housing versus Subsidized Housing

PUBLIC HOUSING	SUBSIDIZED HOUSING
Publicly funded	Partially publicly subsidized
Owned and managed by local housing authority (government agency)*	Owned and managed by private firm or non-profit organization
All units serve households making less than 50% of Area Median Income**	Can include a mix of market rate units and units for households making less than 80% Area Median Income
Often, housing of last resort—serving the neediest and those hard to house	Depending on the program, the affordable units may target those making less than 80%, 60%, or 50% of Area Median Income
Permanently affordable	Length of time of affordability restrictions may vary, typically 30 years

*Some public housing units are managed by private sector entities.

**For a discussion on Area Median Income see Chapter 6.

Profile of Public Housing Today

The public housing program provides rental housing for eligible low-income families, the elderly, and persons with disabilities. The public housing program is administered by the U.S. Department of Housing and Urban Development (HUD) (U.S. Department of Housing and Urban Development n.d.). In the United States, there are roughly 1.2 million households living in public housing units, managed by some 3,300 public housing authorities. These local authorities vary greatly in size. Close to half of local housing authorities manage less than 100 units of public housing, with another 40 percent of local housing authorities overseeing 100–500 units of public housing. On the other end of the size spectrum are some extremely large housing authorities—the New York City Housing Authority alone manages 15.5 percent of all the public housing in the United States (Schwartz 2015).

The public housing stock is quite varied. While the highrise housing families has been made infamous in news stories and films, public housing includes single family homes, scattered site duplexes, row houses, walk-ups, and elderly highrises. Table 9.2 indicates the breakdown of the public housing stock by generalized housing types.

Table 9.3 presents a profile of the households served by public housing. This data from the HUD indicates that one-third of households in public housing are working, and only 5 percent receive welfare. Also noteworthy is that around one-fifth of these households have a member who is disabled, and roughly one-third are headed by someone over 62 years of age.

The History of Public Housing

The history of public housing begins in the 1930s, as detailed in Chapter 4. The Housing Act of 1937 allowed for the construction of housing by the government in part to provide jobs but also to upgrade the housing stock. Initially, the federal government oversaw construction, but due to a court ruling, the program was altered so local housing authorities would be the public housing developers. One assumption many people make today is that the public housing program has always been focused on serving the poorest part of the population, but in fact, its original focus was on offering housing assistance to

Table 9.2 Public Housing Stock: Housing Types

HOUSING TYPE	PERCENT OF PUBLIC HOUSING STOCK*
Detached, single family	2.7
Row Housing/ Townhouses/Semi-detached	32.5
Walk-up	11.4
Highrise/Elevator	30.3
Mixed	23.0

Source: Included in *Housing Policy in the United States*, Third ed., Alex F. Schwartz, 2015, cited as from Public Housing Operating Cost Study: Final Report by Harvard University Graduate School of Design, 2003.

*Note that this data set is from 2003; the demolition of public housing in subsequent years has changed these percentages.

Table 9.3 Profile of Households in Public Housing (2015)

Total served:	1,047,231 households
Household income:	$ 14,368 average
	78% of households make less than $20,000
Rent payment:	$310 average household contribution
Major source of income:	30% Wages 5% Welfare 60% Other
	(Other may include: Social Security, Social Security Disability, Alimony, Pension, etc.)
Race and ethnicity:	45% Black, 28% White, 23% Hispanic, 3% Asian/Pacific, 1% Native American
Disability:	21% of households have a member with a disability
Age:	32% of households have a head of household over 62 years of age
One-person household:	34% of all households have only one member

Source: Data from Picture of Subsidized Households available at: www.huduser.gov/portal/datasets/picture/year-lydata.html#data-display-tab

working class households experiencing a temporary economic setback. It was specifically created to address the needs of the middle class who found themselves outside the labor market during the post-Depression period (United States 1937; Stoloff 2004). The original legislation set a cap on the cost per unit to limit federal spending and also to reduce competition between public housing and the private sector.

Initially the income of tenants was limited to no higher than five times the rent cost of the unit they lived in. Beyond income limits, tenant screening was conducted to identify potential renters who were of good character, employed, and able to reliably pay rent. Types of tenant screening have varied over time in public housing. When the housing was developed in the 1930s, qualitative screening was the norm (Marcuse 1995). During these times, unwed pregnant women may have been evicted, and eligibility was limited to two-parent households with an employed head of household and a record of good housekeeping skills. In the 1960s, tenant screening evolved in response to criticisms about practices such as these, complaining that some housing authorities were too strict and moralistic (Hays 2012). From the beginning through the 1960s, housing authorities also actively segregated their housing units, sorting residency in buildings along racial lines.

The Housing Act of 1949 reiterated support for public housing but also introduced other subsidized housing programs. Priorities were set for public housing to serve very low-income people, and for rents not to exceed a maximum level (rents were required to be 20% less than lowest market rates) (United States 1949). This benefited business interests by limiting the program to the very poor and leaving the working class to be housed by private builders, ensuring noncompetitiveness with the private sector.

Additionally, this Housing Act married public housing to urban renewal efforts: public housing units could only be built where the same number of substandard units were to be demolished (Jackson 1985). Urban renewal was a program steeped in the idea of modernization. Public housing projects of this period were designed as modern highrises, set apart from the rest of the city, and echoed the famous architect Le Corbusier's Radiant City ideas. Vertical towers of residential units were built with open space for recreational activity at the ground level between the buildings. These towers of glass, steel, and concrete stood as the very embodiment of a contemporary society moving away from the backwardness of its former dilapidated housing. But embracing modernization only went so far; racial segregation by tower continued to be the norm.

The Housing Act of 1949 led to a concentration of public housing in urban areas, with urban renewal often displacing poor communities of color, although those that were displaced were given priority for the new public housing units (Vale 2002). This urban concentration was reinforced by the exclusionary choices of suburban areas: few of these communities established a local housing authority, as they were not interested in siting housing for the different races and classes served by public housing.

After World War II, programs were established to allow working class people to buy their own homes through low-interest mortgages (see discussion of FHA and VA programs in Chapter 4), and these benefits were targeted to white households—allowing them to move to the suburbs and keeping black households concentrated in cities. The

Figure 9.1 Highrise Public Housing in New York City
Source: Image © Robert Elliott, used with permission

result was the outmigration of white working class households from public housing during the 1950s and 1960s, leaving behind households without the same means, and households of color shut out of the suburbs by discriminatory practices. In the same period, income limits for public housing residents meant they could be penalized or evicted if their incomes surpassed the upper limit, effectively discouraging upward mobility and replacing successful families with struggling households (Stoloff 2004).

Conditions in public housing changed rapidly over the twenty-year period of 1940–1960. The tenants served became poorer, building conditions deteriorated, tenant morale dropped as mobility remained stagnant, and public housing, along with its residents, became stigmatized (Goetz 2013). Public housing faced many challenges—some internal and some external. Mismanagement and fiscal constraints contributed to a decline, as did the national economic restructuring that resulted in a loss of manufacturing jobs. Another factor contributing to the decline was the rise in gang activity and illegal drugs. Lawrence Vale, who has written extensively on the history of public housing, notes that public housing came to symbolize violence, drugs, and societal dysfunction. He writes, "as a symbol and symptom of these broader societal problems, public housing has been blamed for contributing to them" (Vale 2002, 7). Public housing did not create these problems, yet they thrived within some public housing.

Two key types of challenges to understand about the history of public housing are the *financial* challenges it faced, and the challenges posed by the *design* of public housing structures.

Financial Challenges

The major financing challenge faced by public housing has been the tug-of-war relationship between having sufficient funds to cover operational and maintenance costs and keeping rents low enough for low income tenants. The original financial premise was that federal funds would cover the acquisition of land and the cost of construction, and tenant rents would cover ongoing operational and maintenance expenses, including the cost of utilities, landscaping, grounds keeping, and the routine replacement of features worn through use. Over time, the incomes of tenants declined, and in turn the rent paid (based on a percentage of these incomes) also declined. Tenants' incomes declined as Congress passed regulations to give priority for the limited public housing units to the neediest households. Policies were put in place to first house the homeless, those paying more than 50 percent of their income towards rent, and those with very low incomes. Ironically, the stream of funds for maintenance was falling just as the useful life of the initial building systems was coming to an end. Housing authorities found themselves trying to do more with less and delaying larger expenses, such as installing new roofs or upgrading heating systems.

Infamous examples of public housing in failure include the high-rise projects of Pruitt Igoe in St. Louis, Missouri; Columbia Point in Boston, Massachusetts; and Cabrini-Green in Chicago, Illinois. Conditions spiraled out of control as inadequate maintenance led to increased vacancies, which had the double effect of decreasing funds available for maintenance and increasing opportunities for vandalism. These buildings became uninhabitable: elevators stopped working, garbage was left uncollected, mold flourished where pipes leaked, and the infiltration of criminal activities jeopardized the safety of residents. In some cases, the poor services and deplorable conditions led to widespread tenant discontent and rent strikes, eventually leading to the passage of the Brooke Amendment to the 1969 Housing Act, which capped the public housing rent at 25 percent of income

(30 percent since 1981) and provided subsidies to help housing authorities pay for deficits and capital improvements (Hays 2012). For much of this housing, the Brooke Amendment was too little too late and did not solve the problems this public housing faced (Stoloff 2004).

In the 1970s, public housing received little attention as the HUD pursued alternatives to what was now widely seen as a failure of both approach and execution. Since 1981, there has been no large-scale funding for new public housing at the federal level. Local governments have built some public housing, usually on the scattered site model, and public housing has been used selectively as part of other housing projects. As of 2003, the bulk of the federal housing money is spent on tenant-based housing vouchers, where a recipient pays 30 percent of their income towards rent and the voucher covers the difference between that and the rental price of a housing unit in the private sector (see Chapter 6).

Design Challenges

Poor design has historically shared the blame for many of the problems public housing has faced. In the 1940s, planners and architects believed that highrise buildings could provide a healthy living environment that would work favorably in comparison to the slum areas they would replace. However, the design features associated with highrise housing had pros and cons. Positive attributes of highrises include space efficiency and maximizing the use of costly land. Yet highrise housing is not the most efficient use of funds: in terms of cost per unit, it can be significantly more expensive to build than other housing types. In addition, in attempts to save money, a good portion of the highrise housing that was built in the 1940s was designed poorly—sacrificing amenities and using inferior building materials—and thus the housing did not stand up well to regular use (Stoloff 2004).

The highrise housing was also famously appraised by architect Oscar Newman as lacking "defensible space." From visits to the Pruitt Igoe housing project, he noted that individual housing units were often well-maintained, but the exterior common spaces were filthy and dangerous havens for crime (Cisneros 1995). Newman characterized the ground level common areas as no-man's lands, and wrote about how the main elevators were difficult to monitor for people who did not belong. His work has led to improved site and building designs that consider the potential for criminal activity and how residents can gain control with clear visibility and markers of ownership.

Beyond the building layouts, the site design of highrise public housing was also problematic. For example, the towers were often purposely set apart from the surrounding neighborhood, with buildings placed on diagonals in contrast to the existing grid street pattern, or built as "superblocks" closing off and covering several regular sized city blocks. These developments had a massive institutional look that made it easy to identify, and in turn stigmatize, them as public housing (Franck and Mostoller 1995). Because of the serious problems that plagued highrise buildings, by 1968 HUD prohibited the building of highrises for family public housing, but high rises have continued to house the elderly more successfully (Stoloff 2004).

Blaming the Victim

Historically, and even today, blame is also put on residents of color who are depicted as not taking care of the properties or are characterized as being inherently problematic tenants. Arguably, in many cases, resident uprisings were in response to their basic needs not being met, but subsequently such uprisings were used against residents to perpetuate stereotypes about poor people of color not being desirable tenants, committing vandalism, and generally causing the problems that public housing faced. Criminal elements did exist in the housing and vandalism did occur, but many of the tenants were victims of the life-threatening conditions. Yet these residents had no alternatives for relocating. Historian Kenneth Jackson has summed up public housing failure this way, "Actually, the fault was not with public housing or with the tenants, but with the expectation that any one solution could so vastly reduce poverty and social pathology" (Jackson 1985, 229).

The New Philosophy of Public Housing Today

In 1992, the HUD completed a report on public housing to gauge the amount of "distressed" housing that persisted. From this report, the HUD began to target the most problematic housing for demolition in a program called HOPE VI. The HOPE VI program became an avenue for eliminating decrepit public housing and replacing it with new, urbanist-designed, mixed-income neighborhoods. This is consistent with a philosophy change within the federal government, which now favors approaches that support the deconcentration of poverty and developments that combine public housing with market rate units. New urbanist design emphasizes walkability, through street connections to the surrounding neighborhoods, quality architecture, and features, such as porches and small parks, to promote social interactions.

The HOPE VI approach was largely shaped as a response to the failures of inadequate maintenance funding, poor quality construction, concentration of poverty, and a lack of support services. The mix of subsidized units with market units is used to ensure that funding is available for maintenance and to raise the quality of construction. As the developer is competing with market developments, the design and construction must meet private development standards. Mixed-income developments prevent the isolation of lower income residents in places of concentrated poverty. HOPE VI also provided funding for social services to be provided on-site. The evaluation of the success of HOPE VI is still underway, but a main critique has been that not all removed public housing units are rebuilt. Some displaced public housing residents have not been able to return to the new improved development. An additional concern is that the approach often undervalues the rich social networks that exist in public housing. Residents of public housing often have developed "communities of mutual support that are important in helping them meet daily needs" (Goetz 2013, 24). In some areas, HOPE VI was in fact a second round of housing demolition aimed at upgrading the housing stock (the first being the creation of the public housing project). The higher quality housing put in its place serves residents but also adds to the property values of the area.

Redevelopment can be a long and complex process, and meeting the needs of all parties involved requires collaboration. Read the sidebar about Lyman Terrace in Holyoke, Massachusetts.

In 2010 the Choice Neighborhoods Program was developed by (HUD) to go beyond public housing redesign, to comprehensive neighborhood transformation in places with distressed public housing. This program brings key people together to create and implement a plan that transforms housing in great need of improvement and to address challenges in surrounding neighborhoods. These parties include local leaders, residents, public housing authorities, cities, schools, police, business owners, nonprofits, private developers and others. The program also focuses on making improvements to important neighborhood resources such as vacant properties, schools, and other local services (U.S. Department of Housing and Urban Development 2017).

Choice Neighborhoods is focused on three core goals as stated by HUD:

1. Housing: Replace distressed public and assisted housing with high-quality mixed-income housing that is well-managed and responsive to the needs of the surrounding neighborhood;
2. People: Improve educational outcomes and intergenerational mobility for youth with services and supports delivered directly to youth and their families; and
3. Neighborhood: Create the conditions necessary for public and private reinvestment in distressed neighborhoods to offer the kinds of amenities and assets, including safety, good schools, and commercial activity, that are important to families' choices about their community.

(U.S. Department of Housing and Urban Development 2017)

To achieve the above stated goals, communities must develop a comprehensive neighborhood revitalization strategy, or Transformation Plan, as a guiding document (U.S. Department of Housing and Urban Development 2017). Currently, the future of the Choice Neighborhoods program is uncertain.

Box 9.1   Lyman Terrace, Holyoke, Massachusetts

Figure 9.2   Lyman Terrace, Holyoke, Massachusetts

Source: Photo by A. Gross Reproduced with permission

Figure 9.3   Lyman Terrace, Holyoke, Massachusetts, after redevelopment
Source: Photo and redevelopment design by DHK Architects, reproduced with permission

Lyman Terrace, located in Holyoke, Massachusetts, was originally constructed in 1939, making it one of the country's oldest public housing projects. The development has 167 apartment units that serve some of Holyoke's neediest families. While the demand for this affordable housing resource is great within the City of Holyoke, the property had deteriorated over time and needed a vast array of improvements to effectively support the families that reside there. Located in downtown Holyoke, Lyman Terrace is part of a community struggling economically in a post-manufacturing environment. Lyman Terrace's redevelopment has become important to the community character of Holyoke overall.

Efforts to redevelop Lyman Terrace have been ongoing for more than a decade. Originally, the Holyoke Housing Authority (HHA) planned to improve the property using the HOPE VI program (U. S. Department of Housing and Urban Development n.d.). Despite submitting several funding applications between 2006 and 2011, HHA was unsuccessful in securing funds for the redevelopment. After these attempts, the HHA moved forward with a plan that proposed demolition of the property and replacement of the existing buildings with new construction. The residents living at Lyman Terrace, who had strong attachments to their homes, objected to the plan to demolish and replace the property and felt that their housing could be preserved. Lyman residents came together and sought the support of Holyoke's Mayor, Alex Morse, who brought together the Department of Housing and Community Development, Massachusetts Housing Partnership, and MassDevelopment to evaluate the potential of rehabilitating the units. Residents feared redevelopment would mean fewer affordable units and the dismantling of their tight-knit community. A feasibility study prepared by these agencies confirmed the viability of preserving the existing structures, and also recognized that significant infrastructure work would be required and that the costs to renovate the structures would be high.

Using this feasibility study, in 2013 the HHA issued a request for proposals for a development partner for Lyman Terrace and in early 2014 selected The Community Builders, Inc. (TCB), whose mission is focused on building and sustaining communities where people of all incomes can achieve their full potential. Subsequently, TCB and HHA worked to develop and advance a redevelopment strategy for Lyman Terrace, and the project was awarded resources through the Low Income Housing Tax Credit program in 2015. The redevelopment plan for Lyman

Terrace maximizes the number of affordable housing units that will be preserved on the site, making use of the housing already in place, and complementing other strategic investments underway by the City and the State to support the revitalization of downtown Holyoke overall.

Throughout the redevelopment, TCB and HHA have worked diligently to involve residents, consulting a resident advisory committee on key issues and conducting regular resident meetings. After years of effort on the part of many, groundbreaking on the redevelopment at Lyman Terrace began in January 2017.

(The Community Builders, Inc., Crowley, R., Datta, E., and Gross, A., 2015)

Conclusion

Today, HUD has a variety of programs for renovating and replacing public housing. Funding for these efforts falls short of the demand as local housing authorities face unfunded major renovations to this aging—yet critical—infrastructure. The struggle to maintain this aging housing stock will continue. Although public housing is only a relatively small percentage of the overall housing stock, it fulfills an important need. Many of these public housing developments are well-run and provide decent, secure housing with an affordable rent for Americans with no other choices. The loss of this housing stock means even fewer choices for those the market does not serve.

Questions and Activities

1. How is public housing discussed in the media, including films? Do you think the discussion of public housing in the news, on television, or in film has influenced your perception of public housing and whom it serves?
2. Public housing was established partially in response to the undesirable tenement-style housing in cities where residents were living in extremely poor conditions. Watch *The Pruitt Igoe Myth* (Freidrichs 2011).

   - What did you find most thought-provoking about the film?
   - What was your view of public housing before watching this film? Did this film influence your view of public housing?
   - In the film, you saw interviewees talk about the poor living conditions and dangers of living in Pruitt Igoe. You also saw interviewees talk about their attachment to living there, the desirable living space, sharing strong and important personal memories. How do you reconcile the difference between these two views? (Broadman 1982)

3. How might public housing contribute to segregation in terms of class and/or race?
4. In 2015, the *Washington Post* published a story on very over-income families residing in public housing called "A family in public housing makes $498,000 a year. And HUD wants tenants like this to stay" (Rein 2015). Read the article and consider the following questions:

   - What might be the motivations for these families to stay in public housing even though they make enough money to leave?
   - Do you think the HUD should change their regulations and force families out of public housing once they make a certain amount of money?

• In the article, Milan Ozdinec is quoted as stating, "There are positive social benefits from having families with varying income levels residing in the same property." Do you agree with this statement? What are the social benefits you can think of? Are there negative aspects to people with extreme income differences living in the same property?

5. Watch *Down the Project: The Crisis of Public Housing.*

• The film contains a voiceover of a news announcement from the 1930s: "Down they're coming, the cold-water, no-light tenements. Down are coming the bad living conditions that produce bad citizens." Explain this quotation.

• An excellent accompanying study guide for this film is available free of charge online at: www.der.org/resources/study-guides/down-the-project-study-guide.pdf (Broadman and Bratt 1982).

6. Watch *Imagining Home* about a HOPE VI project in Seattle, Washington (Arbuthnot and Wilhelm 2009).

• What types of things form the basis of residents' attachment to Columbia Villa? What is it the residents value?

• Compare the experience of being displaced from the perspective of a child and that of an adult.

• Do you see any tensions in New Columbia, and if so, what is the basis of these tensions?

• Are there any personal stories you would consider a "success" and why?

References

Andersson, Fredrik, John C. Haltiwanger, Mark J. Kutzbach, Giordano Palloni, Henry O. Pollakowski, and Daniel H. Weinberg. 2013. *Childhood Housing and Adult Earnings: A Between-Siblings Analysis of Housing Vouchers Versus Public Housing.* Center for Economic Studies CES, 13–48. Washington, DC: U.S. Census Bureau.

Arbuthnot, Sue, and Richard Wilhelm. 2009. *Imagining Home.* Directed by Sue Arbuthnot and Richard Wilhelm. Produced by Hare in the Gate, Producers, LLC.

Broadman, Richard. 1982. *Down the Project: The Crisis of Public Housing.* Directed by Richard Broadman. Produced by Documentary Educational Resources.

Broadman, Richard, and Rachel G. Bratt. n.d. "What Happened to Public Housing? A Study Guide for the Film Down The Project: The Crisis of Public Housing." http://der.org/resources/study-guides/down-the-project-study-guide.pdf.

Cisneros, Henry. 1995. *Defensible Space: Deterring Crime and Building Community.* Washington, DC: U.S. Department of Housing and Urban Development.

Franck, Karen A., and Michael Mostoller. 1995. "From Courts to Open Space to Streets: Changes in the Site Design of U.S. Public Housing." *Journal of Architectural and Planning Research* 12(3): 186–220.

Freidrichs, Chad. 2011. *The Pruitt-Igoe Myth.* Directed by Chad Freidrichs. Produced by First Run Features. Performed by Sylvester Brown and Robert Fishman.

Goetz, Edward G. 2013. *New Deal Ruins: Race, Economic Justice, and Public Housing Policy.* Ithaca and New York: Cornell University Press.

Hays, Allen R. 2012. *The Federal Goverment & Urban Housing,* 3rd Edition. Albany and New York: State University of New York Press.

Jackson, Kenneth T. 1985. *Crabgrass Frontier.* New York: Oxford University Press.

Lotzar, Charles. 2015. *What Is the Difference Between Public Housing Vs. Affordable Housing?* February 17.

Marcuse, Peter. 1995. "Interpreting Public Housing History." *Journal of Architectural and Planning Research* 12(3): 240–258.

Rein, Lisa. 2015. "A Family in Public Housing Makes $498,000 a Year. And HUD Wants Tenants Like This to Stay." *The Washington Post*, August 17.

Schwartz, Alex F. 2015. *Housing Policy in the United States*, 3rd Edition. New York: Routledge.

Stoloff, Jennifer A. 2004. "A Brief History of Public Housing." *Office of Development and Research, U.S. Department of Housing and Urban Development, Washington, D.C.*

The Community Builders, Inc., Eliza Datta, Rachana Crowley, and Alina Gross. 2014. Revelopment Narrative of Lyman Terrace. Boston: The Community Builders, Inc.

United States. 1937. "United States Housing Act of 1937." Vol. 50. no. Part 1.

United States. 1949. "United States Housing Act of 1949." Vol. 63. no. Part 1.

U. S. Department of Housing and Urban Development. n.d. *HOPE VI*. Accessed November 5, 2016. http://portal.hud.gov/hudportal/HUD?src=/program_offices/public_indian_housing/programs/ph/hope6.

U.S. Department of Housing and Urban Development. 2017. *Hud.gov*. June 22. Accessed 2017. https://portal.hud.gov/hudportal/HUD?src=/program_offices/public_indian_housing/programs/ph/cn.

U.S. Department of Housing and Urban Development. n.d. *HUD's Public Housing Program*. http://portal.hud.gov/hudportal/HUD?src=/topics/rental_assistance/phprog.

Vale, Lawrence J. 2002. *Reclaiming Public Housing: A Half Century of Struggle in Three Public Neighborhoods*. Cambridge, MA: Harvard University Press.

Vale, Lawrence J. 2007. *From the Puritans to the Projects: Public Housing and the Public Neighbors*. Cambridge, MA: Harvard University Press.

10

State and Local
Housing Initiatives

The Constitution of the United States specifies *federalism*, shared governance between the federal and state levels of government. The federal government has authority in a few specific areas, while the remaining matters of government are under the control of each state. In this system, states hold a lot of power. When it comes to housing development, yet a third level of authority can be involved—local communities. Municipalities only have the power granted to them from their home state, and this varies greatly among states.

We know from Chapter 4, History of Federal Involvement in Housing, that the federal government plays a significant role in housing. Wide-ranging initiatives—from federal tax policy to the HUD programs, banking regulations, and the Justice Department's fair housing prosecutions—are all part of federal housing policy. But increasingly, states and local governments have become active in the production, preservation, and improvement of affordable housing. States and local communities stepped up activity as federal funding declined in the 1980s and housing needs expanded (Nenno and Brophy 1982). In some ways, establishing housing responses at the local level is consistent with what we learned about housing markets in Chapter 8 (Housing and the Economy)—these markets are best understood at the smaller regional or local levels. This is true despite the reality that some forces and trends—such as changes in the finance system, demographic shifts, and tax policies—are beyond local control.

Here we will present the major ways states and local communities use their resources and power to address the need for affordable housing. For each of these two levels of government, we consider the planning, funding, and regulatory mechanisms available to further the objective of decent housing for all.

States

Planning Mechanisms

Many states complete a housing analysis as part of a statewide comprehensive plan for development. Such documents study the nature and extent of housing needs, analyze demographic trends, and propose actions to meet the needs in that state. This data and analysis can be very useful to municipalities, where there may be less research capacity due to smaller budgets and fewer staff positions. Additionally, HUD block grant programs require participating states to develop plans to establish "data-driven, place-based" responses to housing needs (U.S. Department of Housing and Urban Development n.d.). These housing planning efforts can determine where funding should go within the state and, increasingly, are coordinated with investments made by other state agencies. As an example, a state may coordinate the construction of a new railroad line or the extension of a water main with the development of surrounding land into new housing.

States recognize that economic development is connected to housing availability. Companies are less likely to relocate or expand in locations where housing costs are extremely high or housing choices are very limited. Businesses seek out places where their employees can live comfortably on a set salary, and in a location reasonably accessible to their jobs. States have come to see new housing—and a choice of accessible and affordable housing types—as a critical piece of being competitive when trying to appeal to businesses. In fact, a 2003 task force report prepared for the then Governor of Massachusetts stated,

> The lack of affordable housing in Massachusetts continues to be the greatest threat to our economic vitality. Massachusetts will continue to lose population and fail to attract and retain highly skilled labor if our housing affordability crisis continues.
>
> (Department of Housing and Community Development 2003)

Funding Mechanisms

States use their taxing power, which far exceeds that of municipalities, to generate funds for a variety of housing related programs. All states have housing finance agencies that issue tax exempt bonds to raise funds to expand housing opportunities (Iglesias and Lento 2011). These funds have been used to provide first-time homebuyers with low interest mortgages and to offer low interest construction loans to developers of affordable multifamily housing. Such funding is an important part of the complex financing packages needed for the development of new affordable housing. Not-for-profit and private for-profit housing developers may apply to state agencies for these funds.

In addition to selling tax-exempt bonds, 47 states have established housing trust funds that can contribute dollars for the development of affordable housing. Housing trusts are funded in a variety of ways. Some states allocate dollars through a line item in the general budget (e.g., New York, Texas, Utah), others collect a small tax on the transfer of real estate (e.g., Vermont, South Carolina, New Jersey), and others tack an extra fee on the recording of documents (e.g., Massachusetts, Ohio, Oregon, Washington) (State Housing Trust Funds n.d.). Like funds raised by selling tax exempt bonds, not-for-profit and private housing developers can apply for these housing trust funds to develop affordable housing.

Many states also have historic preservation tax credits that can be used for adaptive reuse projects that create affordable housing units. These tax credits are often an important part of the overall package of funding needed to complete expensive, historically appropriate renovations. Developers receive credits towards taxes owed, thus saving funds that can offset the lower rents or sales prices for affordable units.

Regulatory Mechanisms

We introduced the issue of building codes in Chapter 8, Housing and the Economy. States have building codes that set standards for the structural integrity of buildings and the safety of building systems (e.g., plumbing, fire, electrical). In Chapter 8, we also discussed how these standards can increase the cost of housing. In 1998, New Jersey pioneered the adoption of a sub-code on housing rehabilitation that aimed to minimize the cost of creating housing units in older buildings. This sub-code provides flexibility for adapting older buildings as it may not be possible to meet modern code requirements at

Figure 10.1 Rehabilitation of this historic mill, Lippit Mill in West Warwick, Rhode Island, is planned using the historic tax credits. The mill will be converted into affordable housing units

Source: Image © C. Bull, used by permission

Figure 10.2 Accessory apartment over a garage in a predominantly single family neighborhood

Source: Image © Radcliffe Dacanay, used with permission

a reasonable cost. The rehabilitation of existing structures can be a more cost-effective way of adding to the housing stock than building new units, so the flexibility of the code supports new affordable housing. Before the adoption of the rehabilitation sub-code, much of New Jersey's older building stock stood vacant, but the state saw a substantial increase in rehabilitation once the sub-code was in place (Building Technology 2001). Other states have followed New Jersey's lead, including Rhode Island, Maryland, and Minnesota (Iglesias and Lento 2011).

Another state level regulatory approach that supports affordable housing is the concept of *fair share housing*. Fair share is defined as "the portion of a region's housing needs for which a municipality must create realistic housing opportunities for low- and moderate-income households" (Kinsey and Gallo 2015). While the specifics of this approach differ greatly among the states that have adopted it, they all embrace fair share as an anti-exclusionary approach. No community is an island unto itself, as residents benefit from the development and offerings in surrounding areas. Also, communities receive federal and state grants that provide services and improvements for residents but which are funded by all taxpayers in the state. Each community, then, should be open to all households by supplying a portion of the region's needed affordable housing. New Jersey has a long history with the concept of fair share housing, much of which has played out in the state courts. In New Jersey this concept is known as the Mount Laurel Doctrine, which has enabled this state to calculate specific targets of affordable housing units for each community. In Massachusetts, the approach is simpler, with the flat goal of 10 percent of a community's housing stock being permanently affordable. Other states that have adopted a fair share approach are Rhode Island, Connecticut, Pennsylvania, Illinois, and New Hampshire. For communities in each of these states, there is a process for overturning a community's denial of a permit for an affordable housing project if the community fails to meet its "fair share" of affordable housing (Mallach 2009).

Municipalities

Planning Mechanisms

Approximately half of all states mandate a municipal planning process to develop a master plan with a vision for the future. The required master plans must take a comprehensive approach and include a chapter on the community's housing. This work considers existing conditions, future needs, local constraints, and opportunities for providing diverse housing types (Mallach 2009). Housing needs for low and moderate income households, as well as other special needs groups, are addressed in this analysis. Many affluent suburban communities find that the group consisting of entry-level municipal employees (teachers, police officers, firefighters) is priced out of the local housing market and starting salaries make them eligible for affordable housing.

In addition to this technical review of the issue, communities lead by developing community support for housing initiatives. Often the housing element recommends the creation of a committee to oversee the implementation of the recommended actions. This is an opportunity for residents to work together and collaborate with other groups, such as the business community, faith-based groups, and civic organizations, on initiatives to expand housing opportunities for low and moderate income households. Building local support and a group that can advocate for housing can be critical to overcoming local opposition. At the local level, affordable housing can be met with fierce hostility, as property owners seek to "protect" their property values and reject what they perceive as people unlike them from moving in to the area. Often, communities experience organized opposition to affordable housing despite the fact studies have established that this housing does not lower property values, and after-the-fact neighbors who resisted projects find few of their fears come to pass (Bratt et al. 2012). Such resistance can also have racism and classism at its root, with existing residents holding and perpetuating negative stereotypes of low and moderate income households and people of color.

Partnerships between municipalities and not-for-profit housing developers are a way to build capacity for successful projects. Groups like Habitat for Humanity and other local community development corporations work with neighborhoods and municipal leaders to expand housing opportunities for low and moderate income households. If the community has formed a Housing Authority, they are a natural partner for affordable housing programs. While local communities are not often in the position to contribute large amounts of funding to housing projects, as partners they can offer technical assistance and a thorough knowledge of the development process.

Funding Mechanisms

Another way cities and towns can help affordable housing is by providing affordable housing projects some relief from fees. To keep development costs down, municipalities can waive permit application fees, sewer or water connection fees, or school impact fees, for eligible housing projects. Affordable housing often pays reduced property taxes—or none at all. Also, like states, many local communities have housing trust funds. These funds can grow through payments from other development. Boston, Massachusetts, has a well-known program called "linkage" that works this way. Developers of commercial properties are assessed a fee and contribute payments to the housing trust fund, so the city can provide funding support for affordable housing projects. The linkage program is based on an argument that the success of the business is correlated with housing for employees of all types from top management to the maintenance personnel. Housing Trust funds can be used to cover the cost of land, design, construction, and more associated with affordable housing development.

Another common way for local communities to lower development costs is by donating land for affordable housing development. An inventory of municipally owned land often identifies vacant lands that are not needed and can be declared surplus. Municipalities may also offer property the community now owns because the former owner failed to pay the property taxes or abandoned the property. Developing housing at an affordable level is more achievable if there is no cost for the land.

Finally, many local communities are receiving the federal funds described in Chapters 4 and 6, and using these for a wide variety of authorized housing assistance, including construction subsidies, land purchases, development costs such as land surveys and environmental tests, down payment assistance, low interest rehabilitation loans, homeownership counseling, homelessness and foreclosure prevention, weatherization and energy efficiency improvements, and more.

Regulatory Mechanisms

There are several ways local regulations can expand affordable housing options. For certain communities, changing zoning to allow apartments by-right in some residential areas is a step in the right direction. Others have established programs that make it easier to develop accessory apartments (also called mother-in-law apartments) in single-family neighborhoods. These new, smaller units add housing choice and can benefit both those that rent the apartment and the homeowners who collect the rent. Some communities require these new apartments to be rented at affordable rates. Municipalities have also allowed affordable housing more flexibility in site design, such as permitting reduced frontage requirements, lower lot area minimums, or approving clustering of housing to save money. Some pioneering communities are experimenting with "tiny homes"— stand-alone housing units of 150–700 square feet, including designing communities composed of a group of tiny homes, or buildings of micro-apartments in urban places like New York City or Seattle.

Another regulatory mechanism for expanding the supply of affordable housing is *inclusionary zoning*. Begun in the 1970s, it is estimated that between 300–500 inclusionary programs have been adopted by local and regional levels of government (Calamia and Mallach 2009). While program details differ, inclusionary zoning generally requires new residential developments to set aside a portion of units (10–20 percent) as affordable to low and moderate income households. Some communities offer density bonuses to help offset these costs to developers, and others offer construction and fee waivers to reduce the developers' costs.

Not surprisingly, inclusionary zoning is not popular with the development community, which feels it places the bulk of the cost of affordable housing on developers. But

Figure 10.3 Repurposing of an outdated firehouse into residential space

Source: Image © Chris Bull, used by permission

Figure 10.4 An Inclusionary Zoning Example: Bonus Square Footage in Exchange for Affordable Units

Source: Graphic © Roger K. Lewis, used with permission

as an approach to increasing the supply of affordable housing, inclusionary zoning has some strengths:

- it ensures, as the overall housing stock grows, the number of affordable housing units also expands;
- it creates mixed-income development (an approach favored by HUD; see Chapter 6), and means households of different income levels will have shared access to the same quality services (see Chapter 7);
- it uses fewer public subsidies to create mixed-income communities than other approaches to affordable housing development; and
- it can be used in neighborhoods experiencing gentrification (see Chapter 8) by ensuring affordable units are part of the development mix.

(Office of Policy Development and Research 2013)

These strengths are not guaranteed, however, as many inclusionary programs also allow developers to make a payment to a housing fund, rather than incorporate units in their development. These payments are then used to support affordable housing, but the development may not be in the same area, or may not happen at the same time.

Another local regulatory mechanism for trying to lower housing costs is by streamlining the permitting of projects with affordable units. As discussed in Chapter 8, Housing and the Economy, time is money for housing developers. While a project is going through the local review and permitting process, the developer is accumulating costs through interest on loans to purchase the property or fund pre-permitting work. Some communities have worked hard to design a process with greater coordination and shorter timelines to keep these costs down for projects that include affordable units.

Other, much less widespread local level regulations for promoting affordable housing include negotiating community benefits agreements (CBA) and adopting rent control. Because state and municipal laws differ, these two approaches are not always determined to be legal. CBAs establish a process for developers to sit with local neighborhood groups and negotiate what the developer will provide the neighborhood where a large project is proposed. The project could be commercial, residential, or mixed use. In some places, the CBA agreement becomes part of the municipality's formal permitting process, in others it is an outside agreement between the developer and the community groups involved. How much developers are willing to negotiate is in part related to the permitting process of the community. If the local municipality has discretion in issuing the permit, or if the developer is seeking many waivers or variances from the regulations, the leverage the municipality has in issuing the permit can influence the developer to negotiate. In exchange for the developer coming to an agreement with local groups, these groups offer support at municipal hearings for the developer's project (Salkin 2007). The benefits community groups negotiate may include affordable units, neighborhood amenities, jobs for residents, or public access to private spaces. In general, the use of CBAs has been restricted to large urban areas such as New York, Boston, Los Angeles, Atlanta, Chicago, Denver, Seattle—locations where developers stand to make large profits on projects (Partnership for Working Families 2016).

Rent control is a regulation that sets limits on how much landlords can increase rent. The use of rent control is quite limited, and in some places, it has been determined not to be legal. Limiting the rent landlords can charge is not popular with the real estate community. Additionally, rent control is not always effective at targeting its benefits—affordable and stable rent levels—to those that most need them. New York City and several California communities use rent control to counter speculation among real estate investors and offer a degree of protection to the many tenants living in these communities.

One final local level affordable housing technique is that of alternative ownership models. These programs are typically championed by local not-for-profit organizations such as land trusts and coop-housing groups. Under these models, the ownership of land and buildings is commonly held—not privately assigned. The common ownership provides a mechanism for taking the land and sometimes also buildings, out of the speculation of the market. Residents in the housing are only paying for the building—not the land.

As an example, land trusts purchase land and hold it in perpetuity. The land trust rents the land—at an affordable rate—to households who build or rent homes on the land. In this model, the cost of the land is separated from that of the building, making the housing less expensive. Also, by removing the land from speculation, the cost of the housing does not increase dramatically as demand grows.

Coop housing is similar in structure to land trusts. Households form an association that holds the land and maybe some shared buildings in common, lowering the overall costs to all. These common forms of ownership can limit the selling price of the housing to affordable levels. This is a way of de-commodifying housing—seeing it not as a product to be sold at its highest value, but rather a place to live, and be part of a community.

Conclusions

While the federal government brings the most overall funds to affordable housing, states and local governments are also active in the development and preservation of quality housing for all economic classes. Through planning, funding, and regulating, states and municipalities increase the understanding of housing issues and add to the count of affordable units. These three functions are themselves complementary, as plans highlight the needs and generate ideas for affordable approaches, and funds and regulations can move these ideas to reality. There is great variation in approaches but also a sharing of success stories, as state and local communities contribute to the national goal of a decent home for all.

Questions

1. There are federal, state, and local responses to the need for affordable housing. Write down some of the strengths and weaknesses you think each level brings to the development of affordable housing.
2. This chapter notes that many states see housing and economic prosperity as tightly linked. In your own words, explain the argument made in this chapter, declare if you agree or disagree, and connect this to issues discussed earlier in this book about housing and the economy (see Chapter 1).
3. Consider local opposition to a proposed affordable housing project. Using the news article below on a project under a fair share regulation, or one from your local area, identify the different sides of the issue. Summarize the motivations and concerns of the different actors. How do you think the conflict should be resolved?
4. Get a copy of the housing plan/chapter for your hometown or nearby municipality. List some of its objectives and summarize one of the recommended funding and one of the recommended regulatory actions for meeting the affordable housing needs described.
5. Habitat for Humanity is the largest not-for-profit housing developer in the world. Research and summarize its sweat-equity approach to affordable homeownership. What do you think are the strengths of this model?

Article on Affordable Housing Project

From: Daily News of Newburyport, www.newburyportnews.com/news/local_news/neighbors-oppose-proposal-for-project-on-mullen-property/article_57902f8b-5f0d-538b-b164–975a1b85adb9.html

Published: September 19, 2008 Neighbors Oppose Proposal for Project on Mullen Property by Jennifer Solis Correspondent

WEST NEWBURY—Town officials are considering a plan to sell 34 acres of municipal land to a private developer as a way to add much needed income-restricted and age-restricted homes to the town's housing stock.

But many abutters to the Mullen property off Church Street say the plan, presented in draft form to selectmen on Wednesday, unfairly skirts local regulations and is not in the best interests of the town.

Appointed in June 2007, the Community Housing Committee has worked closely with consultant Nick Cracknell of Horsley-Witten Group to analyze the Mullen site and review permitting options under both Chapter 40R and Chapter 40B state regulations. The plan they presented to selectmen this week is one of three concept designs discussed at a public hearing last winter. It included a draft of a 12-page guideline for requests for proposals from developers.

With less than one-third of town employees and only 15 percent of the local teaching staff living in town, CHC Chairman David Houlden said the need for reasonably priced housing is "huge." Other members of the panel are Patricia Reeser, Brian Murphey, Marge Peterson and Gail Majauckas.

If selectmen agree to include it on the warrant, voters at a Special Town Meeting on Oct. 20 will be asked to surplus the land—the first step in allowing a private developer to purchase it. Approval requires a two-thirds majority. A simple majority vote is needed to approve issuance of the request for proposals. A final version of the document will be posted on the town's Web site (www.westnewbury-ma.gov) with copies available for review in the selectmen's office and the GAR Memorial Library.

The plan calls for the town to invite developers to propose a so-called "friendly" Chapter 40B affordable housing development, though neighbors argue that just how friendly the development is depends on how close you live to the parcel.

Adopted in 1969, Chapter 40B, also called the comprehensive permit, is known as the state's "anti-snob zoning" law. It allows developers to build at a higher density than is normally permissible under a town's zoning bylaws, provided that at least 25 percent of the units have long-term affordability restrictions.

According to state guidelines, West Newbury must increase its 26 units of affordable housing stock to 140 units by the next census or risk losing out on some state funding.

With a comprehensive permit, a developer can side-step the local regulations, a strong concern for the 25 residents who attended Wednesday's meeting.

Proponents of the plan argue it offers a way for the town to be proactive in controlling the type of 40B housing developments that are coming to West Newbury one way or another. A 40-unit intergenerational village that includes 25 affordable units buys the town two years of protection from the state mandates.

The proposal divides the property into two pods. One section has 12, 600- to 1,800-square-foot starter homes and eight over-55 units of between 600 and 1,400 square feet accessed from Church Street.

A second pod consists of 20, 900-square-foot senior rental apartments housed in a structure no more than two stories high. Access through an extended driveway on Main Street should minimize traffic impact to the neighborhood.

According to MassHighway regulations, the driveway would need a 74-foot radius, but the property only has access to 50 feet of frontage on Main Street. The developer would need to get approval from the state for the reduced curb cut. At 20 feet, the width of the driveway falls short of the 24 feet pre-ferred by the public safety department for emergency vehicle access.

All the senior rentals and five of the starter homes would be reserved as afford-able units. The affordable starter homes would sell for $160,000 to $170,000, with the market rate stock estimated to sell for under $400,000. The over-55 housing would have a market value of $350,000 to $485,000, said Houlden.

A shared water waste treatment system located near the Church Street end of the parcel would handle 10,000 gallons daily. It meets state requirements that a septic system is set back 50 feet from bordering vegetated wetlands, but not the town's 100-foot setback requirement.

"As a sponsor of the project, doesn't the town have an obligation to comply with its own rules and regulations?" asked Peter Flink, a vocal opponent of the plan whose Main Street home abuts the proposed access driveway. Last month the Board of Health stated it would not support any project that did not adhere to local rules and regulations.

"Why are selectmen going over the heads of the Board of Health and usurping their power?" Flink asked.

Further controversy stems from the committee's recommendation to set a min-imum bid price for the 34-acre parcel at $400,000—considerably less than the $1.2 million price tag the town paid for it. Selectman Glenn Kemper admitted that the deflated land costs were "a hard one to swallow" and wondered if putting off the project until the economy turns around might be worth con-sidering. But Holden said in order to provide the type of low-density housing project most residents want, the town is going to have to take a hit on land cost.

"The fewer units we build, the less value the land has (to a developer)," he said.

Voters will have a chance to vote on the final proposal, Houlden stressed, not-ing that "any and all bids can be rejected" if they don't meet 100 percent of the standards set in the request for proposals.

The developer must submit to an extensive permitting process, with opportu-nities for residents to weigh in at public hearings as part of that process. All permitting approvals must be in place prior to the conveyance of the land.

Peter Haack of the Planning Board labeled it "arrogance" to assert that this was the only viable use for this land. "Perhaps we do need housing, but I don't think this is the right place for it."

But Selectman Dick Cushing complimented the committee, saying, "These people are working for us, they are not trying to sell us something."

"This is our recommendation," said Holden, "But it is up to the will of the town as to what is ultimately done. It needs to be a community process."

The committee continues revising the bid document at its next meeting on Sept. 23 at 7:30 p.m. in the first floor hearing room of the 1910 Building.

References

Bratt, Rachel, Alexandra DeGenova, Brendan Goodwin, Moriarty Shannon, and Jeremy Robitaille. 2012. "Fear of Affordable Housing: Perception vs. Reality." *Shelterforce*. Accessed February, 2018. https://shelterforce.org/2012/10/10/fear_of_affordable_housing_perception_vs-_reality/

Building Technology, Inc. 2001. *Smart Codes in Your Community: A Guide to Building Rehabilita-tion Codes*. Washington, DC: U.S. Department of Housing and Urban Development.

Calamia, Nico, and Alan Mallach. January 2009. "Inclusionary Housing, Incentives, and Land Value Recapture." *LandLines*: 15–21.

Department of Housing and Community Development. 2003. *Chapter 40B Task Force Findings and Recommendations*. Boston, MA: Commonwealth of Massachusetts. http://archives.lib. state.ma.us/bitstream/handle/2452/38695/ocm52598238.pdf?sequence=1.

Iglesias, Tim, and Rochelle E. Lento, eds. 2011. *The Legal Guide to Affordable Housing Development*, 2nd Edition. Chicago: ABA Publishing.

Kinsey, David N., and Vito Gallo. 2015. *Developing Effective Municipal Housing Plans*. Trenton, NJ: Fiar Share Housing Center, Housing and Community Development Network of New Jersey.

Mallach, Alan. 2009. *A Decent Home: Planning, Building, and Preserving Affordable Housing*. Washington, DC: American Planning Association.

Nenno, Mary K., and Paul C. Brophy. 1982. "Housing and Local Government." In *Housing and Local Government*, edited by Mary K. Nenno and Paul C. Brophy, 181–190. Washington, DC: International City Management Association.

Office of Policy Development and Research. 2013. "Inclusionary Zoning and Mixed-Income Communities." *Evidence Matters*, Spring. www.huduser.gov/portal/periodicals/em/spring13/highlight3.html.

Partnership for Working Families. 2016. *Common Challenges in Negotiating Community Benefits Agreements and How to Avoid Them*. Oakland, CA: Partnership for Working Families. www.forworkingfamilies.org/resources/publications/common-challenges-negotiating-community-benefits-agreements-how-avoid-them.

Salkin, Patricia E. 2007. "Understanding Community Benefit Agreements: Opportunities and Traps for Developers, Municipalities and Community Organizations." *SSRN*. https://papers.ssrn.com/sol3/papers2.cfm?abstract_id=1025724.

State Housing Trust Funds. n.d. *Center for Community Change*. Accessed February 20, 2017. http://housingtrustfundproject.org/wp-content/uploads/2016/10/State-htfund-revenue-sources-2016.pdf.

U.S. Department of Housing and Urban Development. n.d. *Consolidated Planning*. Accessed February 20, 2017. https://portal.hud.gov/hudportal/HUD?src=/program_offices/comm_planning/about/conplan.

11

HOMELESSNESS

Having a roof over our head is something that many of us take for granted but the reality is that a significant number of people do not have a home of their own or even a consistent place to seek physical shelter. As of January 2015, approximately 565,000 people were homeless in the United States (National Alliance to End Homelessness, 2016). This also means they do not experience the feelings of belonging, refuge, security, and privacy that we have learned come with stable housing. As some advocates have put it, homelessness "can be seen as a metaphor for disconnection from family friends, caretakers, reassuring routines, belongings, and community" (Bassuck & Olivet, 2012, p. 286). Being homeless is not, however, an identity—we should not use the label "homeless" to describe people. It robs them of dignity and reduces them to being just a condition. Within our society there are many people facing homelessness, including men, women, children, veterans, immigrants, and people with mental or physical disabilities (Figure 11.1)—people who are someone's parent, child, grandchild, cousin, or friend, and they should be treated as whole people facing challenging circumstances.

Imagine being a child without family to care for you and being on your own without a place to call home. One of the most sobering statistics in today's homeless population is the number of young children and youth that are unaccompanied—living without an adult—and homeless. In 2016, 36,907 (or about 6.5 percent) of the total homeless population were unaccompanied youth and children, of which 4,467 were unaccompanied children under the age of 18 and 32,340 were unaccompanied young people between the ages of 18–24 (National Alliance to End Homelessness 2016). These figures, of course, do not include the thousands more children *within* family units who are also homeless. Here, we delve into some of the specific experiences of being homeless. This chapter will examine the issue of homelessness by offering key statistics, considering the variety of contributing factors, and exploring the ways all can attain and sustain a place to call home.

Why Are People Homeless?

There are a number of reasons why individuals can find themselves homeless. Some of the leading causes of homelessness include a lack of affordable housing, insufficient income, unemployment, domestic violence, mental illness and lack of appropriate mental health care, and addiction (National Law Center 2015). Several categories are used to classify the factors that lead to individuals being homeless. These categories include *structural factors, system failures,* or *individual/relational factors. Structural factors* that cause homelessness may include economic and societal issues that limit opportunities and shape our social environments, such as a lack of income, discrimination, a debilitating physical or health disability, and an insufficient supply of affordable housing. A *system failure* is a cause when systems of care or support failed for an individual, leading to his/her becoming homeless, such as a transition from the child welfare system or inadequate discharge planning from a hospital or mental health facility. *Individual* or *relational factors* include personal circumstances of an individual, such as a traumatic event, personal crisis, or mental health or addiction challenge (Gaetz, Donaldson, Richter, and Gulliver 2013).

These factors cut across the various groups shown in Figure 11.1. In addition to the children and young adults noted above, these 2015 figures indicate that 38 percent of those that are homeless are part of a family, and 8 percent of those that are homeless are veterans.

While there has always been homelessness in our society, it reached a crisis point in the 1980s. At this time, the gap between income and housing costs became so great that many families experienced loss of employment, eviction, or foreclosure. Previously, families were not a large portion of those experiencing homelessness. In this way, the "face" of homelessness changed from that of a lone adult to one that includes parents with children. Such instability affects the young through disruptions in school attendance, inability to concentrate on school work, emotional stress, and hunger. These can have long-lasting negative effects as these children become adults (Institute of Medicine (U.S.) Committee on Health Care for Homeless People, 1988; Mallach 2009). Adults, too, face disruptions and hardships that come from lacking a stable place to live. The lack of a home address can make finding work difficult and put one at greater risk of illness, mental stress, and crime (Schwartz 2015).

A report by the Institute of Medicine concerned with the severe health impacts of homelessness noted a distinction between those who face *temporary, episodic,* and

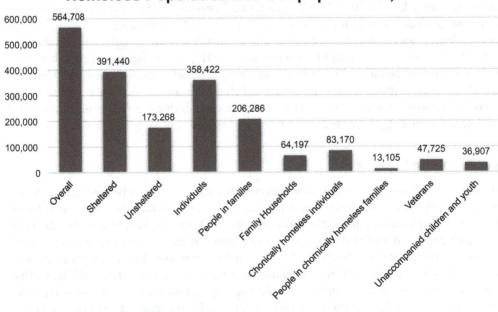

Figure 11.1   Homeless Populations and Subpopulations, 2015

Source: National Alliance to End Homelessness (2016)

chronic homelessness (1988). *Temporary* loss of housing can be due to natural disaster (fire, hurricane, etc.) or man-made causes, such as employment layoffs, and quick intervention can get people back on track. *Episodic* homelessness can be associated with funds that periodically run out, health conditions that flare up, or people who bounce back and forth between their own domicile, "doubling-up" with others, and emergency shelters. *Chronic* homelessness, long-term periods of living in makeshift accommodations or in emergency shelters, is more prevalent among those with mental illness or drug and alcohol addictions. If stability is not quickly restored, people are more likely to lose much of what is needed to regain normalcy, such as health, income, and strong community ties.

Homelessness and Deinstitutionalization

Besides skyrocketing housing costs and a shortage of affordable housing, another contributing factor to the increase in the number of people facing homelessness was the deinstitutionalization of those battling mental illness. From 1900 to 1950, the majority of people who were mentally ill were confined to state mental hospitals where conditions for patients were often inhumane. The majority of these institutions provided few to no opportunities for education, employment, and recreation, and also performed procedures such as lobotomies (altering part of the brain) which are now seen as medically abusive and unsound, worsening mental illness in patients, and often reducing individuals to a vegetative state. Around 1955, a movement began toward deinstitutionalization, reducing the usage of state hospitals and reintegrating mental health patients back into communities. The number of new patients admitted into state hospitals also went down dramatically from the 1950s through the 1990s (Messinger, Committee on Temporary Shelter 2010).

While closing these institutions was important because of the abusive nature of the "care" occurring there, a lack of social services and support for the reintegration into communities was a problem for mental health patients. Many patients were released without proper plans for care or resources to go to when they needed help with their condition. This problem has never been fully resolved. Currently, about a third of individuals facing homelessness are identified as mentally ill (Messinger, Committee on Temporary Shelter 2010).

Aging Out of Foster Care

Each year in the United States more than 20,000 young people "age out" of foster care and need to find their own places to live. This population is extremely vulnerable, with studies reporting that in the first few years after leaving foster care, one in four youths will end up homeless for at least one night, about half will be unemployed, only half will graduate from high school, and as many as 6 out of 10 young women will become pregnant. The level of continuing support for youths leaving foster care varies by state, but, in many cases, 18–21-year-olds who have not graduated from high school are expected to pay for their own place to live. These types of expectations and lack of support put this population at risk of being unable to adequately care for themselves (Reed n.d.).

Veterans and Homelessness

According to the National Alliance to End Homelessness, in 2014 about there were about 50,000 homeless veterans in the United States, accounting for roughly 9 percent of the

homeless population overall. This was a substantial (67 percent) decrease from the number of homeless veterans that were counted just 5 years prior, suggesting that the U.S. is
making significant progress towards ending veteran homelessness. Homeless veterans
are usually male (91 percent), single (98 percent), living in a city (76 percent) and many
have mental or physical disabilities (54 percent). In recent years as troops have returned
from Iraq and Afghanistan, the demographics of homelessness has started to change,
with more being younger, female, and head of household. Despite these recent shifts,
however, homeless veterans are still most likely to be men between the ages of 51 and 61,
having served in the Vietnam War (The U.S. Department of Housing and Urban Development 2013; National Alliance to End Homelessness 2015).

Because of their military service, the veteran population is at higher risk for having traumatic brain injuries and post-traumatic stress disorder (PTSD), both of which are among
the most significant risk factors for homelessness (Metraux, Clegg, Daigh, Culhane, and
Kane 2013). Among the more recent Iraq and Afghanistan veterans, who are more frequently female than older veterans, the experience of sexual trauma while serving in the
military greatly increases their risk of homelessness. There are also challenges for veterans associated with returning to civilian life or seeking employment outside the military
(National Coalition for Homeless Veterans, n.d.). These types of factors put veterans at a
greater risk of homelessness than the general population, and have led to veteran-specific
programs (Fargo et al., 2012; National Alliance to End Homelessness 2015).

Homelessness and Domestic Violence

National studies indicate that domestic violence is one of the leading causes of homelessness for women and children (The Washington State Coalition Against Domestic Violence 2013). Securing safe housing, and monetary resources to maintain safe housing,
are two of the most important concerns for abused women who are planning to leave or
have recently left an abuser (Clough, Draughon, Nije-Carr, Rollins, and Glass 2014). In
addition to needing to escape abuse, survivors of domestic violence may find themselves
cut off from support networks and financial resources by the abuser. This puts them at a
greater risk for homelessness, along with their own lack of income, employment history,
credit history, or landlord references. Other symptoms that women in these situations
may suffer include anxiety, panic, depression, and substance abuse (National Alliance
to End Homelessness 2017). Studies have also suggested that many women experiencing
homelessness are survivors of domestic violence, even if such violence is not the cause of
their homelessness. Another notable fact about this issue is that 38 percent of all domestic violence victims become homeless at some point in their lives (Baker et al. 2003)
(Administration for Children and Families 2016).

Attaining and Sustaining a Home

As a society, we have responded to homelessness with a variety of initiatives. One of
the most immediate types of responses is the provision of emergency shelter. Homeless
shelters are a type of Band-Aid, as they are simply short-term physical accommodations.
Generally, shelters are open for limited hours, have strict rules, can be chaotic, and are
not equipped to work with attendees on the underlying causes of their homelessness.
People using shelters still lack a place to prepare food, store belongings, and enjoy privacy. In a few instances, places have mandated the provision of emergency shelter. The
State of Massachusetts, for example, guarantees all families have an indoor place to stay
on any given night. New York City also has what is called "the right to shelter," and it

extends to every eligible man, woman, and child. Other places, such as Washington, DC, limit the right to shelter for those nights when the temperature drops below freezing, and Nevada guarantees shelter for unaccompanied youth (Mass Legal Help 2017; City of New York 2017; Hodges 2015; Eliminating Homelessness Among Nevada's Youth Know Your Rights 2017). Not everyone is aware of, or exercises, these shelter rights.

The federal government made a major commitment to ending homelessness with the 1987 McKinney-Vento Homeless Assistance Act. This legislation drew attention to homelessness as a reality in one of the wealthiest countries in the world, yet competition for funding is still intense, as the needs far exceed the resources. Beyond shelters, non-profits, faith-based groups, social service providers, and housing developers all run *transitional* housing programs to serve as a temporary bridge between emergency shelters and permanent housing. People in transitional housing work with social service counselors on "housing readiness," which addresses obstacles to obtaining and maintaining housing, and can include attending drug or alcohol rehabilitation programs, achieving a GED, or developing work skills (Bassuck and Olivet 2012).

When discussing solutions to homelessness, it is important to remember that people have varying views on if, when, and how the situation should be addressed. For example, the political views addressed in Chapter 3 also apply to potential solutions for homelessness. Individuals coming from a more liberal political viewpoint may be in favor of developing comprehensive programming, including governmental intervention, to help the people get out of homelessness for the long term, while a conservative viewpoint may emphasize personal responsibility and private or charitably funded solutions to the problem.

New Solutions for Homelessness: Housing First

One of the more recent developments in programming to help alleviate homelessness turns the housing readiness approach on its head. The *Housing First* form of homeless assistance instead moves people directly from the street or a shelter into their own apartment. The principle behind this approach is that a homeless household's highest need is housing, and that other issues that can affect the household's stability can be better addressed only after housing is secured. Once in permanent housing, households can benefit from the qualities of privacy, routine, good health, and stability while working on the factors that contributed to their homelessness (Homelessness and Reed 2014). Figure 11.2 presents the contrast between "Housing Readiness" and "Housing First."

Conclusion

The focus of this book has been the commitment we as a nation have made to ensuring all have access to stable and healthy home environments. Homelessness is in part related to a lack of affordable housing. While we have spent considerable time discussing how to make housing affordable so households do not have to choose between housing and other needs, and on locating affordable housing in areas of opportunity, homelessness is about the most vulnerable of our society and those facing the starkest realities in terms of shelter. As we noted in the opening to this book, one way to consider how much housing provides is to consider the absence of home. There can be significant and long-term consequences for those Americans who experience the reality of not having a personal residence. The statistics on homelessness in America indicate that children and adults suffer from physical, mental, and emotional stresses related to a lack of housing. Homelessness "is a state, not a trait" (Bassuck and Olivet 2012, 287). As such, it is something policies and programs can address.

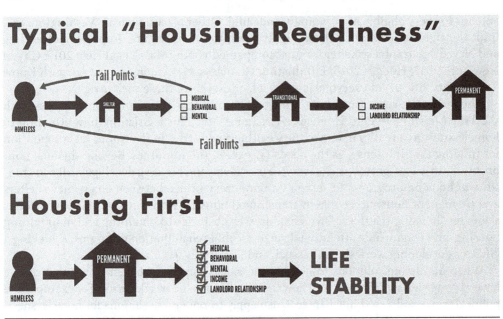

Figure 11.2   Housing Readiness versus Housing First

Source: Graphic by Abode Services, the West Coast's largest Housing First provider, used by permission

Chapter Activities

1. Complete this exercise developed by the National Healthcare for the Homeless Council as part of a curriculum, "Outreach to People Experiencing Homelessness" (Kraybill 2002).

    > Hand out a blank piece of paper. Have the students fold the paper in four—crease well.
    >
    > In each quadrant write *one* of the things housing provides—consider what we covered early on:

    > Safety
    > Identity
    > Asset
    > Pride
    > Stability
    > Privacy
    > Place to Rejuvenate
    > Place to Be a Family
    > Refuge / Be Yourself

    Rip away the first one you could most readily part with, continue one by one through all four being stripped from you. Check in with each other after each choice—ask about reasoning. Compare which is the last one each person is left with. Ask: How do people experiencing homelessness try to recreate some of these aspects of home?

2. Discussion Question Set: The following questions about one's perception of the homeless are part of longer list originally published on The Kindness Blog and

then by the Huffington Post (O'Connor 2014). Use these questions to reflect on how you perceive the homeless and consider whether reading this chapter may have changed any of your views. Go through this list question by question or focus on a few to carefully consider and discuss.

- When you see a homeless person, do you look the other way and keep on walking? Do you avoid making eye contact?
- If you do ignore a homeless person's request for help, just how quickly does the incident evaporate from your mind? Seconds? Minutes?
- What is your honest opinion of people in these circumstances?
- Do you think they could get a job if they wanted to? Do you think it would be easy to get a job without a permanent address?
- Have you considered that there are homeless people who have regular jobs?
- Does your suspicion that some people might be pulling a con stop you from helping any of them?
- Do you think the homeless are beyond our ability to help?
- Are you fearful, rather than empathetic, of some behaviors exhibited by those with mental health challenges?
- Are you immune from losing everything that you care about?
- Are you somehow better than the homeless or just better off?

3. Film: Watch the documentary *athome* (Alpert and Hoffman 2013) or the documentary *Our Journey Home* (Moreau and Romslo 2015). Utilize the accompanying discussion guides found at http://athomedocumentary.org/s/home-discussion-guide.pdf and www.rethinkhousing.org/meet-the-characters.

4. Discussion Question: Domestic Violence and Homelessness

The ACLU Women's Right's Project reported that a significant portion of landlords are unwilling to rent to a woman who has experienced domestic violence. A 2005 investigation of a fair housing group in New York found that 29 percent of landlords either flatly refused to rent to a domestic violence victim or failed to follow up as promised when contacted by an investigator posing as a housing coordinator for a domestic violence survivor assistance program. (Anti-Discrimination Center of Metro New York 2005; American Civil Liberties Union Foundation 2008).

- What are some potential reasons that landlords might refuse to provide housing for victims of domestic violence?
- What could be done to combat this problem?

5. Walk in Another's Shoes Writing Activity- Homeless Reality: Moving to a Shelter

Imagine you are a single parent of one 8-year-old working full-time as a housekeeper for Holiday Inn Express. Your annual salary is $21,000. Last year when your landlord raised the rent you applied for a Housing Voucher, only to find your name was added to a waiting list that could take 4 years to open up. Your child has asthma and your medical bills have been rising, even though you go to the sliding fee clinic.

When not at work, you have been desperately looking for a new apartment because your landlord sold the house and you moved out March 1. You have had no luck finding something you can afford. You moved in with your best friend, but after three weeks tensions are high in the apartment and her landlord has made it clear they want you to move on.

You turn to your last resort—using the homeless shelter located across town. The location of the shelter means that, rather than a 15-minute trip to work, you will need to transfer buses, so depending on the time of day, it will take 45 minutes to one hour to get to and from work. Also, technically the shelter is not located within the district of the elementary school your child attends. The shelter has 40 beds (15 reserved for men and the others for women and children). The beds are arranged in an open dormitory style (little privacy), and there is more demand for beds than availability, so a line forms for first-come first-served around 3 PM.

Despite the set of rules (see the following page) meant to keep guests safe you have many concerns about the shelter and, in particular, the safety and health of your child. You are not sure if he will be able to sleep under the conditions; the coughing and apparent illness of other guests worries you; you know some of them are addicts and desperate; and, in general, it is hard for you to know who to trust.

Write a page about your life at the shelter. To help you outline what a day will involve, think about your schedule and your child's; think through your own day (the real you) and then imagine the fictional person's comparable activities. What will the rhythm of your life be like? How might this affect your child and the things 8-year-olds like to do? Be sure to think about the issues of transportation from place to place; things like belongings, laundry; doctor appointments and medicine; homework; your child getting together with friends or participating in activities; looking for a new place to live; etc. What are the challenges you will face? What creative ways can you come up with to meet some of your needs?

Rules of the Home Shelter

- The HOME Shelter is for those 18 years and older who are homeless, able to care for themselves, and not a danger to themselves or others.
- No one will be admitted to any shelter site that is under the influence of drugs or alcohol to the point that he or she is unaware of surroundings or is unable to walk unaided.
- Guests must be in by 10 p.m. and leave by 8 a.m. (Doors open at 4 p.m. and often beds fill quickly.)
- No pets or visitors are allowed.
- The shelter is a temporary home, and the staff and volunteers will provide information to help those who use it find permanent housing.
- Men and women may not stay together. Mothers may stay with their children.
- HOME Shelter personnel reserve the right to search belongings.
- You may not leave belongings in the shelter during the day (staff cannot be responsible for them).
- Weapons are not allowed in the shelter or on shelter property. All knives are considered weapons and must be given to shelter staff for safekeeping for the night. Guns will be given to the police.

- Neither alcohol nor illegal drugs can be brought on shelter property. If they are found, they will be taken and not returned. The police will be called if illegal drugs are suspected.
- Verbal attacks are not allowed. Physical attacks in any form against other guests, shelter staff, and volunteers are not allowed.
- There is no smoking in the shelter. Smoking breaks are allowed outside the shelter with the security intervention assistant. Smoking will be allowed for a 10-minute period before every hour until 11 p.m. and again at 6 a.m. in a designated area.
- If a guest is asked to leave the shelter for violating rules and refuses, the police will be called.
- Lights are out in the sleeping area at 10 p.m. and in the dining area at 11 p.m. They are turned back on at 6 a.m.
- A weekly shower is required. Showers are available at The Presbyterian Church on Monday mornings and Thursday evenings.

References

Administration for Children and Familes. 2016. "Domestic Violence and Homelessness: Statistics (2016)." *Family and Youth Services Bureau.* www.acf.hhs.gov/fysb/resource/dv-homelessness-stats-2016.

American Civil Liberties Union Foundation. 2008. *Domestic Violence and Homelessness.* American Civil Liberties Union Foundation.

Anti-Discrimination Center of Metro New York. 2005. *Center Finds Significant Incidents of Discrimination of Survivors Against Domestic Violence.* New York: Anti-Discrimination Center of Metro New York.

Baker, Charlene K., Sarah L. Cook, and Fran H. Norris. 2003. "Domestic Violence and Housing Problems: A Contextual Analysis of Women's Help-Seekng, Received Informal Support, and Formal System Response." *Violence Against Women:* 754–783.

Bassuck, Ellen L., and Jeffrey Olivet. 2012. "Homelessness." In *The Encyclopedia of Housing*, 2nd Edition, edited by Andrew T. Carswell, 285–290. Thousand Oaks, CA: Sage Publications.

City of New York. 2017. "Shelter." *NYC Department of Homeless Services*, March 17.

Clough, Amber, Jessica E Draughon, Veronica Nije-Carr, Chiquita Rollins, and Nancy Glass. 2014. "'Having housing made everything else possible': Affordable, safe and stable housing for women survivors of violence." *Qualitative Social Work* 13(5): 671–688.

Fargo, Jamison, Stephen Metraux, Thomas Byrne, Ellen Munley, Ann Elizabeth Montgomery, Harlan Jones, George Sheldon, Vincent Kane, and Dennis Culhane. 2012. "Prevalence and Risk of Homelessness Among U.S. Veterans." *Preventing Chronic Disease 9.* http://repository.upenn.edu/cgi/viewcontent.cgi?article=1161&context=spp_papers.

Gaetz, Stephen, Jesse Donaldson, Tim Richter, and Tanya Gulliver. 2013. *The State of Homelessness in Canada 2013.* Toronto: Canadian Homelessness Research Network Press.

Hodges, Lauren. 2015. "As Temperatures Drop, Shelter Needs for Homeless Families Rise." *National Public Radio*, February 6.

Institute of Medicine (U.S.) Committee on Health Care for Homeless People. 1988.

Kraybill, Ken. 2002. *Outreach to People Experiencing Homelessness: A Curriculum for Training Health Care for the Homeless Outreach Workers.* Produced by National Health Care for the Homeless Council. Nashville, TN. http:// nhchc.org/wp-content/uploads/2012/02/OutreachCurriculum2005.pdf.

Locke, Mary. 2015. *Our Journey Home.* Directed by Patrick Moreau. Produced by Patrick.

Mallach, Alan. 2009. *A Decent Home: Planning, Building, and Preserving Affordable Housing*. Chicago, IL: American Planning Association.

Mass Legal Help. 2017. "Basic Shelter Rights." *Mass Legal Help*, March 17. www.masslegalhelp. org/homelessness/basic-shelter-rights.

Messinger, Alex, and Committee on Temporary Shelter. 2010. "Deinstitutionalization and People Without Homes." In *Unsheltered Lives: Teaching About Homelessness in Grades K-12 An Interdisciplinary Activity Guide*, p.35. edited by Alex Messinger. Burlington: Committee on Temporary Shelter.

Metraux, Stephen, Limin X Clegg, John D Daigh, Dennis P Culhane, and Vincent Kane. 2013. "Risk Factors for Becoming Homeless Among a Cohort of Veterans Who Served in the Era of the Iraq and Afghanistan Conflicts." *American Journal of Public Health* 103 (Supplement 2): S255–S261. (American Public Health Association).

National Alliance to End Homelessness. 2015. "Fact Sheet: Veteran Homelessness." *National Alliance to End Homelessness*, April 22. Accessed June 26, 2017. www.endhomelessness.org/ library/entry/fact-sheet-veteran-homelessness.

National Alliance to End Homelessness. 2016. *The State of Homelessness in America 2016*. Washington, DC: Homelessness Research Institute.

National Alliance to End Homelessness. 2017. "Domestic Violence." Edited by *National Alliance to End Homelessness*. Accessed January 27, 2017. www.endhomelessness.org/pages/ domestic_violence.

National Alliance to End Homelessness and Martena Reed. 2014. *Why Housing First Benefits Everyone (Not Just Homeless People)*. Accessed 2017. www.endhomelessness.org/blog/entry/ why-housing-first-benefits-everyone-not-just-homeless-people.

National Coalition for Homeless Veterans. n.d. "Background and Statistics." National Coalition for Homeless Veterans. Accessed June 27, 2017. http://nchv.org/index.php/news/media/ background_and_statistics/.

National Law Center. 2015. "Homelessness in America: Overview of Data and Causes." *National Law Center on Homelessness and Poverty*, January. Accessed January 24, 2017. www.nlchp. org/documents/Homeless_Stats_Fact_Sheet.

O'Connor, Mike. 2014. "The Homeless - 39 Questions for Your Reflection." *Kindness Blog: Kindness Images, Videos, True Life Stories, Quotes, Personal Reflections and Meditations*. Accessed January 22, 2017. https://kindnessblog.com/2014/10/01/the-homeless-39-questions-for-your-reflection/.

Reed, Karaim. n.d. *Housing First: A Special Report*. http://npr.org/news/specials/housingfirst/ whoneeds/fostercare.html.

Schwartz, Alex. 2015. *Housing Policy in the United States 3rd Edition*. New York: Routledge.

U. S. Department of Housing and Urban Development. 2013. "The 2013 Annual Homeless Assessment Report (AHAR) to Congress." *Office of Community Planning and Development, U.S. Department of Housing and Urban Development*. https://hudexchange.info/resources/doc uments/ahar-2013-part1.pdf.

The Washington State Coalition Against Domestic Violence. 2013. "The Intersection of Domestic Violence and Homelessness." *Domestic Violence Housing First*. http://ncdsv.org/images/ WSCADV-VAHFP_Intersection-of-DV-and-Homelessness_6-2013.pdf.

12

CONCLUSION

Our journey has established housing as central to the quality of our lives. While the need for shelter crosses all boundaries, there are some uniquely American aspects of housing related to cultural attitudes, historical development choices, distribution of political power, and heavy reliance on a regulated market. These forces shape the housing needs many in our society face as well as the nature of our responses. The American approach to providing decent housing for all is a palimpsest created through choices. Choices can be modified; we can expand our means for meeting housing needs. The American approach leaves a sizeable group without homes, others suffering from residential instability, and many locked out of areas of opportunity. Access to decent housing is not equitably distributed, and federal financial benefits lopsidedly favor wealthier and white households. Nearly 70 years after the 1949 national commitment to decent housing for all, the commitment remains unfulfilled not due to impossibility, but to a lack of political will.

One theme in this book is that we have multiple conflicting objectives for housing. We view it as a home, with all the attendant emotional power, as physical shelter, and as a reflection of our own worth. At the same time, housing is an investment, income generator, and national job generator. These multiple objectives serve different groups and can lead to conflicting government policies. For example, policies that subsidize the construction of single family houses for the middle class may reduce focus on and funding for affordable rental units in safe and stable neighborhoods. Some suggest that, ironically, acting on behalf of housing as a home is weak in America due to the very strength of the correlation between home and the individual: an American ethic of individualism ties success to abilities and grit—thus if housing reflects the self, it must be the product of your own work and not in some way supported through government intervention (Iglesias 2007).

Additionally, Americans choose, in general, to rely on the private market to meet housing needs. The supply of public and subsidized housing in America is strikingly low when compared to European countries. Although we know housing matters, we just can't overcome our faith in the regulated market as the superior way to deliver housing. Fear of government control, in combination with a perceived failure of public housing and racism, has meant a greater reliance on private sector activity and a declining commitment of federal dollars to housing assistance for those who need it. The American preference for as unregulated a market as possible keeps us from demanding living wages that could cover housing costs or creating laws to limit speculation and profiteering in the housing market. We choose not to prioritize housing as home.

Over time, housing initiatives have changed from supply-driven programs that build housing to demand-driven programs that equip households with vouchers for use in the private market. This is, in part, a reflection of the lower costs, but discriminatory practices and market fluctuations constrain the ability of vouchers to provide affordable housing in all areas. Inadequate funding for vouchers means that two-thirds of eligible rental households are not covered, and those who do have vouchers often cannot find units to meet their needs (Steffen et al. 2015). Our current response to housing needs falls short in many ways, and for demand-driven approaches to succeed, greater funding and an opening up of housing markets is needed. This theme is related to the ongoing debate over whether to prioritize people-based approaches or place-based approaches. Most advocates call for both assistance that allows households to move to meet their housing needs, and strategies for revitalizing places where there are unmet housing needs.

We need to face the disturbing truth of housing in America—race and ethnicity persist as forces that limit housing opportunities. Attitudes of past discrimination have created a segregated society that, in turn, perpetuates the attitudes of seeing some groups as inferior and others as superior. The inequality in education, job opportunities, and health among different neighborhoods extends the initial segregation over generations by curtailing opportunities to advance. Fair housing laws have provided tools for righting wrongs, yet studies have documented continued discrimination based on race, ethnicity, family composition, sexual orientation, past convictions, and more. Ironically, the housing voucher program, formerly known as "Section 8," developed to correct for prior government endorsed housing discrimination, has itself become a type of racial slur (Badger 2015). One incident of racial tension in Texas included whites taunting blacks with the words, "go back to your Section 8 housing." Some parts of American society conflate housing assistance with personal failure and racial inferiority. This attitude contributes to a limited national commitment to decent housing for all.

Another theme has been the degree to which American cultural values have shaped our response to housing. American culture has determined the types of housing we prefer, and influenced the means chosen for meeting housing needs. The ethic of individualism mentioned above (and a cultural tendency to equate material affluence with self-worth) has supported the suburban single-family ideal of the American dream. The independent person, in direct control of his/her plot of land, is our cultural definition of success, and our system has not embraced socially controlled housing options.

The overall American commitment to decent housing for all must be called into question when figures show vast unmet need and hardships. If we accept these circumstances, are we really committed to housing? If we are committed to decent housing for all, how can we tolerate homelessness? Why is it that we creep along, accepting such meager efforts at meeting the substantial and deep need for such an essential thing? There *are* success stories related to housing—families who have been able to move to safer places, children who have gained access to quality education, and elderly who no longer must choose between medicine and housing. If such stories are to become the norm, and we hope someday they will, public and political determination is needed to adopt changes and commit funding to successful housing approaches. We argue for a renewed national commitment to decent housing for all. We challenge the reader, having explored housing in America, to assess his/her own conclusions on the national commitment to decent housing for all.

Questions and Activities

1. Housing has been referred to as the physical, economic, and social backbone of a community structure (Iglesias and Lento, The Legal Guide to Affordable Housing Development 2013). Do you agree with this assertion? Be specific in your reasoning.

2. This book was written with the goal of getting you to become an involved citizen regarding housing issues. Some initial ways you might learn about housing issues in your community could be:

   a. Attending a local public meeting
   b. Scanning current newspaper articles for housing related articles
   c. Taking a walk around some different neighborhoods while paying attention to what people have access to and what is harder to get to (grocery stores, open space, hospitals, etc.).

   What are some additional ways that you could learn about and be active in housing issues in your community or state?

3. Consider our cultural norms and federal housing policies. What would it take to change the current distribution of financial resources, or to see a greater role for socially assisted housing in America?

4. Consider the role of the courts in the many aspects of housing covered here. In what ways have legal decisions affected housing in America? Think in terms of establishing and protecting rights, and interpreting local actions, as presented in different chapters of the book.

5. If a friend or relative asked you how this book changed your understanding of housing, what main takeaways would you offer?

References

Badger, Emily. 2015. "How Section 8 became a 'racial slur': A History of Public Housing in America." *The Washington Post Wonkblog.* June 15. https:// washingtonpost.com/news/wonk/wp/2015/06/15/how-section-8-became-a-racial-slur/?utm_term=.602050f8d65b.

Iglesias, Tim. 2007. "Our Pluralist Housing Ethics and the Struggle for Affordability." *Wake Forest Law Review:* 511–595.

Iglesias, Tim, and Rochelle E Lento. 2013. *The Legal Guide to Affordable Housing Development.* 2nd edition. Chicago, IL: American Bar Association Book Publishing.

Steffen, Barry L., George R. Carter, Marge Martin, Danilo Pelletiere, David A. Vandenbroucke, and Yunn-Gann David Yao. 2015. *Worst Case Housing Needs 2015 Report to Congress.* Washington, DC: U.S. Housing and Urban Development.

Index

Note: A page number in *italic* or **bold** refers to a figure or a table, respectively.